Living the Hockey Dream

Interviews and Personal Stories from
NHL Superstars and Other Lovers of the Game

D0774117

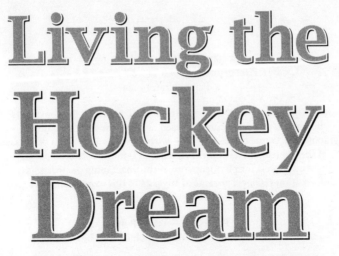

Living the Hockey Dream

Interviews and Personal Stories from
NHL Superstars and Other Lovers of the Game

Brian Kennedy

© 2009 by Folklore Publishing
First printed in 2009 10 9 8 7 6 5 4 3 2 1
Printed in Canada

All rights reserved. No part of this work covered by the copyrights
hereon may be reproduced or used in any form or by any means—
graphic, electronic or mechanical—without the prior written permission
of the publisher, except for reviewers, who may quote brief passages.
Any request for photocopying, recording, taping or storage on
information retrieval systems of any part of this work shall be directed
in writing to the publisher.

The Publisher: Folklore Publishing
Website: www.folklorepublishing.com

Library and Archives Canada Cataloguing in Publication

Kennedy, Brian, 1962–
Living the hockey dream : Interviews and Personal Stories from NHL
Superstars and Other Lovers of the Game / Brian Kennedy.

ISBN 978-1-894864-82-4

National Hockey League—Biography. I. Title.

GV847.8.N3K45 2009   796.962092'2   C2009-900200-0

Project Director: Faye Boer
Project Editor: Kathy van Denderen
Cover Image: Kamchatka/Dreamstime.com
Backcover Image: Photos.com
Author Photo: © Gabriela Moya

We acknowledge the support of the Alberta Foundation for the Arts for
our publishing program.

We acknowledge the financial support of the Government of Canada
through the Book Publishing Industry Development Program (BPIDP)
for our publishing activities.

Alberta Foundation for the Arts   Canadian Heritage   Patrimoine canadien

PC: 6

For my dad, who has given me hockey,
and so much more

CONTENTS

Section Three: Hockey and Family

Section Four: Hockey Friends and Enemies

Section Five: The Wider World of Hockey

Acknowledgments

I want to thank the many people who took the time to tell me their stories for this book. Busy with their lives and the game, they nevertheless allowed me to ask whatever questions I wanted, and they responded with candor. No matter what I asked, not one person told me I was out of line, nor did anyone refuse to answer any of my questions. (Of course, some of what they said, I didn't use, but that's a different matter.) These interviews were conducted between summer 2008 and spring 2009. Some were done on the phone, and some took place in person, but all of them allowed me to enter the lives of the people I spoke with in a way that I hope you will enjoy as you read their stories.

Part of the thrill of writing a book like this, at least for me, was talking to players I had known only as images on TV screens. Many times, the people I interviewed were my childhood heroes. In that group are Bobby Hull, Bobby Clarke, Marcel Dionne, Jim Pappin, Rick Kehoe, Bob Berry, Rogie Vachon, Ian Turnbull, Vaclav Nedomansky, Lorne Henning and Emile Francis.

Although each person I interviewed was generous with his or her time, several made exceptional efforts to make our conversations possible. Jordin Tootoo called me from the Nashville team bus on the way back from practice. Ian Laperriere talked to me as he headed off to pick up his kids from school. Lorne Henning called me from his office in Vancouver rather than having me call him because I couldn't get a phone access card for his area code. Ray Ferraro told me to call him in his hotel room after a game, despite it being 10:30 PM when we started and after 11:30 when we said goodbye. And there's a certain thrill that invades your morning when you pick up your phone and hear, "Brian? It's Bob Clarke," spoken on the other end. I could tell a similar story for almost every one of the people profiled in this book, but I will leave it at "thank you" and hope that their inclusion here serves them well.

Several teams, including the Philadelphia Flyers, Nashville Predators, Los Angeles Kings, Carolina Hurricanes, Phoenix Coyotes and Edmonton Oilers, were especially helpful in connecting me with players and alums.

Media relations people from the hockey clubs, including Zack Hill of the Flyers, Mike Sundheim from Carolina,

Mike Kalinowski and Jeremy Zager of the Kings, Kevin Wilson from Nashville, Alex Gilchrist from Anaheim, Jeff Holbrook from Phoenix and J.J. Hebert from Edmonton, also helped a lot.

I also want to mention my friends in the hockey media who have helped me so much. Ron McLean sent me a very nice email about *Growing Up Hockey* and offered to let me quote him on www.growinguphockey.com (the website I created for the book). Kelly Hrudey was also kind enough to write the foreword for that book. Each of the following people has—in his or her own way—been a shaping force in my hockey writing experience: Kevin Greenstein, Josh Brewster, Gann Matsuda, Kat Kealy, Doug Stolhand, Dennis Bernstein, Keijo Jolli, Graig Woodburn, Charles Smith, Ted Sobel, Rich Hammond, Dave Joseph and Jim Dwyer. Jack Falla, who passed away unexpectedly in the fall of 2008, was my dear friend and mentor. I wish he could have seen this new book.

My colleagues at Pasadena City College, where I serve as associate professor of English, have never wavered in their support for and interest in my work. (Special thanks to Darryl Distin and Bev Tate for all they've done for me.) My students, too, have shared in the joys of my writing life, and I have tried to use this aspect of my career to increase my understanding of their efforts as they work on their own writing skills.

To my publisher, Faye Boer, my editor, Kathy van Denderen, as well as the talented designers at Folklore in

Edmonton, thanks again. *Growing Up Hockey* was a dream come true; this book, a pure pleasure to work on with you.

And, as always, I must say to my wife, Gabriela; my dad, Hugh; my sister, Sandra Reimer; her husband, Phil; and their kids, Daniel and Sarah—thank you for your continued encouragement as I've pursued my dreams. My mom is no longer with us, but everything I write owes a debt of gratitude to her as well.

Preface

Maybe I'm naïve, but, while growing up, I assumed that people who had made it to the NHL had some kind of magical touch on them, that it had always been obvious that playing professional hockey is what they would do. Actually, I didn't believe this only during my youth—I still thought this way as recently as a few years ago, when I did my first NHL interview, with Mark Hardy. I asked him at one point, and only half in jest, "Don't you get the urge standing in a store to yell out, 'I'm Mark Hardy, and I played in the NHL!'?" He laughed and said that it hadn't ever occurred to him.

The reason I asked Mark this question is that I had the notion that hockey players had lives much like those I imagined for my teachers in grade school. When I went home, they seemed to vanish, as though they did not exist anyplace but the classroom. Similarly, I thought that the lives of NHLers were perfect and charmed, and that they existed in only one dimension, where all they did was play hockey.

Perhaps that's why, when I interviewed the Kings' Dustin Brown a few months after I talked to Hardy, I asked him about every moment of his day. Brown was young, living alone, and I wondered whether the team scrutinized his diet, monitoring everything he ate. He looked at me a bit quizzically when I asked him about this, saying, "No, you just do what's best for you, what keeps you feeling good."

Over the past few years, as I've managed to carve out a bit of a career writing about the game, I've put the hockey life in perspective. I have met many of the men who were my boyhood idols, and I've talked to them about life before and after hockey, as well as about their playing days. What I've learned is much more profound than it sounds—these guys are just people.

Maybe you knew that already, at least intellectually. But maybe you hadn't given a lot of time or thought to the fact that players live complicated lives off the ice. That they face difficult decisions. That they don't disappear when the game, or the career, is over. Like anyone else, they have to figure out how to forge meaning out of who they are and how hockey figures into that. It's not automatic, and once they're done playing, they don't sit around all day watching highlight reels of their greatest goals (which is what I'd probably do, had I ever done anything spectacular on a hockey rink).

Hockey players' lives are a lot like yours and mine, and their growing up often resembles what we experienced. That's true even of the superstars. So, as I gathered these stories, I focused on the magic moments shared by all who love the game, and I tried to include a variety of people, not just those with household names. My goal was to talk to players from different eras, people who had varying degrees of success in the game, those who work in capacities other than as players and those involved in other areas of the hockey world than the NHL, to find out what makes hockey special for them.

There are superstars profiled in this book. Bobby Clarke, Marcel Dionne, Mark Howe (who never received the recognition he deserved—look at the numbers and you'll agree), Bobby Hull and Wayne Gretzky all fit into this category. And their stories are heartwarming and real. But many of the people portrayed in *Living the Hockey Dream* are regular folks—players who fulfilled the hockey dream but didn't light the NHL on fire, and people who make their living in and around the game, giving it its character and depth, but whom you might not ever hear much about unless someone took the time to tell you about them.

In my first book, *Growing Up Hockey*, I had the crazy idea that people might want to read about the exploits of a third-line right winger who never went anywhere in hockey. I was convinced that his experiences (actually, my experiences) resembled those of many other folks, and that they were thus worth sharing. Judging by the reaction to that book, I was right, and the best emails I receive are the ones that go something like this: "When you talk about your rink, all I could think of was the corner where we played our games." In other words, people who write to me often don't discuss my stories; they talk about theirs, which was precisely the idea. It's why I often describe the book by saying, "These aren't my stories alone. They're yours, too. I just happened to be the one who wrote them all down."

Living the Hockey Dream extends that attempt to preserve memories by exploring the lives of others involved in the game, while also adding a few more stories of mine. It is my hope that reading about people around the world of hockey will provide fans of the game a larger awareness of what it gives to those who devote themselves to it and a sense of the courage it takes to craft a hockey life.

I went into the interviews with a bunch of facts about each person and a sense of where his or her story would go thematically. From there, I let the person talk, and at times, I think we were both surprised at what dislodged itself from his or her memory bank. As much as I could, I verified the facts, but keep in mind that this book, like my earlier one, is a work of memory first and foremost. The argument for that method, if you need one, is simple—people's thoughts, feelings and emotions about the things they've done are more important than their statistical profiles.

I've really tried to avoid clichéd versions of the past. Some of my newfound friends were better than others at expressing their ideas in interesting ways (and some were simply masters—Ray Ferraro comes to mind), and that's where my job as the shaper of the stories came in. However, I have tried to preserve the voice and character of the person in each story, especially the little details that might have otherwise been lost.

Anyone who lives a hockey life—whether as a player or in some other capacity—will experience twists and turns, mistakes and struggles. In that way, hockey isn't that different from normal life. But in observing how these events were handled by people who are, most of them, only known to us during the 60 minutes that the clock runs 82 nights a year, we learn an important lesson.

Hockey may be a passion, even a religion, to some. However, no matter how we mythologize it, no matter how great we view its greatest players to be, in the end, it is a game played by people subject to the same losses and foibles that the rest of us experience. In that, I think, there is comfort.

SECTION ONE

Hockey Dreams

⌒

The people who make a life in hockey, it turns out, aren't that much different from those of us who don't. Sure, they have a gift for shooting the puck, or stopping it, and that makes them superior to the rest of us regarding what they can do on the ice. But their goals, hopes and dreams aren't any different, and for almost everyone who makes it in hockey, their experiences reflect the common ones of us all: collecting hockey cards, worshipping the players of their era, dreaming of their own chance to one day hoist the Stanley Cup.

Their hockey life starts when they're old enough to skate and, in most cases, develops pretty quickly as they are recognized for their special talents. Most players who make the game a career play above their own age group from a relatively young age. But having said that, their lives are otherwise similar to those of other kids, until they reach their mid-teens. That's when the first big shock comes, when they must leave home to play hockey somewhere else. Many express the feelings they had in those days, and not one says the experience was easy.

One thing to remember is that, despite life making pretty good sense when one looks back on it, looking forward is no clearer for the hockey star than it is for the rest of us. We might look at these guys' lives and think it was a given all along. But that's just not so. Most guys who make the NHL put up amazing numbers in Junior hockey. But so do others whose careers never take them to the pros. What happens to those in the latter group? They don't get the lucky break, don't get drafted by a team that needs them or don't get off on the right foot when they finally make it to an NHL camp.

Part of what makes hockey dreams so precious is that they are so fragile. It's not evident which ones are going to come true, until they do.

⌒

chapter one

The Hockey Gods Are Real

The hockey gods are real. I know this because they've done things for me that can be explained in no other way than by their intervention. One example is the miracle they worked in helping me to get Kelly Hrudey to write the foreword for *Growing Up Hockey*.

The miracle began shortly after I got the contract for that book. I had the chance to attend a conference in Victoria, BC, to read some chapters from the book. After the reading, a man approached me.

"I liked your stories," he said. "I'm a hockey dad." My first thought was that almost any father in Canada could make such a claim, but then I noticed his hands. Better yet, the ring he was wearing. It was large, diamond-studded.

As he reached out to shake my hand, I couldn't help but blurt out, "That's a Stanley Cup ring!"

"Yes, it is. I'm Don Simpson, and my son, Craig, won a couple of Cups with the Oilers," he said, quickly steering the conversation back to my book. "I like your work, and if there's anything I can do to help you, please let me know." He handed me his business card. I took it and thanked him for his encouragement. "Please be in touch," he reiterated.

By the time I got home a few days later, I had figured out that Craig Simpson wasn't Don's only famous offspring. His daughter, Christine, was also involved in hockey, as a broadcaster. At the encouragement of my publisher, I decided to contact Don to see whether Christine would like a copy of my book when it came out. Maybe, we hoped, she could help make people aware of its existence.

I emailed Dr. Don Simpson, who told me that he had given Christine the thumbs-up on the book, and that she would be glad to have me contact her. And, in a pattern of friendliness that I was realizing was deep in her family's way of doing things, Chris, as I learned to call her, was as encouraging as her father had been when I emailed him.

A month later, I had the idea that *Growing Up Hockey* would benefit from a foreword written by a former player. My first thought was that Chris might be able to help me out. By this point, I had figured out that everybody in hockey doesn't automatically know everybody else, but I thought that maybe, as a broadcaster, she might have connections to the person I was looking for. That individual was Kelly Hrudey. He was perfect because he had been a Kings player—one of the all-time favorites—and was now a high-profile figure in Canada as part of the broadcast team for *Hockey Night in Canada*.

I decided that contacting Chris couldn't hurt, so I sent her an email. "I appreciate all your encouragement," I started. "Now, I have just one more favor to ask. Could you by any chance find a way to put me in touch with Kelly Hrudey? My publisher and I agree that he would be the perfect person to write the foreword for my book."

Within five minutes, she replied. "As a matter of fact," Chris said, "I'm sitting at the dinner table with Kelly right now. We're working the same playoff game. His email address is——. He says to contact him anytime." I almost fell off the Ikea desk chair where I sit to do my work.

"The hockey gods," I said to myself. "There's no other explanation." I had seen their work before, and I knew they were powerful, but this? Now, I had to tap them one more time, only this would be for a gigantic task. If Kelly said yes, my book would have a huge boost.

Over the next few hours, I thought about what words to use in my approach to him. I had no idea how many layers of lawyers a guy like Kelly Hrudey had, or how long a contract he might demand for such a favor. Would he send me to his agent, his publicity manager, the *HNIC* top brass? Would he demand some kind of ironclad guarantee as to the contents of the book?

I realized that my speculations were getting me nowhere, so I wrote an email telling him about my book and explaining that I had support from people such as the Simpsons. Toward the end, I asked for the favor I needed. "If you could write a foreword, it would be the biggest help I could imagine," I said.

I sent the email later that night, fully expecting to be contacted by a fancy law firm, if anyone ever responded at all. A few minutes went by, and there it was. "Sure. Just have your publisher send me a copy of the book so I can read it."

What? No contract? No, "I played in the NHL, mister, and I don't do this kind of thing without a big royalty"? Nope. Just a simple promise that he'd help me out, with no strings attached. Talk about something I would have to pay forward!

My publisher sent Kelly the manuscript the next day, overnight delivery, and he read it in the days that followed. Then he constructed a foreword that captured the spirit of the book perfectly, and we talked about it on the phone. I told him how much I appreciated his gesture, and he said that he was glad to do it. But the story doesn't end there.

A few weeks later, I was covering a playoff game in Anaheim, and who gets on the elevator but Kelly Hrudey. I stuck out my hand. "I'm Brian Kennedy, the guy who wrote

Growing Up Hockey," I said. "I can't tell you how much I appreciate your willingness to help me out with it."

Now, if Kelly were a guy with an ego at all, what do you think his first response would have been? Maybe something to the effect of, "Well, you know, I'm super busy but glad to do it"?

He said nothing of the sort. Instead, he said, "Interesting book. How long did it take you to write it?" I was stunned. Here was a guy with a 15-year history in the game and face recognition through being on *Hockey Night in Canada* which meant that he was a star wherever he went in the hockey world, and his first instinct was to talk not about himself, but about me. Wow.

Naturally, I answered his question (two years), and as he got off a floor before me, I thanked him again. Then I said, only half to myself, "Hockey gods, you've done a lot for me. But there's a guy who deserves special merit for the way he helped my dream come true." I'm not sure what favors Kelly may need from the hockey gods in the future, but I hope they won't forget his generosity. I know I never will.

chapter two

Much Bigger Than in Real Life

Bobby Hull

Bobby Hull's exploits in the game will forever be legendary. The curved stick, the wicked shot that terrified goaltenders and the million-dollar contract that took him from the Chicago Blackhawks to the Winnipeg Jets of the WHA are the things that come to mind whenever his name is mentioned. So large is his legend that it almost seems as though he comes from a realm beyond the reach of mortals. However, his past is one shared by a lot of players who have made hockey their life, and one of Hull's most vivid childhood memories includes playing on local outdoor ice, refusing to stop except to eat.

"I was always on my skates as long as there was ice to be had," he says. "Between age 10 and 14, I played organized hockey in Belleville, about seven miles from where I lived, but that was just an hour a week for however many weeks the season lasted. The rest of the time, I was on the open-air ice near my house."

The outdoor spots where he played were in one of two places. Out the door of his home one direction, Hull could cross a field and get to the Bay of Quinte, where kids played hockey much of the winter. Out the other direction, between two rows of houses owned by the local cement company, was a rink with proper boards and nets.

The young Hull got up at 6:00 AM, stoked the wood fire or shook out the coal grate, whichever chore needed to be done, and put on the porridge pot for his family. Although he was only six, he woke up his mom so she could help him get his skates on. He then traipsed over to the rink, where he'd shovel off the snow. "I probably shoveled enough snow to cover half of Chicago," he recalls.

It got to be a familiar sight to many of Point Anne's 500 residents, and people often cornered Bobby's dad to make a simple request. "Mr. Hull," they'd say, "can't you keep that kid of yours in the house at least until 8:00 AM?"

"That didn't deter me at all," Hull recalls. "I'd be out there shoveling. Pretty soon I'd look up, and there'd be a hundred pairs of eyes staring at me, kids who wanted to skate. We'd let them onto the ice to skate for an hour or two, but it was too crowded to play hockey. So we'd kick them off and play."

They'd play until the cement company blew its steam whistle, which occurred at 8:00 AM, noon, 1:00 PM and 5:00 PM. Hull and his siblings, 11 in all, knew that if they wanted to eat lunch or dinner, they'd better be home at noon or five on the dot. "No matter where we were in the village," he says, "we'd beat feet home and eat." When it was winter, he'd go home to eat, but the skates wouldn't come off, and after a hurried meal he'd be back on the rink again.

Hull never saw an NHL game until he was 10 years old, because he grew up in the era before most people had TVs. But the impression of the night he went to Maple Leaf Gardens and witnessed the Leafs playing the Detroit Red Wings never left him. "I decided early on that I was going to play in the National Hockey League," he says. "I don't know how it was for other people, but as far as I was concerned, all my life I dreamed about the NHL. I knew that when I got old enough, I'd play, come hell or high water. I didn't care what team I played for, but that's what I was going to do."

Hull credits his parents for giving him the genetic gift that got him started, but to that he added a will of his own. "I had three things going for me. I could skate, I could shoot, and I was strong. My parents gave me the start, and I put the muscle on my frame and developed my skating ability. When I got open, I could shoot the puck. That's all I needed."

He first played organized hockey close to home. In 1949, at age 10, he heard that a league was starting in Belleville.

He got there somehow. "Whether in the car with my dad or hitchhiking, I don't remember now," he chuckles, "but I signed up." The trouble was, there was no division for his age group. The youngest was Bantam, for kids 12 and 13. It didn't matter, though; he played with the older boys, and that year, his team won the championship. Before too long, he had attracted the notice of hockey people, and he left home at 14 to play. By 1956, at the age of 17, he was in the Ontario Hockey Association and destined for the NHL.

It was a debut he almost missed. He was playing Junior in St. Catharines and going to school, where he was a member of the football team. One afternoon, when he arrived home a little after 6:00 PM, his landlady, Mrs. Christy, met him at the door. "You're in trouble now," she said with a stern look.

"What did I do?" was Hull's automatic reply.

"Bob Wilson has been calling here every 15 minutes since four o'clock," the landlady said, "wondering where you are." It was during the early part of the school year, and the Chicago Blackhawks were holding their training camp in town. Hull had earlier told Wilson, the team's chief eastern scout, that he would be at school until late in the day.

Hull went inside and had just sat down to eat dinner when the phone rang again.

"I'm not going to answer that," Mrs. Christy said.

Hull picked up the phone, and it was Wilson. "Where have you been?" he asked.

"I've been at school, playing football," Hull replied.

"You were doing what? Don't you know that there's an exhibition game tonight against the New York Rangers? You need to get down here as soon as you can," Wilson implored.

Hull ran out the door and made it in time to get dressed, then went out and scored two goals against Gump Worsley. That night after the game, the Blackhawks asked him whether his mom and dad could come up from Point Anne. They did, and the next day Hull was signed to an NHL contract.

At the time, the NHL terms dictated that once a youngster signed a "C-form" indicating his desire to play for a certain team, he would be awarded a bonus when he signed his first NHL contract. Hull had signed the C-form a few years earlier, so at this point, inking the NHL deal, he received $1000, then headed to Chicago. That first year (1957–58), he made $6500 more, playing the full 70-game schedule and scoring 13 goals (13-34-47). He returned home at the end of the season with $3000 and went to work at the Coca-Cola bottling plant in Belleville. To get back and forth to work, he drove a 1957 Chevy that he'd bought for $1400.

It wasn't long before he brought a Stanley Cup championship home with him, after the 1960–61 season. Chicago had gone through Montréal in the semi-finals. "We won the

Cup, really, by beating them," Hull recalls. "We had a long overtime in the third game, and won that, and then Glenn Hall shut them out two games in a row. We knew then that Detroit would be a cakewalk after beating the mighty Montréal Canadiens."

The team won the trophy in Detroit but got snowed in and had to spend the night there. His celebration of the win was tainted a little bit because he got sick. He recalls drinking beer out of Mike Wirtz's "dirty old felt hat" and ending up too ill to celebrate. But there were other triumphs, including several AVCO Cup wins in the WHA in the 1970s. "Whenever you win the championship of whatever league you're in, it means a lot," he says of that time.

He still has the ring from the Stanley Cup win. "[It's] sitting on my bureau right now," he elaborates when asked what he did with it.

Hull sums up his career and his present place in the game by saying, "Hockey has been my life. Being able to play the game professionally as long as I did was fantastic. Being able to enjoy my son Brett play for 17 years was a joy, as well as seeing my other kids do well." He particularly enjoyed watching Brett play in St. Louis with Adam Oates. "It was there that he developed into the great goal scorer that he was. He may have been the greatest goal scorer in the history of the game. He could score so many ways." Hull fondly remembers Brett's

50 goals in 50 games (1990–91 and 1991–92) as well as his 72- (1989–90) and 86-goal seasons (1990–91).

Bobby Hull is certainly one proud dad. "You know what really pops the buttons on my shirt?" he asks. "I've got a VHS tape of all 86 of those goals, back to back." It's something he loves to watch.

Hull now serves as an ambassador for the Blackhawks along with Tony Esposito and Stan Mikita. He cites the recent revitalization of the team as something he values a great deal. "Rocky Wirtz took over, and he is a fabulous young man who knew what he had to do. He has led a resurgence, attendance is way up, and we've got some great young kids with the club." Those young kids, naturally, include Patrick Kane and Jonathan Toews—Kane, particularly, has taken to Hull. "Patrick thinks of me as a big brother. Anytime I'm around, he's right next to me. He loves to listen to the tales that I tell," Hull says. He adds that both kids stand out through their dedication to the game. "I don't have to tell these guys anything about that. They were ready when they came up." So was an 18-year-old from a tiny company town back in the 1950s.

Bobby Hull says he stands 5 feet 9 inches, but with his skates on, he's probably 5 feet 10 or 11 inches. His 195 pounds coupled with tremendous strength and lack of fear yielded a combination that made him a 610-goal scorer in the NHL and saw him get 913 total professional goals in 23 seasons in the NHL and WHA. But, as with many mythological figures, his impact on those who admire him cannot be quantified. As a result, Hull will always remain far bigger in the imaginations of those who watched him play than any human scale of measurement might suggest.

chapter three

Call It a Natural Gift

Marcel Dionne

When he was a kid, Marcel Dionne could look out the windows of his Drummondville, Québec, home and see the two rinks he and his friends played on. One was in his backyard, and the other was in front of his school, which was across the street. Every day during winter, he watched, and when he saw the first few guys, out he went. "If we didn't clean the rink off properly—it snowed a lot in those days—we didn't play," he says. Had anyone else in the neighborhood been looking on when he was on the rink, they would have seen something to remember, because the kid with the uncanny ability went on to become one of the most prolific scorers in NHL history.

When the season didn't permit the kids to play on outdoor ice, they played on the street. "We played all the time, on that ice outside and on the street. We practiced our stickhandling all the time, even when there was no ice. It was a bit different than today, a bit of an advantage," he says. All that practice helps explain his ability to score 731 NHL goals during an 18-year career that spanned from 1971 to 1989, but of course it is only part of the equation. The rest comes down to natural ability and the support of his family.

But it wasn't smooth sailing right from the start. Dionne was eight years old when he played his first year of minor hockey. At the time, he didn't know the difference between the red line and the blue line, because previously he had played only shinny, with no rules. The future superstar learned quickly how to conform to the official version of the game.

By the time he was 10, people could see something in the kid from Drummondville, though Marcel himself didn't anticipate a career in hockey just yet. "People were talking about you, articles in the newspapers, but still, you had to go out and perform. By the time I was 13, 14, I was near the top of the crop along with Gilbert Perreault and Guy Lafleur," he says. The latter two lived in other areas of Québec, but the three competed against one another in tournaments.

Dionne also watched games on TV, but as he says, "It was only one game a week at the time, on Saturday. *Hockey Night in Canada*, French network. We'd also catch games on the radio, though. Of course I'd identify with the Montréal Canadiens, being a French Canadian, but there were only six teams, so you got to know the players real quick, your idols, and that was the thing. You went outside and played hockey, and you became Jean Beliveau, Gordie Howe, Bobby Hull with all your friends and cousins who played hockey. Those were different times."

Although he lived 60 miles or so from Montréal, Dionne didn't go to a live NHL game until he was 15. The New York Rangers by this time were the sponsors of the Drummondville Rangers, for whom he played, and Emile Francis took him to a game at the Forum, and into the Rangers' locker room. Dionne also saw a game against the Red Wings and recalls seeing Gordie Howe on the ice.

"Within four years, I was on the ice playing against those Rangers. Eddie Giacomin, Rod Gilbert. I remember my first NHL game against the New York Rangers, Rod Gilbert said to me, 'I remember you. You were in our dressing room.' It was really good."

None of Marcel's success would have been possible, however, without family encouragement. When he was a kid, his mom had a lot to do with his hockey-playing career. Marcel came from a family of eight, and his dad was always working different shifts at a steel plant to support them. His mom also had a business, but his parents found a way to get him to his games. Back then, it was easier than it might be now, because, as Marcel says, "We used to play maybe 12 games indoors every year, and these days, kids are playing 80 games. My parents were like everybody else, trying to do

their best. My mom was very big to help. It's the same today—
the moms are the biggest part of it."

He tells a story that illustrates his natural gifts. "One
game, I broke my skate blade, and it wasn't like now where
you could replace it the next day. So they got me some other
skates, not new ones, and put them on me to play the next day.
They didn't fit right. I still went out and scored five goals." As
he recalls these events, he laughs, because to him, this is what
kids do. To the rest of us, his talent is something to marvel at.

His career progressed to the point where it was clear
that the NHL was in his future, and thus it was time to play
Junior hockey. Rather than stay in Québec, he decided to
play in Ontario in the fall of 1968, mostly because he knew
that if he learned English, his future would hold more possi-
bilities. "The English wasn't really exposed to us. Now, it's
different, but then, I wanted to become bilingual, and I went
to St. Catharines." His mom helped with the move and she
went to live with him, along with one brother and two sisters.
His mom stayed until about Christmas, and his brother lived
with him for the three years he spent with the St. Catharines
Black Hawks. They stayed in billets after Mrs. Dionne left.

"It was a pivotal moment for me to go out and do
things on my own. I learned at an early age to live on my
own," Marcel says of that time.

The next step was the 1971 NHL draft, held in a Montréal hotel. Marcel was there with some people from the St. Catharines team, but it wasn't the big deal it is today—no one put on sweaters or caps with team logos. It was just the picking of names, and it was inevitable that his would be called first, by Montréal, or second, by Detroit. "I knew if I was not first, I was going to be second, so it was no big surprise." (Guy Lafleur was also in the draft.)

In fact, Montréal had had a deal in place for Dionne the night before the draft. "Scotty Bowman told me just recently," Marcel says, "that they tried everything to get me to be with the Montréal Canadiens." The Habs picked Lafleur, however, and Dionne went to Detroit. "You know what, that's a long time ago. It doesn't really matter today—it's too late!" He chuckles as he says it, and the laugh reveals his easy-going nature.

His career went from one sparkling moment to another, and his scoring set records that stood until Gretzky came along. Marcel still sits fifth on the all-time scoring list, and fourth in goals.

Despite his sterling career, Dionne doesn't live in the past. He's more interested in today. For instance, he won all kinds of accolades and trophies as a kid, but he's not particularly sentimental about them. "Things that you've had for 50 years, I think it's a little bit too much. I told my mom, 'You've got so many grandkids, I think it's time to start putting up some of their stuff.'" At the same time, people have expressed interest in these artifacts, and so he has sold some of them through his sports marketing business and on eBay. "I kept the really special stuff, the Hall of Fame [commemoratives] and so on, but what I really value is pictures—photos of my kids with Gretzky or Beliveau or Gordie Howe. Those matter a lot more to me than certain personal awards that I have won. When people have a tragedy, what do they want to save? The pictures— that's irreplaceable. They tell the story," he says.

Aside from cherished photographs, Marcel has also retained the friendships and memories from his playing days. "I go back to my hometown a lot, but to St. Catharines more. I see the guys a lot, and I never lost touch with anybody. Those were great years, and lots of those guys went on to play pro. We get together now. It's always nice, and believe me, it's always the same stories. We talk about the same thing all the time, and it's always funny."

When the time came to stop playing, Dionne took on the role of hockey dad, moving his family to Buffalo. "My boys wanted to play hockey, so we moved. It made sense for me, being near the border so they could travel, be close to more facilities to train, and so on. Carrying the Dionne name was a bit of a burden on them, but my one son played a year of college and then some more hockey in a semi-pro league, and the other one played a little bit less, but that's fine. They picked up their careers, and they went on."

Twenty years after retiring from the NHL, Dionne remains active in hockey old-timers events and is still a recognizable face to fans of the game. He tells a story to illustrate the funny side of his fame. "I was at a restaurant recently, and the guy picked up my credit card and said, 'You're that Rocket Richard!' I laughed and said, 'OK, if that's what you think.' I enjoy that, but I don't consider myself a celebrity. If people enjoy seeing me, then that's fantastic. But when my career was over, I retired and moved on, and I've never worked for anyone else. I have my own business, and I love what I do.

"Hockey came natural in our family. My dad never played sports, but [my parents] were a part of it with me all along the way. Then my young brother [Gilbert Dionne] won a Cup with Montréal in 1993, and my parents saw that. Their commitment to hockey was fulfilled by him winning the Cup. They got me on the one hand as a Hall of Famer, and they got him on the other hand with his name on the Cup." As he says this, Dionne's smile almost reaches up to his eyes—sniper's eyes that picked 731 holes in dozens of goalies over his time with Detroit, Los Angeles and New York.

chapter four

All He Ever Wanted to Do

Bobby Clarke

The photo of Bobby Clarke taken when he was in Junior hockey shows a young blond kid, smiling with a full set of white teeth. Pictures of Clarke a handful of years later show him clutching the Stanley Cup, smiling just as broadly, but this time with tousled curly hair, longer in 1970s style, and with a huge gap where his four upper front teeth should be. At 24, he was already a warrior. By 34, he was retired from hockey. But for fans who recall the game in the 1970s, or even anyone who cares to look at his career statistics, Clarke's name will always be linked with success. He won the Hart Trophy three times, plus two Stanley Cups and a raft of other awards over a career that spanned from 1969 to 1984.

Conventional wisdom views the ferocity with which Clarke played in the NHL as a product of his upbringing in far-flung Flin Flon, Manitoba, a place so distant that it was said the nearest hockey opponent had to travel the whole day to get there to play. The lore surrounding him suggested that getting out of the city was a prime motivation for the young centerman, and the only way he was going to do that was by being tougher than the next player. In addition to the obstacle of distance, Clarke also had to fight the perception that he might not be able to withstand the rigors of the professional game, given that he was diagnosed with diabetes as a teenager and had to give himself insulin shots every day.

The truth as he explains it isn't quite so gritty. "For whatever reason, all I wanted to do was put my skates on and go out on the ice. I loved hockey, and I would do anything to play hockey," Clarke says. "All day, every day, we played. In the summer, we did other things, like playing baseball, but the hockey sticks were never far away."

Growing up, Clarke got a new hockey stick every Christmas. One year, a pair of gloves was under the tree, too. "I put them on right away, wouldn't take them off. I went to bed with them on that night, the new stick right beside my bed. But that's not unusual. A thousand, a million Canadian kids did the very same thing," he says.

In his hometown, devotion to hockey was not exceptional. "All the kids played. When I was a kid, it was before TV came to Flin Flon, and hockey was our focus. Lots of good players went through the town."

Organized games back then in Flin Flon were played on an outdoor rink, with inside ice available for about 15 weeks per year, and his games were scheduled from eight until nine on Saturday mornings. Between those contests, he spent his time on the city's outdoor rinks. "I'd go down there in the morning and skate by myself. The feel of that smooth ice was like nothing else," he muses.

His idol at the time was Gordie Howe. "I listened to the games on the radio. The nice thing about radio was that you used your imagination, and to me, Gordie Howe was by far the greatest." He adds, "If my parents hadn't made me go to church, Gordie Howe would have been my God."

What Clarke couldn't have known while listening to those late-night broadcasts was that, a few years later, he would get to play against Howe. Clarke's rookie season with the Flyers came in 1969–70, and he says this about the game: "I'm 20 years old, and there he is. And I thought, 'How do I play against him? I can't compete against someone like that.'"

However, he was well prepared to compete at the professional level by playing Junior hockey for his hometown team. "I don't think back then that they had lists of young prospects, and I'm certain there was no draft," he recalls. "But I played well enough to be asked to play on the Flin Flon Bombers squad." His parents, meanwhile, were involved, but not to the point of mania. "They went to games, but it wasn't their whole life," he explains.

His folks, however, did have to deal with their son's diabetes, a diagnosis that came when Bobby was 13 or 14. "My parents were worried, a lot. But I was never scared of needles. I just said to the doctor, 'Can I play hockey?' In my mind, I was a hockey player who happened to have diabetes, not a diabetic hockey player. He told me I could, with some care, and that's that."

His Junior coach, Pat Ginnell, took the young Clarke to the Mayo Clinic for a medical evaluation and clearance to play. This extra effort was perhaps beyond the call of duty, but Ginnell's influence stretched far into Clarke's life. "He gave me the chance to play in the National Hockey League, not just for what he did for me in terms of the diabetes issue. He created expectations that made what might have been a hard workout an ordinary one. He pushed all of us and demanded a lot, and the proof is there—not many Junior teams, especially from a town of 10,000, produced that many NHL players." Flin Flon Bombers alums from Clarke's NHL draft year team in 1969–70 include Reggie Leach, Gene Carr and Blaine Stoughton, with other years equally rich in talent.

As his Junior career progressed, a 17-year-old Bobby sat his parents down at the kitchen table one day for the grand pronouncement that he was quitting school. "I was old enough that they couldn't do anything," he says. "I had a plan. I was going to work in the mines and play Junior hockey, and that's what I did, for three years. I loved it, working with men, drinking beer after work and playing for the Bombers."

His father took the news well, but not without comment. He looked straight at his son and uttered only one declaration: "You get nothing for nothing. You'd better work."

Clarke muses about his dad's comment, "I don't think he gave it to me to remember forever, but I have remembered it all this time."

And if there's anything Clarke did, it was work. Finding himself the captain of the Flyers in 1973, at 23—at the time, the youngest player ever to hold the honor—Clarke was typically first to arrive at practice and the one who applied himself the hardest. Not because he had to set an example, but because he wanted to be as good as he could be.

His reputation as a gritty player was forged early in his NHL career, and some said that he played mean as a way to escape where he came from. This way of viewing Clarke's motivation stemmed from his statement that he'd never have gotten out of Flin Flon unless he had learned to give an opponent a good two-handed whack once in a while.

There's no question Clarke was rough and tumble. But the two-hander comment has an explanation that puts it into another context. "I remember the first time I said that," Clarke explains. "I had won my first Hart Trophy, and I was being interviewed by Red Fisher [sports editor and columnist for the *Montréal Star*]. I was kidding around with him. He had been teasing me about wearing my 'Flin Flon suit' because I'd showed up at the Team Canada '72 training camp wearing cutoff jeans shorts and running shoes. So I said something about learning to deliver a good two-hander as a way to get out of Flin Flon. It was a joke, nothing more.

"Flin Flon wasn't a place I tried to escape. I loved Flin Flon. I love it still. I went back every summer before I had my own kids, and I go back still. But I obviously wasn't going to play NHL hockey there, and that's all I ever wanted to do. At some point, I had to leave."

Some people would love to believe that the Canadian North produces a different breed of player, one cut from rougher stock than your average NHLer. Maybe they think that enduring winters that last for months, with temperatures dipping to dozens of degrees below zero, builds toughness. Or perhaps they imagine that a sense of desperation is forged from looking out over the miles of flat terrain and wondering what's out there in the bigger world and how to get some of it for yourself.

But for Bobby Clarke, none of that led him to the big time in hockey. Instead, his place in the game developed from the passion inside him that wouldn't allow him to do anything else but play. "I always believed that the goal was to get the puck and put it in the other team's net. My philosophy was, 'Don't be afraid to try new things to accomplish that.

Go after the puck and get it.'" He managed to do that 358 times in his career, as well as to notch 852 assists. But his contributions didn't stop there.

Fans who haven't seen a game from before the early 1970s may not realize that until Clarke came along, the art of taking a faceoff looked nothing like it does now. Before Clarke's day, the faceoff was decidedly gentlemanly, with each guy standing well back, his stick extended in front of him. As the puck dropped, the two players seemed to pause a moment, then both reached out, each trying to give the puck a gentle whack to get it to come to his side. The action was done only with the arms, not with the body as is done today.

Clarke's technique in the circle was to shorten up his grip on his stick and put his face right over top of where the puck was going to be dropped. It must have seemed extremely disorienting to his opponents, though Clarke won't take credit for his innovation. "There have always been great faceoff men," he says, "Stan Mikita, Doug Jarvis. It's not something you can practice. I know people do practice faceoffs, but with me, it was just a matter of getting low to the ice. I tried to teach myself how to win that puck every time, but how many faceoffs do you take in a game? 20? 25? You're going to lose your share, too."

Fair enough, but Bobby Clarke remade the art of the faceoff the same way Dominik Hasek reinvented goaltending when he dropped his stick and flipped around on his back to get a puck that was surely going in. And Clarke achieved a lot of other milestones, too, on his way to the Hockey Hall of Fame, which inducted him in 1987.

Clarke still lives in the Philadelphia area, and he now works with the Flyers organization in the front office. He's a long way from Flin Flon, but he hasn't really changed over the years from the boy he was. Anyone who knows Clarke or has followed his career both on and off the ice recognizes that he's a no-BS kind of guy. His passion for the game comes through in his tone of voice and the words he uses when he speaks—hockey means everything.

And as for Flin Flon, he still goes back, but not as the town's hero. "Flin Flon has honored me a lot, and I'm grateful for that, but the greatest hockey played in town was by the Bombers Memorial Cup team of 1957, and the town has honored them as a team. That's the way it should be—it's a team game."

A team game, one might add, that wouldn't have the same passionate history were it not for a skinny blond kid who had to brave diabetes and the wrath of opponents at every turn in order to do the only thing he loved to do.

chapter five

Just Playing the Game
Wayne Gretzky

When you have a hockey career as magical as the one Wayne Gretzky had, your childhood must have been magical, too, right? With that belief, hockey fans and hockey parents the world over have scrutinized Gretzky's younger days perhaps more than those of any other sports star, ever. Their goal? To find the key that turns a seemingly average kid into a hockey hero.

The dilemma is, the harder you look, the more you realize that the young Wayne Gretzky was a lot like most kids who grow up with hockey on the brain. He played, he had his heroes, and he spent time pretending to win the Stanley Cup. Of course, he did the latter on what became the most famous backyard rink in history. And when fans think of Gretzky as a kid, the first thing that comes to mind is that famous saying of his father, Walter, that went something like, "I told him not to go where the puck is, but where it's going to be." It was the mantra that, it is believed, turned the gangly kid into the play-maker and goal scorer he became.

In an interview on his website, www.gretzky.com, Wayne talks about the backyard rink, and in discussing his dad's role, he says, "He would stand in the big window and watch me. The odd time he'd come out and tell me some things, but mostly he just stayed in there and watched." Wayne further says that he was by himself most of the time, and that he was out there "almost all day long." He adds, "It's the best way to learn."

Face to face with me one afternoon after his Phoenix Coyotes had beat the LA Kings, Gretzky says that when he was young, hockey was more than something the kids in his neighborhood did in the winter. "We played hockey all year long. In the wintertime, we played on the backyard rinks and ponds, and in the summertime we played on grass, we played on gravel, we played on anything."

And, of course, he had his hockey heroes. Or rather, he puts it in the singular. "Gordie Howe," he says without hesitating when I ask who his mentors were as a kid. "My dad and Gordie Howe."

Gretzky had the same dreams every other kid playing hockey has: he fantasized about being the player he admired so much, imagining that he was winning Stanley Cups the way his idol had. When asked whether he pretended to hoist the trophy, he says, "Oh, yeah, I think everybody did. For me, it was always the Detroit Red Wings and Gordie Howe, so that was always something pretty special for me, and that's what I always sort of dreamed about being, and it was always fun." As everyone knows, Wayne eventually did hoist the Cup for real, four times to be exact.

Other elements of Gretzky's early life also mirrored the common Canadian experience. Christmas in the Gretzky household was celebrated in much the same way as in other hockey homes. Five kids were not too many for Walter and Phyllis to provide the kinds of things that helped dreams come true, and Wayne received a key gift that he remembers: "Mine was a Gordie Howe number 9 jersey," he says.

Like many other kids in that era and since, Gretzky had the chance to meet his idol. It was the occasion of that famous photograph in which a 10-year-old Wayne is standing next to a seated Gordie. The older man holds a hockey stick in his right hand, with the butt-end down. The shaft is held diagonally across Howe's body, and the blade hooks Wayne around the neck. Howe smiles broadly at the kid, and Wayne looks into the camera and grins as well. Wayne still has clear memories of the day, and he was aware that he would meet his hero. "I was part of the whole show, part of the dinner, and it was an exciting night for me to get a chance to meet my idol, and it was obviously a lot of fun."

According to Wayne's website, the date of their meeting was May 4, 1972, and it was around this time that the boy stopped being any old kid and started playing the game in a way that made him the icon he is. At 10, he had his first national exposure, in the form of a story written about him in *The Star Weekly*, published April 1, 1972. At the time, he was scoring in bunches, and during that season he got 378 goals and over 500 points in 82 games playing for the Brantford Nadrosky Steelers Novice All-Stars (www.gretzky.com has all the details).

Wayne's career continued, and a year or so after his breakout season, a memorable symbol of Gretzky's childhood came into his possession—a white pair of hockey gloves that earned him the nickname the "White Tornado" at a tournament he played in Québec. I ask him whether the gloves were special in some way, maybe a Christmas gift. He laughs, remembering back a few decades. "No, it came down to there were only a couple of pairs of hockey gloves left when I went to buy new hockey gloves for the start of the season, and that was the one that seemed to be the more comfortable, so I ended up wearing those white gloves." He played that tournament at the end of 1974, and by this time, the boy wonder had already scored more than 1000 goals in organized hockey.

In the spring of 1975, he was off to Toronto to play. "Wayne's scoring feats in Brantford upset the competitive balance of the local league," says the bio on his website, and it also rendered his family "unpopular with some." From there, as is well known, Wayne was drafted by the Junior Sault Ste. Marie Greyhounds. In a video interview from that time, Wayne talks about the way his team plays and his part on the squad. He's quiet as he speaks to the off-camera interviewer, and he reflects not just on hockey but on his life with the family he's billeted with as well as on what he's doing in school. As he talks about his team, Wayne seems to be a lot like any player of that time, or today—working hard to get to the next level, never taking for granted anything that he has accomplished. Of course, this belies all that Gretzky had already done in hockey, let alone the numbers he put up over the coming decades.

Most hockey fans happily condense Wayne's career into three words: "The Great One." The moniker rolls off the tongue so easily. But his nickname might better be elongated to "The Great One Whose Numbers You Really Ought To Take Another Look At." About 900 goals and 3000 points in about 1500 games, just to put it in numbers that can easily be remembered. (It's actually 894-1963-2857 in 1487 games.) What's perhaps even more astonishing is that when he was with the Kings, Gretzky often had years when his assists totaled three times his goals. These stats suggest a player who became more crafty as his career went along.

Years later, Gretzky has probably been asked the same questions a hundred times, or a thousand, but he's still willing to answer them for me in his own words, patiently, despite the pressures of coaching and, well, of being Wayne Gretzky. But he's more than a former hockey player. He's a coach and a dad. Now 10 years removed from his career, he is firmly established in the southwestern corner of the U.S., and his family is growing up a long way from the place of his roots. There is no backyard rink at his house—no possibility of it given the weather—so his kids are making their way in the world in a fashion that will not replicate the path he took. His son Trevor, particularly, has shown athletic ability, so it's only natural to ask Gretzky whether he finds it easy to mentor a son whose passion is football and not hockey.

"I think for me the biggest thing that I tell him is that right now you're just 16 years old, and you're a sophomore in high school. Really seize the moment and enjoy the opportunity of being a high school student. Your dream should be just, at this point in time, continuing on in high school and doing well in school. Hopefully, maybe the next step would be to get into college. There's a lot of work that has to go into that," Wayne says. Then he adds, "There are two things that you can't buy. One is size, which he has, and the other is work ethic. He's got good work ethic, and that's what I try to teach him all the time. If you have fun and enjoy and work hard, good things happen. Right now, just enjoy being in high school."

I ask him whether he says the same thing to his players on the Phoenix Coyotes. He smiles at the question and answers without pausing. "Oh, no," he says, "these guys are professionals. I tell them they'd better win."

So there, perhaps, is the secret. Natural ability—size in Trevor's case, amazing vision and plenty of other attributes in Wayne's—has to be nurtured. But at the same time, an element might be missing with a lot of kids who are desperate— or have parents who are desperate for them—to replicate The Great One's feats. The simple secret is that being a kid matters. A time might come when the game is a job, but until then, the key to playing the game is just that—to play the game.

chapter six

Detours and Lucky Breaks
Bob Berry

B ob Berry's NHL career might have ended after only two games—the ones he played in 1968–69 with his hometown Montréal Canadiens—and had he been like most hockey dreamers, that might have been enough. But for Berry, that glorious weekend playing against the Boston Bruins was just a start. Forty years later, Berry is still in the game, having played, coached and scouted in the league during tenures with Montréal, the Kings, Pittsburgh, San Jose and the Blues. As he says it, "It's like my friend Tom McVie always says, 'I can't believe they're still paying me to watch hockey.'" But Berry's is a career that almost never was, and one that was interrupted many times in its early stages. Time after time, however, it was one little thing or another that got Berry to the next step and prolonged his hockey life.

As a kid, and later as a young man, Berry distinguished himself as a multi-sport athlete. Aside from catching the notice of the Habs, who grabbed his rights while he was a teenager, Berry played baseball in the summer and football in the fall. Any of the three sports might have been his future. He spent some time in the Continental Football League, which had teams in places such as Wheeling, West Virginia, and Indianapolis. "I don't know by today's standards whether I could play with those big guys, but at the Canadian level I could catch a ball in a crowd," he says.

Football was not to be his destiny, though. Hockey was, but not without some stops along the way. The first diversion resulted from his parents' insistence that he get an education. "You have to remember that when I grew up, there were six teams," he notes. "And to be a Montréal Canadien or a Toronto Maple Leaf, you had to be a really special person. You went to play Junior until you were 21, and then you made the jump. But the direction I had from my parents was that my odds of playing in the National Hockey League and making a career of it and having a family were not very good. Education was always where my siblings and I were directed."

He began as a freshman at Montréal's Sir George Williams College in the fall of 1963. Only a few weeks into the semester, he reversed course. He had played hockey in Verdun and was a big scorer there, but the Junior Canadiens had a talented team in place, featuring Jacques Lemaire and Serge

Savard, among others, so the Canadiens organization told Berry that if he wanted to play, he should report to Peterborough in the Ontario Hockey Association.

"I left Sir George Williams to go down there, but when I got there I realized that all the kids were going to high school. After about three weeks of that, I thought, 'I'm not going anywhere with this thing.' So I went back and called Mr. Pollock [with the Canadiens] and told him."

Berry resumed his university studies and reclaimed his place on the college hockey team shortly thereafter, and that might have been the end of his prospects in professional sports. But then circumstances took a turn in his favor.

"That next year, Mr. Pollock took an interest in the Sir George Williams team. We ended up playing our games in the Forum. Mr. Pollock was smart enough to know that you don't write people off. People who wouldn't have been assets in a six-team league suddenly were with the 12-team league, and I was an asset," says Berry.

He played out his time at the college (since renamed Concordia University) and graduated with a BA in psychology in 1967. Then he promptly took another detour, this time deciding to try for the 1968 Olympics in Grenoble, France. He and Butch Goring (later to join forces again with the LA Kings) both became members of the Olympic "B" team, based in Ottawa. In the end, neither made the "A" team, and

Berry ended the season playing 40 games in the Québec Senior league. Following that, he returned to Montréal and decided the best course of action would be to let the Canadiens know that he was still available to play hockey if they needed him. "I thought the best thing to do would be to phone Floyd Curry with the Canadiens. I said, 'I would be very interested in the opportunity to turn pro,'" he explains.

He signed with Montréal and played on the club's American Hockey League affiliate in Cleveland. It was from there that he would have his two-game NHL debut. John Ferguson got hurt, and Berry got a call because the Canadiens were playing a home-and-home with Boston. He remembers the games distinctly. "That's when Boston had the big, tough teams. We played Saturday in Montréal. The first time I got on the ice was with Jean Beliveau and Yvan Cournoyer. And then we flew to Boston, which was uncommon. It was right around Christmas, and I stuck around though I never played again, and when Fergie came back, I got sent back down."

The next year, the Cleveland franchise relocated to Montréal, as the Voyageurs. "You want to talk about a good team," says Berry, "look at that bunch. There were about 12 guys who ended up playing in the National League—Mahovlich, Myre, Charron—there were a bunch of them." Perhaps because of that depth of talent, Berry didn't get called up during the 1969–70 season. Then, in the fall of 1970, the team phoned and told him that he'd be going to training camp in Victoria, BC, property of the LA Kings. To this day, he understands why they traded him. "They let me go because they had Rejean Houle and Marc Tardif," he says. "They had players that were better than I was. Plus, they were younger. I was in my mid-twenties because I'd been to university." It was another moment when his hockey career could have stalled. But again he prevailed.

Training camp lasted about five weeks, and the first game was in Vancouver, the first-ever NHL game to be played there. The game was going to be televised across Canada. Berry phoned his parents, who lived in Montréal. "I said, 'I don't know if I'm going to play, or whether I'm going to stay here. I don't have any idea.' That was when you dressed 19 guys," he explains. "Three lines and two extras, plus the goalies. Not like now, when it's 20. Well, I was one of those last two guys, and we won 3–1."

As he tells the story, he pauses and holds up two fingers, indicating that he had scored two of the three goals. "Larry Regan came around the room. He was trying to rebuild the team and get it on track. As he went around, I was about the sixth guy. To every guy he said, 'Good game, good start.' When he got to me, he said, 'If you think you're going to do that every night, you're wrong.'" But Regan's comment was said in jest. "I have all the respect in the world for that guy," he notes.

That performance allowed Berry to stick with the Kings, where he played over 500 games and scored 159 goals.

He remembers the feeling of being so far from where his hockey life started. "I don't think being away from the center of the hockey universe by signing with LA was a concern. I think that the adventure of playing on a team in LA was something special. Guys that I went to school with said, 'You're playing in the NHL? You're going to play in LA!' The West Coast seemed a long way away back then in the age of no cell phones. But I didn't think of it as playing in LA. I thought of it as playing in the NHL. It was kind of magical, since I didn't even know if I was going to be dressing for the first game."

Back in the '70s, NHL careers didn't last into a guy's late 30s. "When you hit 33, 34, you were done," Berry says. "Those days, unless you were Gordie Howe or somebody, you were finished. The careers didn't go 38, 39. And my second deal with the Kings was for five years. The last year, I was 35, so I knew I was done."

But again fate intervened to keep him in the game. "My last year, I was sent down to Springfield, and at Christmas the owner there said, 'Do you want to coach?' I said, 'No, I don't want to coach. I want to play,' but he told me I could do both, so I was player-coach for the last half of the season. At the end of the year, Mr. Cooke [past owner of the Kings] phoned somebody, and they told me that he wanted to see me in Las Vegas. I flew there, and he offered to let me coach the big club."

Berry's tenure with the LA Kings lasted from 1978 to 1981 and ended on a funny note. The Kings were playing in

Pittsburgh and losing. Near the end of the game, Berry noticed that the scorer was letting time run after the whistle. When the game ended, he had to cross diagonally to the gate behind the net at one end of the ice to get to the dressing room. Instead of going there directly, Berry took a detour to the scorer's table and started yelling at the guy. The incident culminated with Berry smashing the clock.

The league demanded payment, and it was over a broken clock that his tenure in LA came to an end. "I quit. I had banged the box or something in Pittsburgh. And they didn't pay it, the team didn't, and I said, 'I'm not paying it.' 2100 bucks. The guy let the clock go in the end of the game. So I said, 'I'm going to quit.' At that time, they'd probably had enough of me anyways, and they said, 'Go ahead and quit.'"

That summer, Berry got a call from Irving Grundman of the Canadiens, asking him if he was available to coach. But he might not have been were it not for that clock-smashing incident.

Before starting work in Montréal, Berry spent some time at language school, learning French well enough that he could do interviews in the language. His time in Montréal, from 1981 to 1984, saw him come full circle, in the sense that he used the smarts he'd gained from his studies as a psych major to revolutionize the Canadiens' practices.

"Years ago, in Montréal when I was there, it was line up and shoot, scrimmage, then off. The Montréal philosophy was that the cream would rise to the top. They had the best players, and they would find ways to win." Berry's approach, however, was more scientific. He used video analysis, which had been recently pioneered by Roger Neilson, and Berry changed the routine at practice as well. "One time, we had the defensemen do the whole practice with their sticks backwards, with the toe of the blade on the ice," he says. "The point was simple—you're not going to get the puck away from a guy that way, so you'd better take the body."

Near the end of his third season with the Habs, Berry was replaced. "I think my biggest failure as a coach and [not] getting to the pinnacle with the players that I had was in not giving my leaders the chance to lead. I should have given that team to Larry Robinson and Bob Gainey and Steve Shutt and Guy Lafleur. I should have given them the team and said, 'Hey, it's yours.' I think a lot of coaches do that. They say 'There's your team,' and they bring everybody with them. I'm not kicking myself, but I think that if I had given more responsibility to those guys, we would have been better."

His life subsequent to being in Montréal saw him as head coach in Pittsburgh, and St. Louis as well. Now, in his mid-60s, he's back with the Kings as a pro scout. Looking back at his life and career, you have to wonder a couple of things. How lucky has this guy been? And why does he keep working after so many years in the game?

"If you would have told me when I was a young kid that I would be 65 years old and still going to hockey games, take my right arm [he gestures], right now. I'm amazed at getting paid to come to games. It took me a while to get focused in to the hockey end of it, but sports have always been my number one passion. Growing up in Montréal, it was like the New York Yankees. It was like, 'I could never play for the Canadiens. How could that happen?' It was so exalted."

Having played with two NHL teams and been part of the staff of five, he says he'll continue to work for the foreseeable future. "You can golf in the summer. Why am I at the rink on game night at five o'clock? I love to come to the hockey rink. It's like the old question, 'How long you gonna play?' and the answer is, 'Until they rip the sweater off my back.' It's a passion."

chapter seven

Hockey in the Present Tense

Lorne Henning

You might think that someone who grew up in a town of 52 people, made the big time in hockey, won some Stanley Cups and has stuck in the game for nearly 30 years since his retirement as a player would forget his roots. Not Lorne Henning.

For Henning, life in Resource, Saskatchewan, had many of the same features as his life as a New York Islander during the team's heyday. Both places thrived on their sense of community, and both embraced a smallish guy who proved his value on the local hockey scene. And in the time since he retired as a player in 1981, despite moving around North America pursuing his hockey dream, Henning has remained true to the values he grew up with.

He played at 5 feet 10 inches and 180 pounds, and he looks much the same now, in his mid-50s, as he did when he was in the NHL. As a boy, he was always known as the small kid in the local outdoor hockey games. They'd play at night on a frozen lake, and it was so dark that the kids could barely see the puck. "That's what developed my stickhandling abilities. If you lost that puck, it took you 15 minutes to find it in the blackness," Henning says.

But when the puck did skitter off, it often fell to Henning to chase it. "I was the smallest guy, so if someone shot wide, it'd be 'Lorne, go get the puck,' since they knew I was light enough not to break through." And he'd go to the place where the ice wasn't as thick as it was near the shore to retrieve the puck.

When he moved on to playing local organized hockey, he remained one of the smallest guys, but that's because he was younger than his teammates by a couple of years. With Henning at center, the local team in Melfort, 10 miles from Resource, won the provincial championship five years in a row, from when he was a Pee Wee, through Bantam, and on to his first year in Midget. That was about the time that bigger-league hockey people started to notice him.

His discovery happened in the way that it does for a lot of small-town hockey prodigies, but the way he recounts it tells you a lot about him, because he deflects the attention away from himself as he couches the story within the tale of a recent encounter with a coach he still very much admires.

"Ernie McLean was my coach my first year in Estevan [Saskatchewan] with the Bruins. He lives out in Vancouver now. He's about 75. I ran into him last night [fall 2008] at the Canucks game, and he told me the story of how he scouted me in Notre Dame, Saskatchewan, when I was 14. He says he came right up to me and told me I should come to Estevan to play. I ended up going to Battleford first with their farm team, then playing with Estevan for the next few years. The last of those, they moved to New Westminster, BC."

For Henning, playing at this level meant he had to leave home, and the costs are something he still remembers. "I'm an only child," he says, "so it was a huge sacrifice for my parents to let me go. I didn't realize it at the time. I was so young. I also had to sacrifice school—I spent half the year at North Battleford and then half the year at home. I took some of my classes at night." The result of the sacrifices he and his family made was what every hockey player dreams of— making the NHL—but Henning found himself on a team that was to be one of the worst in league history: the New York Islanders expansion franchise. He didn't go to the draft, but he got a call the next morning telling him that he had been picked 17th overall, first in the second round. The trouble was, the team was building from scratch. "I had a long first year [1972–73]. I think we won 12 games," he recounts.

Henning retains the feeling of those first days in the NHL. His abiding memory of that time was taking faceoffs against Chicago great Stan Mikita. "I played against Bobby Orr, Hull, those guys, and you'd get to meet them. But Mikita—I liked him so much that I probably had 100 draws against him and won one of them! That was pure talent there."

It didn't take long for the team to change after their early disappointments. "Al Arbour came in. He gave us discipline and direction," Henning recalls. The Islanders went on to perform very well in the regular season. Although at first they didn't do as much as was hoped during the playoffs, they soon became contenders. In 1980 they won their first Stanley Cup. It was a moment that nobody had expected.

Fans might recall the spectacular goal, in overtime, that won the Cup. Henning picked up the puck in the neutral zone and skated back toward his blue line, then wheeled and fired a pass to John Tonelli. Tonelli cruised over the Flyers' blue line on the right side of the ice and flipped a pass to Bob Nystrom, who redirected the puck into the net. The goal set off a raucous explosion of celebration.

"We had no idea it was going to happen, and nobody had planned for what to do after," Henning says. "They opened up the dressing room, and millions of people flooded in—media, family, even fans. It was a mob scene. I didn't move for two hours. I still had my skates and uniform on!"

The unrestrained excitement was a reflection of how the local area had embraced their squad. "We were a part of the community there. Huntington, Candiac Park, these were familiar spots for us. One thing we did was play a lot of softball for charity. We'd be out there and 12,000 people would show up," he says.

Nearly 30 years later and several franchises separated from his playing days, Henning still considers the New York fans among the best. "I was in New York with the Ducks [as assistant coach] in 2002 or 2003, and we were standing outside our hotel. A truck went by and a guy leaned out the window. 'Henning, you still suck!' he yelled. I didn't mind—at least he remembered me. New York is the kind of place where you can walk across the street to the rink, and even though it's cold outside, there will be wall-to-wall people standing there. 'Thanks for the memories,' someone will often say to me."

After the Islanders won the Cup in 1980, Henning took it around to friends, a local sporting goods store and his favorite restaurant. Then he and his wife hosted a party, the kind where they invited the neighbors but also said it was OK if they told friends, who would tell other friends. The Cup win, and the party, took place shortly after Henning's son Brett was born. The new mom and dad put the baby in the Cup. He was about three weeks old. The next year, when the Isles won again, the Hennings did the same thing, getting a kick out of seeing how Brett had grown in the year.

Henning retired as a player after winning the second Cup, but he stayed with the team as an assistant coach.

That year, 1981–82, they won again. This time Brett stood next to the Cup while new brother Garrett, born in January 1982, sat in it. When the Islanders won again the next year, one boy stood on each side of the trophy, not a bad way to measure their progress. Whenever he thinks about those pictures, Henning is reminded of where he started. "My dad still lives in Resource," he says. "He has the photos. They're up in his den, near the TV."

Also in his dad's possession are the rings Henning was awarded as a member of those winning teams. His father wears the first one. The other three are in a safety deposit box at a local bank. "One for each kid," Henning comments, referring to his two boys and their sister, Marissa, who was born just after Henning took the head coaching job in Minnesota, in 1985.

Moving on from the franchise that gave him such great days, Henning worked for the North Stars for two years, the second of which saw him nominated as a finalist for the Jack Adams Trophy, awarded to the coach who has done the most to help his team succeed. But as these things go, "the team tore up the contract. I ended up sticking around, coaching my kids' teams for a couple of years. People used to joke that I was the highest paid night coach in the world," he says with a laugh in his voice. Henning harbors no hard feelings. "Being there also allowed me to go back to university and continue my education.

I had taken some classes when I was on the Island, but I hadn't had time to finish."

His future was to be in hockey, though. He was back with the Islanders as an assistant coach for several years before serving as head coach in 1994–95, and he also did stints as an assistant with the Blackhawks and the then-Mighty Ducks. He is now vice president of player personnel and assistant general manager of the Vancouver Canucks. For Henning, a life in hockey is what's right. "I love the game," he says, "being around the players, the day-to-day stuff."

When he was a boy and the table hockey set came out, Lorne Henning always had to be Frank Mahovlich. "I dreamed of playing in Toronto," he recalls. "The team came through Saskatchewan for an exhibition game, and we went to that." For a kid from a tiny town, attending that game could have been the pinnacle, but Henning has done far more than that in hockey, and he's not finished yet. "I haven't won a Stanley Cup for Marissa," he says, illustrating the point that hockey for him is not a past-tense thing. "You're at a game every night—it's perfect," he says.

chapter eight

The Ironic California Hockey Dream

Josh Brewster

Passion for hockey exists in many forms. Anyone who grew up in an Original Six city takes as a given the game's integration into the fabric of everyday life. Others might remember watching the game take hold in an expansion town. For one Buffalo Sabres fan, the home team started a passion that survived a cross-country move to a place that, logically, should not have been the spot where hockey dreams come true. But the story of how Josh Brewster went from rabid Buffalo fan to hockey broadcaster combines a bit of California dreaming, a lot of hard work and some help from the hockey gods.

"We moved to Williamsville, New York, in 1968, when I was a toddler," Brewster says. "And the Sabres arrived in town in 1970. Many of them lived in my area just outside

Buffalo, and every kid in my school had a story about which Buffalo Sabre lived near his house."

That's probably why Brewster's memories of the team's first trip to the Stanley Cup finals, against Philadelphia in 1975, are vivid but somewhat out of the ordinary. What makes the series live for him is not so much the games themselves as what he was doing during that magical run. "On the day of the first game, I was playing on a mound of dirt near my house, where they were building a new street. It was right near Gilbert Perreault's house. I know that because when he first moved in, he put his name on the mailbox. It didn't take us long to start knocking on his door for autographs. Soon after, the name disappeared. But none of us forgot that he lived there."

Life for Brewster and his buddies revolved around hockey and the local NHL team. However, in their rabid hockey town, tickets were hard to come by. "We'd get seats once or twice a year," he recalls. "First row orange. My dad's friend was a doctor, and he had them. It was the balcony. The seats were six bucks, and my first game was against the Islanders in February of 1974. When you got to those seats, all you could see down below was the giant, double Sabres logos, painted on either side of center ice. The Sabres won 5–1, but what sticks with me is that as my dad was driving out of the parking lot, I kept shutting my eyes. When I did, I could still see the images of the Buffalo Sabres and New York Islanders playing, just as if it were real. I kept doing it to make sure that the impression wouldn't go away."

Although Brewster grew up in the U.S., he, like a lot of American kids living near the border, could catch Canadian broadcasts of *Hockey Night in Canada*. The family watched the game every Saturday night. "I'm very Canadian in one regard," he claims. "I still get chills when I hear that theme song. We would endlessly repeat what we'd heard on the broadcasts, and I became pretty good at saying, in French, 'Le Deuxième Etoile, Steve Shutt,'" he jokes.

For Brewster, on-ice play was restricted to some time at a summer hockey school, but street hockey was, in his words, "how the love of hockey was formulated in all of our minds in my neighborhood." One street would play another in games that were planned days ahead. He played every day from the time he was six until about 16 or 17, often in goal.

As a netminder, Josh managed to get hold of a set of Mylec street hockey goalie pads to accompany his baseball glove and goalie stick. He also had a chest protector. The final touch was a Mylec mask—the hard plastic variety of the period—that he painted to look like the mask worn by Jim Rutherford, who was one of Brewster's heroes. Later on, when Danny Gare got traded to Detroit in December 1981, Josh got a Red Wings Gare sweater to go with the mask.

Josh's goal at the time was to be one of two things— a *Hockey Night in Canada* reporter or an actor and comedy writer. As he grew up, the former dream faded a little bit; a University of Buffalo degree in theater took precedence and led him to Chicago, where he studied and performed comedy for several years.

His stint in comedy led him to California to pursue his acting and voiceover career, and some work in television convinced him to stay. But hockey was never far from his mind, and a couple of years after he'd arrived in LA, he made a decision. "I decided to take a left turn. I was sick of the ups and downs of the acting life, and I wanted to do something that was mine. Hockey was the thing."

He wrote some blurbs about the West Coast Hockey League for *The Hockey News*, then realized that the world was changing with the advent of Internet radio. He became affiliated with a radio school and produced what, as far as he knows, was the first web-based hockey show. He called it the *Western Hockey Radio Show*, and it saw him driving all over Southern California to watch games, from San Diego to Bakersfield. "I wasn't even sure what I was doing," he states. "I just knew that here was a way to be creative, to use my abilities and training to do something I loved."

For three years, he produced radio shows and broadcast them online. Then in 2004 he created a website (www.hockeytalk.biz) and started to do shows from his home studio. A friend of his from Buffalo, Robby Takac, famous as a member of the band the Goo Goo Dolls, gave Brewster an expensive microphone and taught him to edit audio. Brewster really hit on a winning idea when he dreamed up *Hockeytalk Audio Features,* a series of shows in which he interviewed writers and hockey celebrities. Before he knew it, his website was getting more than 300,000 hits per month.

All of that was fantastic, but it didn't make Brewster anything more than a lot of other California wannabe's—until he received one very important phone call.

"I hadn't acted in about six years, but a friend asked me to do a part in a feature he was shooting. I said 'Sure,' and I took a day off work to do the job. As I was wrapping, my phone rang," he says.

"Josh, this is Aaron Teats from the Anaheim Ducks. We'd like to talk to you," the caller stated. Naturally, Brewster asked what was up. Teats responded that the team was planning to start a post-game radio show after the road games, and they wondered if Brewster might be interested in being the host.

"It will stay as vivid in my mind as that day of the finals in 1975. It was 2:00 PM, on a hot California day. Of course I told them yes," Brewster says.

But things got even better. A few weeks into Brewster's second season on the air, the regular color guy for the Ducks' TV broadcast, Brian Hayward, had to miss a game. The radio color man, Brent Severyn, was to take his place. And to substitute for him, the team tapped Brewster. It was a surreal experience.

"You get to the airport, and they wand you and whisk you onto the plane," he recalls. "They ask you what you want to eat. In my case, some of the players came over and asked what was up. When you land, you hear these sirens, and a bus pulls right up to the plane. We got to the Ritz-Carlton in Phoenix, and as we got off, I could see people looking, trying to figure out who it was. They see 25 young, in-shape guys, and it's obvious they are a professional sports team of some kind."

Once checked into his room, Brewster felt the real nerves kick in. "I've been on stage a lot, but this feeling was like the one you'd have the night of a three-hour Shakespeare performance in front of a thousand people. I mean, you look out the window, and you say to yourself, 'This is really the NHL.' There are moments when you're elated, but there are moments when you're terrified, too."

As he does for every radio call-in show, Brewster prepared thoroughly. "My philosophy is that if I don't use nine of ten pages of my notes, that's fine." In the end, the show went well, as did the Ducks' season. Brewster was a part of the team's celebrations after they won the Stanley Cup (in 2007), and he got the chance to buy a ring. It's not the same one the players wear, but it's a treasure nonetheless.

He is still amazed at the almost absurd way in which all of this came about. "I mean, why would you do hockey and

expect to go anywhere in Los Angeles, California? Six years
after driving all over the southern part of the state, for free,
doing a show for a radio school, here I am in the NHL." He
reflects some more, and says, "I didn't move to LA to get
a nine-to-five job. If I wanted that, I could have stayed in Buffalo. If I wasn't going to become an actor, I wanted to become
a hockey broadcaster."

He may yet go further with his career, not ruling out
a move to take a broadcasting job if the right opportunity
comes about. "What I like about sports is that they judge you
by what you do. As an actor, it's 'you're too tall' or 'you don't
have the right look.' But when you do sports, it's the quality of
your work that gets scrutinized," he observes.

If you measure the distance by miles, it's a long way
from Buffalo to Los Angeles, but if you judge it by the size
of a dream, it's really not so far. California is the ironic home to
a lot of hockey dreams. Ironic because in some respects, unless
signed by an NHL team, nobody goes there with hockey in
mind, but some people end up making the NHL anyway.

chapter nine

Leading the Way

Jordin Tootoo

Parents these days seem to have an equation working in their heads. Good coaching plus lots of ice time plus the most expensive gear equals a shot at the NHL. Few realize, when their kids are young, what the real costs of a professional career are. Or maybe they're more concerned with the rewards, which can be considerable. But if money and fame are what they're after, there are two problems with their math: not that many kids make it, and those who do are sometimes the product of anything but privilege.

For many young hockey players and their parents, "sacrifice" isn't sufficiently a part of their vocabulary. They don't realize that a kid with hockey promise often has to leave his family at 16 to play Junior somewhere far from home, effectively ending his childhood sooner than is normal in our culture. They don't think ahead to the homesickness or even to their own loss. But some parents do recognize the sacrifices involved, and they muster up the will to give their children up to their hockey dreams. For most, however, their boy is still a safe few hours' drive from home, and many enjoy jumping in the car and heading off to see their son play.

Contrast the foregoing with the following scenario: a kid of 13 gets on a plane to a city where he knows no one and where the lifestyle is diametrically opposed to everything he's ever experienced, and he plays hockey. He has to play. It's his only shot. That is the story of Nashville Predator Jordin Tootoo. His family made their sacrifice earlier than most, sending their boy off to play hockey in Edmonton, a thousand miles south of his home in Rankin Inlet, Nunavut. When they did so, the change the boy endured was much greater than the shift from rural Ontario, say, to Peterborough, or from the Montréal suburbs to Rimouski. He was in a completely different world. As he says, "What did I know about high-rise buildings and a big city?" What, indeed, coming from a town of 2300?

Good thing for telephones, and Tootoo used them every day his first few months in Edmonton, where he'd been sent to increase his chances of making a life for himself in hockey. "Every day was a battle," he explains. "And I called home every day. But I stuck it out."

The irony is that, looking at the map, you'd think that Tootoo had given up loneliness for company in moving to

Alberta. Rankin Inlet, on the western shore of Hudson Bay, is a town so remote that the only practical way to get there is to fly. The distance from the rest of the world wasn't the point, however.

When Tootoo left home, he had to deal not only with being away from his family but also with the contrast of going from a culture where everything is community-based to one where people live in suburban isolation. He expresses it as never feeling more alone, because he hadn't left nothingness; he had left a "community," a word that comes up again and again as he talks about his home.

"The culture shock of coming from a small community—and getting off in a city where I knew nobody—was huge," he explains. Back home, his network of support extended far beyond his family. "I got support from my community back home." The words he chooses reflect the set of values that formed him. "Coming from a small community," he explains, "you get so used to the mentality of doing whatever you can for the community, you don't think about what *you* might be doing instead."

Take into account, too, that whatever difficulties Tootoo faced on his road to the Western Hockey League— and eventually the Nashville Predators of the NHL—he wasn't "escaping" anything. He was leaving behind a typical, hockey-centered Canadian childhood, ideal in many respects.

After school, he and his friends played hockey on the streets. After dinner they headed to the local indoor arena, which, because of the −20°C (−4°F) weather outside, had natural ice. His dad was involved in minor hockey in the community, and his influence allowed the kids to get onto the ice all the time.

At home, Jordin's bedroom walls were covered with hockey posters, and he collected hockey cards. These he got from the recreation director at the arena. The man often had extra cards lying around, and Tootoo asked for them. He'd take them home and go through them, learning the stats of all the players.

One difference in Tootoo's upbringing from that of kids farther south was that many of the hockey games he saw came via VHS tapes. Another difference, and one that he credits with making him the player he is, was that he didn't always have the newest gear. "Kids today think that if they have the best stuff, they'll be the best player, but it's not that. It's your approach; it's how hard you work," he says. "I always had hand-me-down stuff, but that didn't matter."

What mattered was his spirit, which came from his parents first and his surroundings second. "My dad was a plumber and a good hockey player," he asserts. "My mom was a strong-hearted lady, a farm girl who made it, finding a way to survive." When it came to hockey, his dad's role of getting Jordin on the ice at a young age and helping him pursue his goals as a teenager was complemented by his mom's encouragement. "She enjoyed the physical part of the game," he says, and although I'm talking to him on the phone, I can sense his grin. Tootoo's parents saw promise in their son, and yet they knew that for him to progress he had to play elsewhere, to prove he was as good as he looked among the limited competition at home. Hence the relocation to Edmonton, and the need for those daily calls home, which soon took on a familiar pattern. "I told them that I didn't like the lifestyle," he says. "But they said that this is what I had to do to succeed as a hockey player. Where I come from, there's not a lot of exposure for a kid who plays hockey." So the young Inuk boy persevered, and as he matured, his goals became clearer.

In 1998, three years after he'd moved to Edmonton, he was drafted in the third round of the Bantam draft by Brandon of the WHL, where he played for four years. At that time, his goal was to make the NHL, and he dedicated himself to that goal every day. In talking to him, you notice that his focus is intense, and that he is always concentrating on what needs to be done to stay on task. It's a cliché to say that a person takes one day at a time, but with Tootoo it seems as though that's precisely the attitude that led to his success. He understands that what he does today determines who or what he will be tomorrow.

Now a five-year NHL veteran with a two-year contract reportedly worth almost US$2 million, Tootoo can be viewed in different ways in the imagination of his fans or those who observe his life. He might be taken for a guy whose hardscrabble life has produced the nasty edge that characterizes his play. They might view him as an ambassador for his community back home. They might see him as someone who will forever be displaced in the suburban world of the lower 48 states, given that he did much of his growing up 200 miles south of the Arctic Circle.

When I ask him about these ways of reading his life, he is forthright in explaining how he feels about being a role model. "I enjoy being a role model for the communities I come from. I enjoy being the first, but there need to be other firsts and other kids who do what I did," he says. Tootoo also says that none of that matters when he's on the ice. "What I think about out there is simple: get the puck in deep and get in on the forecheck."

When asked whether his family is able to attend any of his games, he says, "Sure, my parents come down and watch me play. It's not like it's some grand pilgrimage. But at the same time, that's where they're from, and it's a part of them, just like it's a part of me."

He sums up his role-model status by commenting, "I want to be true to my roots. I'm a kid who is doing what he loves, but at the same time, I go home to enjoy the wildlife and the land. That's who I am, and I never want to forget it."

chapter ten

Becoming the Official Kings Press Box Backup Goalie

In the movie *Miracle on 34th Street*, lawyer Fred Gailey has the unusual assignment of proving that a little old man named Kris Kringle is, in fact, Santa Claus. As part of his case, Gailey tells the judge at one point that he'd like to submit some evidence concerning the Post Office, an official agency of the U.S. government. He points out that the agency is bound by law to deliver mail to the person it is intended for, and then he introduces three letters into evidence. These, he says, "have just now been delivered to Mr. Kringle by bona fide employees of the Post Office."

When challenged by the state's attorney, who says that three letters hardly constitute enough evidence, Gailey has the courtroom doors opened, and a line of men, each carrying two sacks of mail, dumps letter after letter onto the judge's bench. After the pile grows so large it's impossible to see His Honor

Henry X. Harper, Gailey says, "Your Honor, every one of these letters is addressed to Santa Claus. The Post Office has delivered them. Therefore, the federal government recognizes this man, Kris Kringle, to be the one and only Santa Claus."

The judge pushes aside the stack of letters so that he can see the people in the courtroom. "Since the United States government declares this man to be Santa Claus, this court will not dispute it. Case dismissed."

It was logic something similar to this movie's plot that allowed me to become the official press box backup goalie of the Los Angeles Kings. At least, that's how I interpret the events of the night of December 15, 2008. Let me explain.

That evening, Kings goalie Eric Ersberg left the game against the San Jose Sharks with a groin injury. I watched through my binoculars from the press box, seeing him leave the bench and go down the tunnel to what I assumed was the treatment room. It seemed obvious to me that because he was injured badly enough to leave the game, he would remove his equipment for medical evaluation.

The backup goalie, on this night Jason LaBarbera, took to the net and finished the game. But I couldn't help wondering aloud, "What happens if he pulls a groin or gets a puck in the throat or something?" I wasn't wishing any ill will on the guy; I was just curious as to how an unusual situation like that would be handled, both in terms of the rules and the procedure the team might have in place. After all, I was covering the game for *Inside Hockey*, and their motto is, "Get Inside!" So it was kind of my job to ponder such things.

Having become comfortable asking questions in the post-game press conference in what was my fourth season covering the NHL, I naturally asked the Kings' coach, Terry Murray, what happens when the backup goalie gets hurt.

He responded by saying that as far as he knew, one of the other players would probably take over the position. He believed that the rules allowed for some time to get the guy properly suited up, given the unusual circumstances.

The National Hockey League's *Official Rules* Section 8.2, "Injured Goalkeeper," shows surprising silence on the possibility. It merely suggests what must happen when the netminder on the ice at a given time is hurt. According to the rule, "If a goalkeeper sustains an injury or becomes ill, he must be ready to resume play immediately or be replaced by a substitute goalkeeper." That goalie, if it's pre-season, gets a two-minute warm-up. During the regular season or playoffs, he gets no extra time. Further, he is said to be subject to the same rules and also to be "entitled to the same privileges" as the regular goalkeeper. It doesn't say anything about who that extra goalie is, although naturally it's the other man in pads when the one hurt is the starter. I began to wonder if there was an "unofficial official" rule about who the job goes to next.

I asked Coach Murray, "Is it kind of like when a baseball team runs out of pitchers, and they call the left fielder to the mound because he pitched a few innings in college?" He must have thought that "left field" was more likely the place my question came from. But he pressed on politely nonetheless.

"Well, there's no guarantee that any of the guys on the bench would want to do it, in which case we'd probably look to one of you up in the press box," Murray replied.

Now, Terry Murray is one of those guys whose humor might best be described as "Canadian." He's deadpan. He never gets rattled. He waits for you to get the joke, but even then he won't let on that he's pulling your leg. So as he said this, he cracked only the slightest of smiles.

This joke might have been the end of the exchange, the question unanswered in any serious way, except that Gann Matsuda, one of my colleagues in the press corps, pointed at me and said, "He's played in goal." Gann said this because he has read *Growing Up Hockey*, and he knows that, more than 30 years ago, as a Bantam, I had a quite respectable stint as a goaltender for my All Saints team and for another team in my league, St. James United. I was good enough that I was asked to be their regular netminder, but, scared that my skills would mysteriously desert me, I went back to my position on right wing.

My eyes flashed from Gann back to Murray. As the coach continued to talk, he looked right at me. "Well, then, I guess it would be up to you," he said.

Now to most people, Murray's statement wouldn't mean much. And you know as well as I do that they're never going to call me down from the press level of Staples Center to strap on the pads. But in my heart of hearts, I don't want to see it realistically. I want to see it in the same way that Fred Gailey saw his little white-haired old man. I want there to be a Santa Claus. So whatever the truth, I choose to believe that I am now a presence on the Kings' roster on any given night. And here's why I can say that.

Murray made his statement during an official post-game press conference, a sanctioned meeting held by the Los Angeles Kings. And Murray, as an officer of the team, is just like those postal employees who delivered all that mail to the judge's bench. He speaks in an official capacity. So, as far as I'm concerned, that makes me the team's official backup backup goaltender.

If you ever look at an official Kings lineup card, the one the coaches fill out and that is kept forever by the NHL afterwards, you won't see my name. But it's there nonetheless. It's there in spirit, or maybe better, in a kind of shadow form of invisible ink. And should you go to a Kings game or see one of their home contests on TV, you now know that high above the ice surface, I'm watching what happens.

And on the odd occasion when a Kings goalie goes down, I stand up and walk back and forth from my familiar chair to the table where the brownies are. What I'm doing, although I try not to make it obvious to my press colleagues, is gently limbering up my legs. I'm hoping that, should the moment come when someone from the GM's suite walks up to me and says, "Kennedy, the backup goalie can't go out for the third period, you need to suit up," I won't be altogether unprepared.

Hockey Hardware and Software

Which of us hasn't dreamed of winning the Stanley Cup, accepting it from the league's commissioner, then skating it around the rink? We've not only dreamed it but also done it, in our imaginations and with upraised arms as we've run around our driveways or streets or skated around our backyards or corner rinks. But how many people actually get to do this for real? In history, somewhere around 2000 individuals have won the Cup, which means, strictly speaking, that they are the only ones who should ever have touched it, aside from its caretakers. Of course, in reality, millions of hockey fans have shunned superstition and placed a hand on the trophy.

The old saying "You don't get something for nothing" is probably no more true than in hockey. Everyone in the game gives a lot, but for those few who earn the right to hoist the Cup, no sacrifice is too dear, and the memories created are never destroyed.

Hockey hardware is not only about the Stanley Cup, however. It's also about all those items the players take from the game. In the case of a lucky few, it will be a ring or two, a sweater from their All-Star appearance, maybe a puck that signaled the 100th—or 500th—goal. But for others the remnants of a hockey career are found in the form of bodies patched up with various surgical techniques and devices. For these guys, the hardware that holds them together is a badge of honor.

Fans, too, have their own hockey hardware. They treasure the artifacts that come to them—the first mini-stick bought by a parent at a game, the ticket stub of their team's greatest game, an autograph or other personal memento that indicates that, for a brief moment, they had the attention of one of their heroes. Maybe it's just a story about "the time when...." All of these items are the hardware and software that live long after the games themselves are over.

elevenchapter eleven

Holding On to Something Eternal

I've touched the Stanley Cup, but I've never won one, and I never will. That's because I was never all that good a hockey player. I have managed to get closer to the game than I ever thought I would, by creating a side career as a hockey writer, and in that capacity I get to share in a lot of players' moments of triumph. Whenever I do, I remember my own meager athletic achievements and the importance of my trophies, no matter how trivial they are in the overall scheme of sports history. I won four of them in my youth, and they mean as much to me now as they did 30 years ago.

Aside from being only so-so at hockey, I was also a terrible basketball player, but I won a trophy in the sport. Sometimes I tell this story to the college students I teach, and I ask them what they think I won it for. "Most Valuable Player," someone always says.

"You flatter me," I respond. "That's an automatic 'A' in the class. But no, I wasn't most valuable. In fact, I wasn't very valuable at all." (They know I don't mean it about the "A," either. That, they have to earn.)

"Most Improved Player," someone else will chime in. The fact is, I was as bad at the end of the season as I had been on day one. "Wrong again," I say. "I didn't improve at all. I still couldn't do a lay-up at the end of the year." But it is true that I won a trophy, and it's a pretty nice one. I still have it, and I'm proud to say that it wasn't a team-awarded cup. It was a tournament-wide award, and I was shocked to hear my name called during the ceremony at the end of the weekend and to be named the guy with the most team spirit.

I also have a soccer trophy, symbolic of my team having won the citywide championship in Peterborough the year I was in grade 10. Most of the guys from the team also played soccer for Crestwood Secondary School, which I attended, and I somehow attached myself to them and was invited to participate. I stuck out the whole season, barely played a minute and was clearly the worst player. But none of that mattered to me. It was obvious from the first that we were a stacked team and were going to run away in our league. I knew that as a member of the squad, I could lay legitimate claim to a championship, and that's precisely what happened.

Standing on the stage at the season-ending banquet, I looked out at the crowd of kids assembled and then glanced over at my teammates. I hadn't done much to deserve to be in the company of these guys, and I knew that they thought the same thing. But the other people in the banquet hall had no idea, and so when everyone on the team raised their trophies with one hand and held up the medals around their necks with the other, I did, too. And the only thing that went through my mind as I surveyed the faces below was, "I'm up here, and the rest of you aren't."

The next day, I wore the medal to school, concealed under my shirt. The only person who saw it was a guy I sometimes hung out with and other times hid from, one of those fringe kids whose friendship was more convenience than anything else. "You won that?" he asked me while we stood in front of our lockers.

"We didn't lose a game all year," I said, not sure whether to elaborate for fear of getting asked what part I had played in the championship. When he didn't press me, I let it drop. That night, at home, I took the medal off and hung it on the trophy shelf my dad had built on the wall next to my bed. It stayed there until my parents moved a couple of years later, then took up a similar position in the next house, though by that time, I was only home for the summers, having left for college.

Hockey never brought me a similar moment. The best I ever did with a team on the ice was contend for, and lose, the Peterborough Church League championship playing for Immaculate Conception during grade 12. But two hockey trophies still reside in my dad's basement. One has a tiny gold player mounted on a wood base, the other a silver puck mounted on a square, black block of particleboard. And though both are more than 30 years old, and the bedrooms where I lived are now occupied by other families whose kids probably have their own shelves of awards in them, I still keep the trophies and the memories attached to them.

The first hockey trophy I won was the best. I was about nine or ten, and for some odd reason the presentation ceremony—if you could call it that—took place in our living room one afternoon after I got home from school. I think the team's banquet had collided with my family's commitment to a church event, and my dad managed to get the coach to come to my house to present my trophy to me. It was before the banquet, as is obvious by the pictures that show a card table set up in front of our fireplace, laden with enough trophies for an entire team.

Of course, I couldn't keep the fact that I was winning something from my friends at school, so I found myself blurting it out that afternoon while a bunch of us waited for the bus. "I'm getting my hockey trophy when I get home," I stated.

I immediately regretted my choice of words. You didn't get your hockey trophy at your house, or "after school" in the way we thought of the routine of our days. You got it on the weekend, at a banquet, the very event that I couldn't attend. I changed tactics immediately, saying, "The coach

wanted to give it to me specially, with my whole family there."
I knew it still sounded slightly off, but nobody seemed to care.
They were too interested in knowing why I was getting a trophy.

"Are you MVP?" someone asked me. I vaguely knew
what that meant but was pretty sure I wasn't most valuable
anything on the squad.

"You're not a goalie on the ice, are you?" another kid
asked. The boys at my school knew I was pretty good in the
nets on the street. It was the one thing I could brag about, and
back up, and so I talked about my skills a lot at school.

"You're not getting a Vezina?" Clearly, some kids knew
more about the awards system in the NHL than I did at this
stage, which was my second year in organized hockey.

"No, I'm not a goalie, and I'm not sure what the trophy's
for," I said, knowing that if I didn't put a stop to this soon, my
story would start to look pretty flimsy. But I was telling the
truth, and one of the most frustrating times in a kid's life is
when he tells the truth but it doesn't come across as if he is. In
situations such as these, you often end up inventing something
to embellish the facts, which makes things even worse.

"What time do you get the cup?" one voice asked. Of
course he didn't mean the Stanley Cup, but the tone of reverence in his voice suggested that any trophy was somehow
related to winning the greatest one of them all.

"I'm not sure, but it's today," I replied. And sure enough, when I got home, everything was set up, and there was my dad, camera ready, with a big smile on his face.

I walked to the table and looked at the arrangement of glory that it held, and my first thought was, *Which one's mine?* A couple of them looked bigger than the others. I stole a glance at those two trophies, hoping. But some other boy's name was on one. The other was, as my friend had suggested earlier that day, for a goalie. It had a tiny netminder on top to signify it as such.

I looked at the other trophies, probably 12 or 15 of them. All of them were alike, and all were small by the standard that I had come to measure such things, which was, naturally, the "lift it up over your head" factor. I had seen the Stanley Cup winners, the Montréal Canadiens, do this with the Cup the spring before. Now, looking at these tiny statues in front of me, I couldn't imagine picking any one of them up over my head the way NHL players did. But my tinge of disappointment was salved when I noticed that each trophy had a name on it. It occurred to me that one of those names must be mine. I quickly scanned the table again, trying to pick out the trophy that I would be given.

Just then, my coach interrupted my thoughts. "You know that our team did very well this year," he began, his voice sounding formal in a pre-game speech kind of way. I immediately and instinctively snapped to attention. "Each of you boys did his part. You scored a couple of goals, and you added some assists." I thought of the puck upstairs in my room, the one I had hand-lettered in model paint the year prior as a remembrance of my first goal ever. Then I briefly reviewed in my head the two goals I had scored this season.

"So I would like to present this to you on behalf of the team…" my coach added. He then reached into the middle of the table, selected one of several identical small trophies, one I quickly saw had my name on it, and handed it over.

For an instant I wondered what I was really getting it for. Although I'd been watching the NHL for only a couple of years, I already knew that those guys got trophies like the Lady Byng and the Art Ross for their spectacular play, not to mention the Conn Smythe (which my hero, Ken Dryden, had won the previous spring while leading the Canadiens to the Stanley Cup). Even at this age, I had grasped the concept that you got a trophy for something. *What have I done to deserve this honor?* I thought. I couldn't come up with anything specific.

I shook the coach's hand and posed for some photos. Then he and my dad packed up the other awards on the table, and my coach left. I phoned my grandmother to tell her the news, fully aware that I didn't really know why I had been given a trophy. But I realized that I'd better have some way to explain it, if not to her, then to the guys in my school the next day. Back then, winners were winners, and there was no such thing as a participation trophy.

In my heart, I knew I didn't have a lot to celebrate about my play, but at that moment it didn't matter. Nor did I give much regard to my vague suspicion that my dad, as an assistant coach on the team, had probably cooked up the whole idea, and paid for the trophies, too. What mattered was that, for this day anyway, I had something eternal in my hands—and it had my name on it.

Would I trade this trophy for a Stanley Cup? In a heartbeat. I'd even give it up for one NHL shift. But saying that does not diminish its value, nor the memories it evokes of that day and the next, when I had something that all my friends desperately wanted and when my dreams of making the NHL had not yet been dimmed by the reality that would set in over the next few years of my hockey life.

chapter twelve

Not Hoisting the Cup
Phil Pritchard

Most hockey fans have lived their whole lives with the dream of winning the Stanley Cup, and in their fantasies they have probably scored the goal that won it, too. After that, the scene goes like this: you skate over to the table where they present the Cup, take it and hoist it overhead as you skate around the rink. In the version most of us live, that "rink" is the driveway or backyard where we play shinny, but it doesn't matter—we lift the imaginary trophy, our minds fill in the gaps, and the dream becomes almost real.

For some, the dream becomes more tangible with a visit to the Hockey Hall of Fame or an All-Star game where the Cup makes an appearance. Pictures are taken, and hands touch the coveted trophy in defiance of the superstition that says only those who win it should place a finger on it. But from a fan's point of view, these moments are the chance to be just one step away from the heroes of the game—Gretzky, Howe, the Richards or whichever player a person most admires.

Fans can't even imagine what it would feel like to have the Cup for themselves for a day, the way winners have since 1995, but if given the opportunity, most would pick it up like the captain of a winning team and carry it around over their heads.

Doing this would cause them to break the unwritten rule that says that only those who have won the Cup on the ice have the right to hoist it past shoulder height. So strong is this prohibition that even Phil Pritchard, known to many as the "Keeper of the Cup" and certainly the man who has spent more time with it than any other human being, alive or dead, has never raised it over his head. And it's not as though he hasn't had his chances.

Pritchard has had a lot of private time when he could have fulfilled such a fantasy. As a vice president and curator at the Hockey Hall of Fame, he is the man responsible for taking the Cup around for 100 days each summer when the winning team has it and for supervising many of its other appearances. As such, he goes to bed with the trophy beside him about 160 nights per year. But the Cup is not just sitting there, shining in the moonlight of his hotel room. It's locked securely in its case. After the day's events are over—the family pictures, the parades, whatever it might be—he takes the Cup back to his room and gives it a cleaning. Then he locks it up for the night.

Pritchard makes it clear that his time with the Cup has bred a reverence in him. So deep is his respect for the trophy and what it means that it extends to the time when the day's festivities are over and it's just him and Lord Stanley's trophy, alone. "The rule about not lifting it over your head is not written anywhere," he explains. "But it's paying homage to history. For me, I haven't won it, so I won't pick it up. I have handled it a lot, but I do that with white gloves on, to pay it respect."

But surely there are moments when, in the privacy of his hotel room, he's tempted to prance it around like he's won it? It's something that he confesses he did in his imagination as a kid, as all of us did. So I ask him why he doesn't, especially since nobody would ever know. "That's something reserved for winners only. I knew long ago that I wasn't good enough to make the NHL," he says. And as a result, he wouldn't even think of taking a privilege reserved for those players who become Stanley Cup champs. "In fact, not even all of the winners lift it up," he adds.

The example he gives is of Jakub Kindl, who won the trophy with the Red Wings in 2008. "We took the Cup to his home in the Czech Republic, but he didn't want to pick it up, though he had the right to. But he hadn't been a central part of the team, more a black aces kind of guy. He'd been up and down from Grand Rapids to the Red Wings during the season. 'This is not how I envisioned winning it,' he said to me. 'I want to do it again, and then I'll bring it home and carry it all the way down my street over my head.'"

Most players, in fact, have the same level of reverence for the trophy. "I take it to them, for their day, and the first thing they do is look for names," Pritchard reports. "Sometimes, it's of a favorite of theirs from the past. Sometimes, they look for famous mistakes, like the 'X'-ing out of Peter Pocklington's father's name from the Oilers' dynasty years.

"What happens is invariably the same. You show them all the little details, the way history has imprinted itself on the Cup, and they go from being the four-million-dollar Stanley Cup champion to being a kid in school. You end up teaching a course on the Cup right there in their living room, with all the family joining in. And you explain that they are now a part of this history," Pritchard says. Of course, their own names are not yet on it. That happens after the summer's grand tour is over.

Usually the Cup makes an appearance at the winning team's training camp. But sometimes things happen a little differently. The year the Ducks won (2007), for instance, the league opened the season the next September in London, UK, and the Cup was put on the back of a double-decker bus, where it was sitting when the players came out to see it for the first time. Pritchard remembers watching as the players exited the arena and approached to find their names on it, and he recalls seeing Brad May standing off to the side to give others their go before he took his turn.

"'B. May,' how are they going to screw that up?" the affable left winger commented. "Let Ilya Bryzgalov in there first—a guy like that has to check the spelling."

The point of the story, and of Pritchard's telling it, is simple. As he says, "Brad May is a guy who gets what this means."

The same could be said of Pritchard. He is, after all, the human being closest to the trophy, spending so much time with it that it's almost alive to him. But when reminded of this, again his respect shows through. "You know what, it just doesn't seem right," he comments. "I mean, who am I?"

Romanticism aside, he is the person who knows every nick and bump on the Cup, including the ones put on it during its yearly travels around the world. He explains that the Cup goes in for maintenance twice a year: once when it's engraved, and one other time, often before it begins its round of All-Star game appearances (not only in the NHL but in many other professional leagues as well). "It's old," he says, "you've got to tighten things up."

When the Cup is taken to the silversmith, Pritchard provides a list of the scratches and bangs it has acquired since its last repair, and the silversmith decides whether they can be polished out. For his part, the Keeper of the Cup does not regret these slight flaws. "It's a living thing—hey, you and I won't be in that kind of shape when we're 116," he observes.

Pritchard's travels throughout the world leave him with not only treasured memories but also a set of artifacts reflecting his time with the Cup, though you have to look in an odd place to find these goodies—his sock drawer.

"All my other drawers are neat," he explains, "but where the socks go, I have about 50 pairs of white gloves, including all the ones I've used to present the trophy at center ice since we started doing it this way in 1994." Each pair of gloves is carefully labeled. But even though the gloves signify a closeness with the Cup, they also suggest a distance, because they are, after all, a barrier between him and the trophy itself. "Growing up, I loved the game at every level," Pritchard says. And though it goes without saying that he loves his job, he adds, "But I'd trade it for one day with the Cup if I could see my name engraved on it as a winner."

His reverence for the history behind the trophy and the game is reflected in his answer to my question of which player on the Cup is his favorite. It's not one of the guys he has seen play, nor one of his idols from the Montréal Canadiens of the '70s dynasty. Instead, he says immediately, "Cyclone Taylor." Then he explains his choice: "Think back to the golden age of the game, and he just seems to be the guy. He started here [Ontario] and ended up in Victoria. He followed his dreams all over the country. That's not a bad description of what Phil Pritchard does too, except that these days, the dreams that accompany the Cup extend much farther than ever before.

chapter thirteen

The Hockey Face

Ian Laperriere

With some people, you can tell what kind of job they have just by looking at them. Think of wrestlers with their cauliflower ears. Or boxers with their noses smashed flat one too many times. And hockey players, especially the old-timers, often lacked at least two, if not four, front teeth. Their noses were twisted masses of flesh. Their eyes sported the scars of late-night stitches, done quickly so that they wouldn't miss a shift. Watching them on TV or seeing them in old black-and-white photos, you felt as though they wore the truth of their sacrifice like a badge of courage.

Not many hockey players look like that today, maybe because the protective equipment is better than in the no-helmet, no-mouthguard days. Or more likely, players these days aren't warriors like the players of days gone by. But nobody sent that memo to Ian Laperriere, who, as of the summer of 2009, was the veteran of 14 seasons and more fights, scraps and shoving matches than almost anyone in the NHL, ever. The evidence of his career in hockey is right there for all to see in the form of a nose that Laperriere describes as "almost touching my right ear."

It's not quite that bad, but the bend is serious enough that it even fooled a medical professional. "One night in Vancouver," he says, "I went to see the doctor after a game. I'd had a fight, and I was concerned that I might have a cut on my hand. You have to be careful to avoid an infection. As he was looking at the hand, he seemed to be rushing. I thought, 'That's funny, I wonder why he's not paying so much attention to this?' Then he reached up and tried to put my nose back in place. The trouble was, nothing had happened to it since a long time before. I told him, 'You're not going to fix that tonight.'"

Laperriere plans to get his nose straightened sometime after he stops playing. In the meantime, he appreciates the symbolism of having a face that has seen many wars. "I do have a hockey face, and I don't take pride in it," he says. Then he rethinks his answer. "Well, in a way I do—it's from how I play. I got that because I do what I do." What he does, of course, is protect the scorers on his team from the cheap shots of opposing players.

Every team needs a guy to fill that role, though it's not one that many players envy, especially when practiced night after night. But Laperriere understands the importance of his job, and a quick visit to any Internet site carrying videos of hockey fights proves his proficiency. His list of opponents reads like a rogue's gallery, and he's been at the game so long that you almost expect to see the great names from the past on it—such as Tiger Williams, who retired when Laperriere was still in elementary school.

With a record like that, and a face to match, you'd think Laperriere lived on the edge, too. In fact, he's mild-mannered. Not quite soft-spoken, he might be better described as polite and deferential, the kind of guy you would chat with when in line to pay for your grass seed at the hardware store.

Growing up, Laperriere wasn't a kid you'd ever imagine might turn into an NHL scrapper. He had the odd fight, but his life was consumed with school and hockey practice. As with every boy, he idolized the best players in the game. He was a Montréal Canadiens fan, but the posters in his bedroom were of Mario Lemieux and Wayne Gretzky. "I never turned out to be them as a player, but they were my idols," he explains.

One Christmas, Ian received a pair of hockey gloves in Montréal Canadiens colors. He was in Pee Wee or Bantam at the time, and his team also shared the bleu-blanc-rouge. "I wore them around quite a bit, and I couldn't wait to get to practice," he says. His father always made sure Ian had the right equipment. He even worked overtime to provide it for his son. "I knew that, too, and it made me realize that I had to work extra hard," he muses. He lost his dad, whom he describes as "a huge presence in my life," a few years ago.

Ian's father also contributed advice to the cause when Ian was young. "He said you need to be physical on the ice, and I always have been. He told me to go out there and finish my check." However, the elder Laperriere knew that his son had to do much more than be rough if he was going to go anywhere in hockey. When Ian was drafted into Junior hockey to play for the Drummondville Voltigeurs in the Québec Major Junior Hockey League, he commented to his father that he'd now be able to fight on the ice. "He looked at me and said, 'If that's what you're planning to do in that league, I'm not going to watch you play.'" The words stuck.

"He didn't want me to go there and be a meathead. About that time, I was figuring out that you need to get points to get noticed and get drafted [into the NHL]. You couldn't be a one-dimensional player." Laperriere found his scoring touch, netting 140 and 150 points, respectively, in his last two years in Junior. "Every guy on an NHL roster," he says, "was among the best players in the league he was in before. Everybody has had lots of points at the level before. These guys are the best in the world, playing in the best league."

As his career in Junior progressed, his parents did watch his games. His father, according to Ian, was "a quiet man who enjoyed seeing me perform on the ice." The first year Laperriere was in Junior, his parents traveled all over

Québec to follow the team, missing only three or four games all season.

Laperriere was drafted in 1992, and in 1993, between his last two years in Junior, he went to his first NHL camp. He continued with the Voltigeurs for the 1993–94 season but also played one game for the St. Louis Blues late in the year. That fall, he was in camp again, at which time he believed he could play at the level of the guys in the NHL. He played 37 games for St. Louis in 1994–95, getting 27 points (13-14-27). But he also racked up 85 penalty minutes, and his role as a middle-weight (he weighs about 201 pounds) started to develop.

His NHL tenure since then has seen him play the majority of his games with the LA Kings and Colorado Avalanche. As of spring 2009, he has over 300 NHL points in just over 1000 NHL games, and his penalty total is almost 1800 minutes. He says this of his role as enforcer: "There are hockey rules on paper, and there are rules not on paper. Those [latter] are the rules I believe in. You get involved at the right time and for the right reason. I'll be there for my guys. The day I see something happen and don't do anything about it, I'll retire. I won't be effective anymore."

Laperriere's final word about his nose puts his career into context. "It's not a trophy. It's more like a business card. It tells people what I do. They ask, 'Are you a boxer?' And I say, 'No, I'm a hockey player.' I like it when people ask me that." Along with a nose that has been broken seven or eight times, he's had more stitches than he can count, and, similar to the great hockey players of old, he's lost his four front teeth, though a bridge now fills the gap.

When asked what he thinks when he passes a mirror these days, he laughs out loud. "I'm beautiful," he says. One day, when it's time to retire, he'll get that nose fixed. "There's not much point in doing it now. I'll wait until I'm done doing this thing. And maybe if I get tired of my bridge, I'll get some teeth screwed in there, too." When he does, he'll erase some of the easy-to-read signs of what he accomplished on the ice, but his legacy will never be erased.

His contribution to the game, although different from those of the players he idolized as a boy, will remain important to the guys he played with. "You're just not going to bother one of my guys," he says. "I had 20 majors last year [2007–08] and I'm 34 years old. But this is how I play. If I stop playing this way, I'll be done. It's my game."

chapter fourteen

A Religious Ring Indeed
Jim Pappin

When a player leaves the game, he can take two things with him—memories, and whatever artifacts remain from his successes in the sport. Jim Pappin has both, which is not to say that the course of his hockey life has been all smooth sailing. It doesn't matter, though, because he looks at things with a refreshing, devil-may-care honesty.

Pappin scored the goal that won Toronto its last Stanley Cup, in 1967, but even then, he didn't know whether he'd have a job in the NHL the next fall. Indeed, he started in the minors the following season, the one that saw six new teams (and hence, double the number of players) enter the league. But that was fine with him.

"I hated [Toronto coach Punch] Imlach so much that it didn't really bother me, and I liked Joe Crozier, the coach in Rochester [of the AHL]. I had a lot better friends, teammates, in Rochester. Toronto was sort of cliquish; they had their basic team. The money wasn't that much different. I was making $7000 playing in Rochester and $8500 in Toronto. You basically had one-year contracts, one-year pro contracts," he recalls.

You can search for a long time, but you're probably not going to find a more honestly outspoken man than Pappin. While you're at it, you might also look for a guy who dealt with the twists and turns of a hockey career with greater equanimity, and you'd fail there, too. Take his approach to spending the early years of his pro career bouncing between the AHL and NHL. "The years we won in Rochester, they never won in Toronto," he says. "In Toronto, we got $7000 [bonus] to win the Stanley Cup. In Rochester, we got $5000 to win the Calder Cup. So I got a good playoff check every year." Pappin was on the Leafs teams that won in 1964 and '67, and the AHL squads that won in 1965, '66 and '68.

His career began with great promise, as he was named an All-Star in his first season, 1963–64. "That's when the All-Stars played the Stanley Cup champions. We tied 3–3. I got two goals. Gordie Howe was first star, I was second star, and Jean Beliveau was third star. That was a thrill, standing between those two guys."

That same year, he won his first Stanley Cup. "The Leafs called me up on the day President Kennedy got shot, November 22, 1963. I played quite a bit until Ronny Stewart came back. Imlach's way of doing things meant that you never lost your job because you got hurt. If you went on the shelf, and you were gone four, six, eight weeks, it didn't matter. When you got in condition and got back, you had your job back. It didn't matter how good the guy they brought up was or what happened. Anyway, I played a lot until Stewart got back, then I sort of bounced around, playing right wing with Red Kelly and Frank Mahovlich and left wing with Bob Pulford and Stewart. Then I went to the end of the bench with Eddie Shack. We were just extras in the playoffs, so I didn't get much ice time. We did win the Stanley Cup, and I was dressed for all the games."

The next NHL thrill for Pappin was that '67 Cup victory, and the goal. "Ah, it was a bit of a fluke goal," he says. "I was a right winger, and I picked the puck up on my side of the ice. Somehow I got over the blue line and Stemmer [Pete Stemkowski] cut in front of me. So I cut over to the left side and took a backhand shot. I was actually trying to pass to Stemkowski, but I got it directed towards the net, and it hit Terry Harper's skate and went in. It would give us a 2–0 lead. Later, our fellows scored into the empty net, which was a big relief." The game ended 3–1 in favor of Toronto.

Pappin also led the playoffs in scoring that year, but the irony of that season is that he had spent time in the minors. "Imlach had sent me down to Rochester that year," he recalls. "I had seven goals in February. He sent me down, and in a week I scored four or five goals in five or six games.

They called me back up, and Imlach got sick and went in the hospital and King Clancy took over as coach." The team had three established lines, which left Pappin and Stemkowski as the two extra guys. One day during practice, King Clancy told Pulford to go with the two kids and be the fourth line.

Pappin describes the ensuing events by saying, "Anyway, the following night we were playing Montréal and we were losing 2–0, in Toronto, and it was the end of the first period. Or second. Clancy told Pulford, 'You and the two kids get out on the ice.' So we went out and scored a goal to make it 2–1. He played us a regular shift, and we scored another goal in the third period to make it 2–2. I know I had a goal and an assist. And we just went from there."

Pappin got called back up with 20 games left in the season, and he scored 15 goals. As he recalls it, seven of them were game winners. "We went from fifth place to third place. So we became one of the regular lines and never missed a shift after that. We outplayed everybody in the playoffs. Our line was far and away the best of all the playoff teams."

But if you think that's what he remembers most vividly about his 14 years in the league, you'd be wrong. "I remember certain things about the Cups I won, and everything about the ones I lost," he comments. "There were two of them. Winning takes away a lot of memories, but when you lose, you never forget. We lost in 1971 and 1973, in the finals. I remember 1971 because we were up two games to nothing, three games to two, and we lost two one-goal games. We had the lead in both games. The final two games, we had the lead going into the third period of both games.

"Ken Dryden [of Montréal] made some great saves. He beat me with a minute to go. I had a goalmouth pass come across. It didn't come across real quick, but I thought I had scored. I got a good shot away, and I saw the empty net, and I thought the puck went in, but somehow he got his leg out. He stretched his leg out, and he was a big man. That was in the final game, the seventh game."

He says that this type of event stays with a player long afterwards. "You're in a bit of a state of shock. You're mad that you lost. You don't get chances to win that often, and we were so close. For about three or four years, our team could have won any year. Boston, Chicago or Montréal. There weren't really many other teams that were challenging in those days."

But back to those wins. Because Pappin's name is on the Stanley Cup, you'd imagine that he has two rings to show for it, right? Not so. "I only got one," he explains. "They used to take the ring back and give you a bigger diamond. They were too cheap to give you another ring." He laughs as he says this. "That's another thing in Toronto. They said they put a bigger diamond in it. Guys that won four times only got one ring, but it had a one-carat diamond in it. You started out with a quarter carat, and they'd keep taking the ring back and making the diamond bigger."

Even that ring has a long and perilous history behind it. "I gave it to my then-father-in-law when I got traded to Chicago. Since I was going to Chicago, I wasn't going to wear a Toronto Maple Leaf ring. He lost it in the ocean, swimming, in 1972. Never told me about it. When I got divorced from his daughter in 1982, he gave me back [what looked like] the same ring, but he had borrowed someone else's ring, and he went to the same jeweler and had another one made. When he gave it back, he told me what happened."

Two and a half decades later, the original ring was found by a treasure hunter searching the water after Hurricane Katrina stirred up a lot of ocean sand. The ring was wedged under an outcropping in the rocks. The fellow's metal detector kept going off, though he couldn't see anything there. He was in water up to his knees, and he just reached down and picked something up. He still didn't know what it was. He first thought it was a religious ring, since its features were obscured by a layer of mud.

He put it in a little pouch and went for a beer. When he pulled it out and showed the bartender, she said, "You've got a Stanley Cup ring there." Luckily, she was from Michigan, so she knew what the Stanley Cup was about. The treasure hunter kept the ring for a couple of weeks, then told a newspaper in Florida, mentioning that Pappin's name was engraved on the inside. The water had not damaged it.

"The ring is in the same shape it was brand new. I guess it was covered up pretty good. So the newspaper in Florida called the *Toronto Star* to see if they knew where I was. Through the Maple Leafs Alumni, they found me," says Pappin.

"It was unbelievable. It was impossible. So he says, 'I really want you to have it back. I've turned down $20,000 for it.' I said, 'I've got a Stanley Cup ring, I'm not paying $20,000 for it.' But he said, 'No, no, I really want you to have it. I want you to have it back.' So I told him, 'I'll tell you what, I'll find out what this ring I've got is worth, and I'll give you whatever you want when I sell this ring.' I talked to my friend Louie Angotti in Florida, and he'd read about it, and he said, 'I wouldn't let this guy have the ring too long. He might be getting better offers for it.'

"So I called him back and told him if I sold the ring for $15,000, and the dealer kept 30 percent, he'd get $12,000. That might take a month, it might take who knows how long. But I've got a fellow in Florida who will give you $10,000 in cash tomorrow and take the ring. He said, 'I'll take that.'"

Pappin now has the original ring and says that he wears it in the summertime. "I play golf a lot in the wintertime, so I don't wear it—taking it on and off—I wear it more when I go back to Canada. A Stanley Cup ring in Palm Desert, California, doesn't mean anything."

He sums up his career, which spanned nearly 800 NHL games and over 275 goals, by saying, "I'm just happy that

I played. Some guys don't even get close, don't even play in a Stanley Cup game, let alone win it. I've had a lot of luck. I've been lucky my whole life. You live life, you get a lot of good breaks. I could have gone to Hamilton and played Junior, but I got sick with the flu in Detroit's training camp, and they sent me home. I ended up going to the Toronto Marlboros, and they had good teams, where Hamilton had terrible teams. I would have ended up playing for the Detroit Red Wings, and they had terrible teams. It took me longer to make the Leafs. My first year pro, my first year out of Junior, they won the Stanley Cup, so I knew I was going to be in the minors for two or three years, whereas in Detroit I would have been called up a lot sooner. I got lucky. I played on a lot of good teams. I played 15 years, probably 10 of those years on first place, second place, championship teams."

Pappin retired in 1977. His career yielded four Cup appearances, two wins and that ring. It wasn't always an easy ride, but it was one that ended where most who play the game can only dream about.

chapter fifteen

Reworking the Software
Emile "The Cat" Francis

H e has one of goaltending's greatest nicknames—"The Cat." And no, he's not the guy who played for Toronto and other teams in the 1990s. Call him "The Cat's Cat," the original. Emile Francis earned the name because he was a lithe, small man at 5 feet 7 inches and 155 pounds. His relative slightness allowed him to move over the ice and track the play in front of him with the agility of a feline walking along the top of a fence. But Francis is known for more than just his skill in net.

He also is credited with an innovation that may have changed his position as much as the subsequent invention of the goalie mask in the late 1950s and the lightweight and shrapnel-proof equipment of the present day. His contribution to the game was in revolutionizing goaltenders' gloves. At the time, the new gloves marked a change second in importance only to the rule that allowed the goalie to drop to the ice to make a save, and that dated back to 1917–18.

He began playing goal when he attended Catholic school in Saskatchewan. His uncle was the coach of the hockey team, but when he went off to war in 1939, Francis, then 13, took over as manager of that squad as well as the baseball team. In this role he could do what he wanted on the ice, so he decided to play half the game as forward and half in net. "I was the best scorer on the team," he states, "so I'd go out and score a couple of goals. I'd tell myself, 'If I have a two-goal lead, I can win this game.' Then I'd go into the nets." His uncle eventually came back from the service and told him he had to choose a position. "I stayed in net because I wanted to play the whole game," he says. "Pretty soon, I was asked to play in Moose Jaw. One night, Scotty Melville of the Regina *Leader-Post* was there, and he wrote, 'Moose Jaw unveiled a new goalkeeper, and he's as quick as a cat.'" The name stuck.

Francis' goaltending style was the product of the equipment he wore. "When I was playing in school, there was only one set of pads. They were so big that I thought if I went down, I'd never get up, so I learned to stay on my feet." His career took him from the amateur ranks to the minor professional leagues. He made his NHL debut with Chicago in 1946–47.

Look at a picture of any goalie before the mid-1940s, and what do you see? Two big mitts that are identical.

Francis himself cites Bill Durnan as a guy famous for wearing gloves of this type. The good thing about them was that they were ambidextrous, allowing the goalie to catch with either hand. The bad thing, according to Francis, was that "the little cage where the puck went was too small." Every time a goalie caught the puck, he got it right in the palm. "I can still feel it hitting me there to this day," he adds.

His move to change the gloves was prompted by a desire to maximize one of his strongest assets, a good catching hand. He spent his summers playing professional baseball, and one year, he took a first baseman's mitt to the hockey rink to see whether the trainer could adapt it for goaltending. The trainer helped Francis graft the pocket section onto a regular goalie glove. This change allowed him to use his catching hand with greater range and confidence, shifting the advantage on any shot to his left side from the shooter to himself.

Everything was fine until he and the Blackhawks went to Detroit to play the Red Wings. At the time, players came out at 7:45 PM and warmed up, and then at 8:00 PM when the siren sounded, the referee blew his whistle, and the game began. King Clancy was the referee on this particular night, and when he skated onto the ice, Jack Adams, the Detroit coach, was yelling and screaming and pointing toward Francis.

What's going on here? Francis recalls thinking. *What's he pointing at? Is the goal judge missing or something?* He turned around to look but could see nothing out of the ordinary.

Clancy skated over to him and said, "That glove you've got on—it's too big. You can't play."

"If I can't wear this, then you don't have a game tonight," Francis replied.

It took Clancy only a second to realize that he meant it. He relented, but said, "Where are you going next?" As it happened, the Blackhawks were headed to Montréal. "OK, then. When you get there, you're going to see Clarence Campbell [the president of the NHL]. You'll show him the glove, and we'll see what he says about it."

Francis duly showed up at Campbell's office a couple of mornings later, feeling as if he was attending an inquisition. The questions came fast and furious. "Where'd you buy that glove? How much did you pay for it? Who put that cuff on there?" As he shot out the questions, Campbell looked the glove over, turning it this way and that to see what the big fuss was about.

Francis, meanwhile, answered each question with the simple truth that he had dreamed up the idea himself. In the end, Campbell agreed that it was fine to carry on playing with the mitt, and the modern catching glove was born.

The only regret Francis has, 60 years later, is that he didn't protect his idea. "Within 30 days, everyone was making a copy of it and selling it, CCM, everyone. I had no idea what a patent was back then. I should have done something like that," he says.

His innovations didn't stop there. He also invented the modern blocker. That glove, like the catching one, was made of leather with a felt pad inside. It, too, provided little protection against a hard shot. So Francis took a big sponge and the front part of a leather shinguard and taped them to the glove for protection. "I was always afraid of getting my hand broken," he says. He did this the first year he got to Chicago, because, as he says, "These guys could shoot so much harder than where I had come from."

One of those hard-shooting guys was Gordie Howe, and Francis' first recollection of him was when someone he didn't recognize came down on right wing. As the player got near the net, Francis says, "He switched hands on me and put the puck inside the far post. 'Who the hell is that guy?' I asked John Mariucci. Mariucci replied, 'Some kid they brought up a couple of days ago.'"

Francis never wore a mask in his hockey career. His nose was broken eight times, and he had over 200 stitches, which leads to a logical question: In terms of protection, why did he worry about his hands and not his face? He had, after all, played baseball, and the idea for the glove had come from there, so why not adapt the catcher's mask for hockey? "It just never occurred to you at all," he says. He remembers the first masked goalie he saw. Francis played against netminder Jacques Plante in an American Hockey League game when Emile was playing for Cleveland and Plante for Buffalo, in 1953–54. "I looked at him, and I said, 'That guy's got no balls putting that thing on. But he's got some brains, I'll tell you!' "

Goaltending back then was a treacherous business. Playing the game with neither a mask nor a man sitting on the bench in the role of backup was only for the bravest. Francis' worst injury occurred when he was playing for the New Haven Ramblers, the farm club of the Rangers, in the late 1940s. A big defenseman had been standing in front of him, a guy who was about 240 pounds but who couldn't move all that fast. As a result, he screened his goalie. Francis recalls with pride that he was an extremely agile player, and so if he ever got hit with a shot, it was always on a deflection. Not this night.

Terry Reardon of the Providence Reds wound up from the blue line and shot. The defenseman ducked but didn't give Francis time to see the shot. The puck hit him square in the face, breaking his nose and taking out five front teeth. The next thing he knew, he was back in the dressing room.

Frank Boucher, who was his coach, asked the doctor, "Is there a bar in here?" When he got an affirmative answer, Boucher said to someone standing nearby, "Go out and get a glass of brandy right away."

Francis drank the brandy, and the stitching started. Half an hour later, the repair work was done, and out he went to resume the game. "I had never had a drink of whisky in my life," he recalls. "I was half in the bag. I swear, if I'd gotten hit in the head again, I wouldn't have noticed." He went home after the game, and when he woke the next day, his nose was three inches from where it should have been, and his eyes were black and almost shut. He spent "one horrible morning" at the doctor's office getting further treatment for his injuries.

He sums up that experience and his position by saying, "A goalkeeper is like a race car driver. When something happens, you get back in there as quickly as you can, or else you'll lose your nerve. You get back in and face the bullet." But Francis also says with regret that a lot of guys were chased from the game by their injuries.

In addition to the danger, goaltending in his day was something of a lonely position. Back then, nobody gave the goalie any advice—not even the coach—and there were no tapes or books to give the netminder any pointers. Everything he learned about the position, Francis acquired on his own. But the one thing a goaltender could do was ask other goalies for some advice. One night, while playing against netminder Frank Brimsek of the Boston Bruins, Francis skated past him at center and said, "Can I meet you after the game?"

Brimsek agreed to meet with him, and Francis asked him why he was getting beat to the side of his catching hand.

It was especially troubling, since Francis always prided himself on having a good glove. Brimsek asked him whether he played baseball, and Francis naturally replied that he did. "What position?" He told Brimsek he was a shortstop.

"That's the problem. You're playing the shot like you're charging a grounder. You're moving out too fast as the shooter comes toward you and backing in. You're so far back when he lets the shot go that you're missing it by a couple of inches," Brimsek said. "You need to slow yourself down, and by the time the guy is in shooting range, 20 or 30 feet out, you'll be right on the corner of the crease where you need to be."

He followed up by asking Francis what lie of goal stick he was using. "An 11," The Cat replied.

"I use a 13," Brimsek countered, "and I think you should try it. It will make you stand up more, lifting your body up higher. You'll cover more net." Francis thanked the two-time Vezina winner, and the men parted company, each again alone to face his dangerous and uncertain job.

Francis played professional hockey for 15 years, retiring in 1960. He then went on to coach and manage his way into the Hockey Hall of Fame in the Builders category. His recollections of that golden era of hockey are rich and specific, including the names of people and the dates of significant events.

His most vivid, and horrible, memory is when he had to identify Terry Sawchuk in the morgue in New York City the morning after he died as a result of what has been described as a playful fight with a teammate.

"I went in there, and all I could see was his head. This was on Memorial Day weekend, and there were probably 30 or 40 people who had died in New York, shootings and all kinds of things, and I saw this bag that looked like a hockey bag, the kind we carried sticks around in," Francis recalls. "I saw his head, and the tag they'd tied on him. 'That's him,' I told them. I went home, but I didn't sleep for three days thinking about it."

Emile Francis can be credited with three things—his innovations of behalf of goalies, his place in the administrative end of the game and a memory that lets him recall events as clearly as if they happened yesterday, not half a century ago. When I mention this to him, his response is immediate. "Thank God all those hits to the head didn't blank me out," he says with a laugh.

chapter sixteen

Always Cool and Relaxed
Rogie Vachon

Where Rogatien Vachon grew up 400 miles north of Montréal in the 1950s, there was no indoor rink, so his brothers and cousins played in one of two places—on the frozen river near the family's dairy farm or on a local outdoor rink. Whenever they gathered, "Rogie," as he would later be known to the hockey world, would turn up, eager to play. He was one of the smaller kids, so his brother would tell him that he had to be in goal.

The kids didn't have any equipment, so Rogie strapped the biggest Eaton's catalogs he could find to his legs. His gloves were oversized mittens. Of course, at that time, goalie masks weren't used, and in net, he didn't wear skates but played with boots on. The kids also made their own sticks, either by nailing some pieces of wood together or going out in the woods and finding a curved branch, which they stuck into the furnace until it was pliable then bent it into the shape they wanted.

Vachon must have been pretty good in the nets, because by the time he was 12, he was playing organized hockey—against men. No kids' leagues existed where he lived, but each village had a team made up of area farmers, and Vachon played on his local team. "There were not many guys crazy enough to be a goalie and stand out there in the minus 10-degree weather for 60 minutes," he says. "I would, so I had the job."

His skills were impressive enough that in two years, when he turned 15, he made it onto the radar of the Montréal Canadiens. It was the team he had grown up idolizing as he and his seven siblings sat by the big battery-powered radio in their living room on Saturday nights and listened to *Hockey Night in Canada*. "There were bird-dogs in every town who would see you play. Then, the idea was that the NHL teams would get you to sign the C-Form, and that committed you to them forever. You might not make the [NHL] team, but you belonged to them," Vachon explains. So it was that Cliff Fletcher and Ron Caron drove 400 miles up from the big city to lock up Rogie's services. Vachon and his parents sat at the kitchen table, and he signed. He didn't get any money for making the commitment, but it meant that he might have a future in hockey.

All he was hoping for was to imitate his idol, Terry Sawchuk, his hero since Rogie was small. "Maybe it was the name itself," he says, "but he seemed to make more saves than anybody else on the radio when we listened as kids."

A couple of years after signing with the Canadiens, Vachon was in Montréal playing for the Junior team. After a stint there, he went to Québec of the American Hockey League and then was assigned to Houston of the Central Professional Hockey League. During that season, 1966–67, he got the call every prospective NHLer waits for. "Charlie Hodge was not doing well as the backup to Gump [Worsley]," he says, "so they brought me to Montréal."

He hadn't been there long when, one night before the warm-up, the trainer handed him the puck. Toe Blake was the coach in those days, and that was his method of letting players know who would start in goal. He hadn't given any hint earlier in the day, although Rogie says, "We'd have a good idea. I knew that if Gump had won six games in a row, they weren't going to change anything." That night it was different. "I was in shock," he recalls, "but then I had to go out and do the warm-up."

Starting in net was hard enough to take, but imagine how he felt early in the game when he saw defenseman Ted Harris staying up on the Detroit blue line while Gordie Howe sneaked in behind him. The pass came to Howe, who carried the puck down the wing. He had his head down, but at one point he looked up to pick his spot. His head went down again, and Rogie charged out of his net to challenge the shot. Howe blasted the puck, picking a low corner from 20 feet out. Vachon stopped it with his pad. His summary of the save tells all. "That probably kept me in the league for a while," he says.

The next year, he and Worsley split the season almost exactly in half, with Rogie playing in 39 games and Gump in 40 (the regular season was 74 games, so obviously, they shared a few outings). They shared the Vezina Trophy, and for his troubles, Vachon got a plaque with an image of the trophy on it, which he still has.

Throughout Vachon's early career, his parents took great pride in his success with the Habs. They drove down to see the games, and his mother would sit in the stands, turn to the stranger next to her and say, "See in the goal? That's my son."

Playing for Montréal in those days was such an honor that a player didn't dare ask for anything, especially if he was a backup goalie, which Vachon was in 1966–67, the year he came up. "They gave me number 29, and that's what I wore," he says. "When you become the number one goalie, then you might ask for the number you [wanted]. After I had played a year or two, I asked for number 30." It was the number that became synonymous with his career, and the one the LA Kings retired a couple of decades later, on Valentine's Day, 1985.

Early on in the NHL, Vachon played without facial protection, but he soon changed that. Throughout the 1960s, goalies around the league were experimenting with masks, and Vachon says that the primary reason for using one was to avoid getting hurt in practice. "There were so many shots," he says, "and guys shooting crazy—two-on-ones, three-on-ones. You could get hurt so easily." He went to a fellow in Ottawa who was the master of the trade at the time and had a mask molded for his face. The trouble was that in those days, masks were merely a fiberglass piece. They didn't have padding. "So you'd save a bunch of stitches but end up with a concussion," Vachon says. He had trouble getting used to the mask—the old Toe Blake complaint that vision would be a problem came true in Vachon's case. To compensate, his mask had bigger eyeholes than most other goalies'.

Like goalies do today, Vachon nursed many superstitions in his years between the pipes. When things went well, he ate the same meal at the same time of day as he had when the streak started. He went to bed at the same time every night and took exactly the same route to the Montréal Forum. He also used the same goal stick until it was completely broken. To prolong the stick's playing life, he reserved it for game action only, and he retaped it frequently. "The sticks used to get cracked before they broke," he says, "so I would get an extra-heavy tape and put that underneath, then take the normal hockey tape and use it over top." Once warm-ups were underway, he would take a few shots, then go to the side of the rink, take a few more shots and go to the side again.

Vachon was always cool and relaxed, even during play-off days when he knew he would be in net. "We'd bus out of town to a hotel for the afternoon to rest, then take a bus back to the Forum for the games," he recounts. "I'd fall asleep on the way. I'm still like that, and my wife is always telling me, 'Hurry up.' I'm calm—nothing bothers me."

His four and a half years in Montréal brought him three Stanley Cups, in 1968, '69 and '71, though in '71 he didn't play during the post-season because the team had brought up Ken Dryden. Back in those days, the Canadiens didn't give out rings but instead included extra money in the pay envelope. "A couple more thousand bucks on top of what the league gave to the winners," he says. One year the players also received a color TV and a tiny replica Cup.

The summer after the last of those wins, Rogie went to GM Sam Pollock to ask what his future would be. Pollock told him that Dryden would probably be the team's number one goalie, because he had taken them through the playoffs and won the Conn Smythe Trophy as playoff MVP. Rogie asked to be traded, because he wanted to be the number one goalie somewhere. He went to the Kings in November 1971 and played six and a half amazing seasons for a team that often was not very good in front of him. The team in those days was a freewheeling bunch, until Bob Pulford, who took over in

1972, established his way of doing things as coach. "We had a lot of work to do," Rogie says. "We had to win games, and we needed to build a fan base. Pulford had a system, a boring system that would let us win 1–0, but it worked." Vachon had 32 of his 51 career shutouts while playing 50, 60 and 70 games a year. The best year the team had was 1974–75, when they logged 105 points.

Vachon left California for Detroit when he couldn't come to a long-term agreement with the Kings in 1978. They offered him three years, but Detroit offered five, so he went. He began as a Red Wing wearing number 40. "I had never had it before, so it seemed like a good idea," he recalls. Number 30 was taken by third goalie Ron Lowe. "It didn't work so well, and I got 30 back after that." After two seasons with Detroit, he played another two in Boston, then retired.

Vachon took from the game a lifelong association with the Kings, a team he has worked with for most of the time since he finished playing, and a lot of memorabilia. His last goalie mask was bronzed for him by the players on the Kings team in 1985 and was presented to him during his jersey retirement ceremony. The team also gave him a replica sweater enclosed in a glass frame. And as for the stock-in-trade of the goalie, the pads, he kept the last pair he'd worn in Boston. In those days, goalie pads were leather, and he used to oil them to help them retain their shape. They were stored in his California garage for years, and when he went out to check on them one day, he found that the oil had destroyed them. The pads went out with that week's garbage.

If one piece of hardware is missing from his collection, it's the plaque given to those inducted into the Hockey Hall of Fame. One wonders why he isn't there yet. Most assume it's because he toiled too far from the spotlight during the heyday of his career while in LA. But people who remember the Worsley-Vachon tandem of 1967–68 or recall that he played eight of the 14 games Montréal took to win the Cup in 1968–69, not to mention his almost mythical role with the Kings through the 1970s, will agree that he ought to be in the Hall of Fame.

Ironically, Vachon's first mask has a place in the Hall, and Rogie says with a chuckle, "I'm not in the Hall of Fame, but I've been there before." His comment reveals the relaxed nature that helped him survive the stresses of goaltending in the days of relatively poor equipment, an era when he was constantly tested by increasingly dangerous shots. But to genuine fans of the game, his words also reflect the hope that Rogie will soon find his way back to Toronto, this time as an inductee.

chapter seventeen

What Would You Do with 1500 Sweaters?

Brian Slagel

E very true hockey fan has a game-replica sweater or two. The strategy in collecting them is usually to get one from your favorite team growing up, and one from your newly adopted team if you've moved away as an adult. But how about a guy with something over 1500 hockey jerseys?

It's inevitable with a collection that large that you'd end up reaching into some far-flung spots in the hockey universe, and that's exactly what Brian Slagel has done. Ever hear of the Tucson Scorch? They were supposed to play in the Western Professional Hockey League back in 2001, but after selling a handful of season ticket packages, the team folded without ever having hit the ice. Still, a few sweaters were produced, and Slagel has a couple of them.

He also has a jersey from the Miami Manatees, a team that lasted only half a season in the World Hockey Association 2 back in 2003–04. Add to that the remaining uniforms of the Tucson Gila Monsters of the West Coast Hockey League, whose equipment guy was Brian's friend. When the team tanked, Brian got a call. "You want this stuff? We've got a ton of it." He did, and what he has is stored along with the rest of his hockey memorabilia.

How does a collection grow to such huge proportions? Sometimes, a deal is simply too good to resist. Witness the time he got a call that the Lexington Men O' War had 50 jerseys they were selling off after the team folded following one season, 2002–03, in the East Coast Hockey League. "They wanted something like 200 bucks for the lot," Brian says. "So I said I'd take them. It's a way of kind of keeping the team around."

His fascination with the game began somewhat by accident. He grew up in Woodland Hills, near Los Angeles, and got into hockey when a friend of his came by a pair of Kings season tickets in 1982. The buddy got the seats for having done some work at the Forum, where the team played from 1967 to 1999. He offered them to Slagel for $100, who thought, *Why not?* He had no idea what he was getting into.

Before long, Brian was going to about 100 games a year as the result of holding season tickets with four different teams. He also traveled to see new teams, and he figures he's been to about 200 arenas in both North America and Europe.

He and friends from around the U.S. also exchanged tapes of games in their areas. Slagel's hockey collection includes about 1500 games on VHS from all over the hockey world. They're in a room at his house that functions as the library, along with his CD collection. That, too, is huge, but as much for professional as personal reasons.

Slagel is the founder of Metal Blade Records, which promotes the bands As I Lay Dying and Cannibal Corpse, among others. In the early 1980s, around the time he was falling in love with hockey, he was working at a record store and going to concerts all over the LA area. A bright guy by any measure, he did what other successful entrepreneurs do—he found a gap in the market for a specific product. "Back then," he explains, "there were no A&R [artists and repertoire] guys doing the metal scene, so I started a fanzine. Then I decided to put together a compilation album." And this is where his lucky break came.

"I had a friend who went to a concert, and he saw this guy with a European metal band's T-shirt on, standing in the parking lot. He went up to him, and they talked. The next day, we all hung out together. A while later, the guy called up and said, 'Hey, if I put a band together, could we be on your album?' I said sure." The "guy" was Lars Ulrich, the drummer for Metallica.

In the early days, Slagel worked with such bands as Slayer. Today the company has about 75 acts under contract on its label. Most of them would be unfamiliar to hockey fans of a certain age. However, the music sells, with numbers anywhere from 10,000 records to half a million units for each act that the company handles. He describes the audience as a combination of young people and those who grew up with certain bands and retained their interest in them despite having moved on to subsequent stages of life. The company is now nearing three decades in business, and it is this success that has allowed Slagel to indulge his hockey passion.

At some point, of course, passion becomes mania. Think about it—how much space would 1500 sweaters take up? And where would you store them? Hockey stuff would be flowing out from under every bed and peeking out from every closet. In Slagel's case, he has ways of dealing with the volume of his treasures. His house near LA contains the choicest of his collection, prime NHL pieces to go along with the array of minor-league stuff. He's a fan of both the Kings and the Penguins and has game-worn sweaters from Gretzky, Lemieux and Jagr, as well as rookie cards of all three. He also has a signed Lemieux jersey from the Stanley Cup days of the '91 and '92 seasons.

Recently a friend helped arrange the game-worn sweaters. The rest of his collection is semi-organized, and a lot of it is at another place he owns, in Phoenix. "If you asked me to find something, other than a game-worn sweater," he says, "it might take me 15 minutes to come up with it." It helps that the VHS collection is alphabetized.

Slagel began collecting back when there was no Internet, so he had to seek things out himself, dealing with authenticators and dealers individually. The advent of eBay both helped and hurt his mania for collecting.

"When eBay came along, that was a big problem for me," he says with a laugh. The auction site was an enticing way to gather new stuff, and that's just what he did. But eBay also diminished the challenge, because it suddenly made everything so readily available. This was part of the reason for Slagel's focus on the more obscure corners of the hockey world. He mentions "pucks of teams [that] didn't even exist" as items he looks for to go along with the sweaters.

"Being a huge hockey fan, I am engrossed in any and every part of it. I love it that there are fans in cities where you wouldn't expect there to be hockey," he explains. He is excited about promoting hockey in places where, in some ways, it has no right to exist. He cites spots such as Hidalgo and Laredo, Texas, as examples. "'Tropical Texas,' they call that part of the very southern tip of the state," he says. "Laredo, near McAllen, Hidalgo, these places have teams that develop big rivalries. It's good for the game."

Along with spending less time collecting, he attends fewer games now, maybe 15 or 20 per year, and technology has superseded the need to exchange tapes with friends. Instead, he has two satellite dishes capturing games, including a Canadian one that allows him to keep pace with what the six teams north of the border are doing, but his involvement with the game hasn't lessened, only shifted.

His record company supports minor league hockey in the form of promotional deals. The San Antonio Rampage and the Wichita Thunder wear warm-up jerseys with the Metal Blade Records logo on them, giving the teams much-needed revenue boosts. Recently, his involvement has gone beyond that, into investing in a company related to the Central Hockey League. Its mission is to build arenas in new cities, and they've recently done so in Youngstown, Ohio; Fort Collins, Colorado; and Prescott, Arizona. A side benefit of these 5000–6000-seat venues existing in such places is that concerts can take place there. "These days, you don't sell out a concert in a huge arena, but concerts in those places are sold out in 10 minutes," he says.

Slagel is not certain what will happen to his collection down the road, only saying, "I'm sure somewhere down the line I'll find something to do with this stuff." Running his business takes up most of his time these days, so he hasn't given much thought to what's next.

One can only imagine an archeologist coming upon Slagel's treasures 500 years from now and trying to put together the pieces. "How do the Pittsburgh Penguins and the Lowell

Loch Monsters relate?" might be the question of some far-off academic conference presentation. The answer would be simple: both teams outlived the ruin of the world caused by global warming—all because of the fanaticism of a hockey guy who is probably doing as much to preserve the artifacts of the game at the minor league level as anyone else in Canada or the U.S.

It's a lucky thing that, to Slagel, hockey is much more than the NHL. His passion for hockey artifacts has turned him into a sort of amateur hockey historian, and in the long term it's the game that will benefit from his interest in the distant reaches of the North American hockey scene.

chapter eighteen

Still My Favorite Way to Spend Time

S ince *Growing Up Hockey* came out in 2007, a lot of people have asked me how long I've been writing about the game. My first response is to say, "A few years, since I got the lucky break I talk about in the Mark Hardy chapter." However, thanks to my tendency to obsessively hoard old stuff, and my equally maniacal need to revisit the past every chance I get, I recently discovered that this statement is not true at all. In fact, I started writing about hockey in the 1970s.

There has been no consistency in my efforts from that time to the present, I must confess. Stints as a motorsports journalist and academic essayist, both crafts I still practice, have taken far more of my attention since my early "work" in hockey. But in the interest of fully disclosing the facts and honoring my grade eight Language Arts teacher, Mrs. Wilson, from Queen Mary school in Peterborough, Ontario, I offer this piece of writing, an essay written for her class.

My Favorite Way to Spend Time

My favorite way to spend time is playing hockey and watching hockey. In the summer, my friends and I play road hockey. We get as many of us as we can, and we play. We play on the street, using old hockey sticks from the previous hockey season, or plastic blades which last longer.

The goalie uses an old baseball glove to catch with. We play with a tennis ball. It is better when we have more players, because then the games are more fun. We play a game which goes up to either 10 or 20 goals, depending on the time we have.

Sometimes, we quit when we get tired, or have to go in. For nets we use two pieces of anything we can find or we can use two rocks for posts. The game is fun and it gets you outside. It is good exercise and it helps you develop moves and fakes for when you play ice hockey. It gets you together with friends in something you enjoy.

I don't know why we like road hockey so much, but that's what we do just about all summer.

In the winter, I enjoy playing ice hockey. I play for All Saints. I also enjoy watching hockey on TV. My favorite team is the Montreal Canadiens. I have been to see the

Canadiens play in the Montreal Forum twice. The first time they played the Boston Bruins. They won 6–2. The next time they played the New York Rangers. They won 4–1. I don't know why I do, but I love hockey.

OK. The essay's pretty much crap, but I will say that the editing isn't too bad, especially for a 13-year-old. I thank Mrs. Wilson for that and try to pay it forward with the college students I teach now.

However, aside from noting the good punctuation, I have to say I'm underwhelmed by the lack of passion this piece expresses. Where, I ask myself, is the magic of the game? What about the mounds of detail that I dredged up almost 30 years later when I wrote about our neighborhood games in *Growing Up Hockey*? Where are the people who populated my street and gave life to the games we played? When I came to write down my childhood recollections in what became *Growing Up Hockey*, I found that memories flooded back, mainly because my Montréal childhood was populated by such a vivid bunch of characters. The villains, the loyal friends—they all reappeared in clear detail.

In the piece above, the specifics are hiding, because I'm writing like Ralph Parker does when he composes his "theme" for Miss Shields in *A Christmas Story*. His strategy, watchers of the movie may recall, was to use the essay as a way to appeal to the powers that be for a BB gun for

Christmas. His audience, as he perceives it, is the adults who act as the gatekeepers to the gifts that kids want the most.

In the essay, I'm not quite thinking of Mrs. Wilson as a gatekeeper, but I am trying to show my earnestness, because I want desperately to have her believe that I mean what I say. What I didn't realize at the time was that real details would have won the day more effectively than assertion and repetition that something is true.

Perhaps that day at Queen Mary, I was too close to the moments themselves to see what they meant. Or maybe I was simply unable to marshal the voice to say anything more than what was obvious to me at the time because I had become part of what Ralphie calls "the faceless rabble"—the vast horde of kids who are just average. In hockey terms, by the time I was in grade eight, I was a kid for whom the game would never be more than an amusement, and not something that I could even remotely hope would be my future. That's the difference a few years can make. When you're eight, you're going to be in the NHL. By 12 or 13, you pretty much accept that you won't.

Still, I think two important glimpses into the past are featured in the essay. First, it confirms to me that my childhood recollections are right. The life my friends and I lived was vastly different from the lives that kids live now. We didn't have a pair of nets to play with. We used whatever we could find for posts. (This was in Peterborough, mind you. In Montréal, we had a net, a square aluminum one,

smaller than regulation.) We didn't have fancy equipment—
we played with baseball gloves and whatever old sticks were
left over from the previous season.

Second, I didn't mention the goalie equipment I owned
at the time, the stuff I had so cleverly conned my parents into
getting me over the period of several years during my days in
Montréal. This included a goalie mask, pads and a pair of
gloves. The latter I still have. Why didn't I talk about them?

I didn't mention my new equipment because at the
very moment I was writing the essay, my life as an on-ice
goalie had begun. It was the fall during which I was making
a magical transformation from a street hockey goaltender
into one who played for real, through a series of events that
I describe in *Growing Up Hockey.* In that book, I say something
like this: "I didn't dare tell anyone at school that this
[my success in nets on the ice] was happening." Usually, my
friends and I bragged about our hockey exploits at school, but
I kept my goaltending success to myself, afraid that talking
about it would cause the magic I was marshalling to somehow
disappear.

Writing about it in the essay, or simply stating that
I had a proper, if not complete, set of goalie equipment, would
have aroused immediate suspicion in my classmates. Why, if
I had this stuff, wasn't I willing to bring it out to our street
hockey games? Because I was hoarding it for use on the ice.
But that was my secret.

What I couldn't know back then was that my great days as a goalie, a position I was so good at that I scared myself, were going to be so brief. Had I recognized this reality, I would have probably talked about my success, taking in some of the glamour of playing the position of the great Ken Dryden. But I couldn't, or didn't.

Nor could I have foreseen how hockey was soon to become something that I feared playing more than loved. It was right around this time that the game was becoming too rough for a house-league third-liner like me, and before another year or two passed, I had hung up my skates for the first time.

All of that is absent from the essay, but the one detail I do note is the scores of the NHL games I went to. I reckon that having a record of the scores would help me figure out the exact dates of those games, should I ever need to know them. (And given how I enjoy reliving the past, that's not at all unlikely, though I still have the game-day programs my dad bought me, which would also be a way of retracing the facts.) But aside from that, mentioning those scores shows me that I had thought about those games a lot and talked about them with my friends. After all, they had taken place at least three or four years before this essay was written, but I remembered the number of goals that were scored. And it shows me that, even early on, I was concerned with preserving exact details of the past.

Perhaps equally revealing is the list I made directly below this essay in my exercise book, likely also in response to an assignment my teacher had given. It contains the "Ten Most Important Things in My Life." But rather than 10, I list 15. And rather than decide on the first one, I indicate a three-way tie: "1. Parents, sister, Gran."

I suppose I could have just said "Family," but I chose the break-out method instead, with my grandmother, who had done as much as anyone in my life to instill in me the love of hockey and especially of the Canadiens, coming in at the same level as my immediate family.

Hockey comes fourth on the list, after "God" and "Money." School is fifth. Books are tenth. Girls end up fourteenth—they were originally twelfth, but they got bumped in favor of "Accordion." (Why I quit piano for that instrument is another question I will never have an answer to.) Looking back, I suppose I would say that books should appear higher on the list. Not those I've written, but those I've read. I did end up earning a PhD in English and becoming a professor, after all.

Hockey, however, probably got about the billing it deserved, and anybody lucky enough to have kept it in his top five as I have, despite the pressures of surviving in the adult world, is, to my way of thinking, a pretty lucky guy.

SECTION THREE

Hockey and Family

"Hockey creates family." "The NHL is one big family." I'm not sure if anyone has actually said these things, but if they have, they're speaking a seeming contradiction. How can a game where men skate full speed and smash into each other with the intention of separating another person from the puck give someone a warm-and-fuzzy family feeling? It seems absurd. Yet the dynamic of family is quite important for many of those in and around the game.

Hockey binds people together. It gives them common goals. It makes them a part of something larger than themselves, and for those few who win it all, the game helps them identify with a group of guys (or women) who will always be that team. But before they ever achieve prominence in hockey, players have to deal with the challenges of growing up, and a common thread among many who succeed is strong support from their folks, starting at a young age.

Maybe it only makes sense that a kid can't become good at a game that demands constant practice, a lot of it happening at six or seven o'clock on weekend mornings, without the whole family getting involved. At some point, too, there's no choice—the make-or-break moment comes when the parents have to decide whether giving up a few years' worth of weekends is worth the chance that their kid could be the next NHL superstar. As the pressure mounts, so do the hopes.

You could think about it the opposite way, though. Maybe families grow stronger because of the demands placed on them by the game. Doing so much together, and having such grand hopes riding on what happens, can't help but make them appreciate each other in ways they might not otherwise.

chapter nineteen

Strapping on the Pads
One More Time

W hen I was about eight or nine, a cousin of mine and my aunt came to stay for a few days at our house in Montréal. Before they arrived, my sister and I were prepped for the visit. "Randy is here to go to the hospital," my mom told us. "He's having bad seizures, and they can't do anything for him down home." She meant in Fredericton, New Brunswick, where they lived.

For days I wondered what I might see when Cousin Randy came. Would he have a seizure in our house? What would we do if he did? Would his physical problems be something visible? If that were the case, was I supposed to act as though everything was normal?

The mystery was solved the day my dad brought them home from Dorval Airport. My sister and I peeked out of the upstairs window, the one in her bedroom, watching them in the driveway. Out of the front seat of our Ford Country Squire station wagon popped a woman who looked a lot like my mom. From the back seat came a kid a little bit older than my sister and I. He looked no different from any of the older boys in our neighborhood.

With relief we went downstairs to greet them. After being introduced, I said the first thing that popped into my mind. "Do you like the Montréal Canadiens?" I had no idea what team someone from New Brunswick followed. I had only been to the province once, to see my grandfather, when I was about four.

"They're OK," Randy replied. "But we like the Boston Bruins." I found out years later that if my mom had any team preference in hockey, it was for the Bruins. It stemmed from where she had grown up, in New Brunswick, and the fact that people there were big Red Sox fans in the summer because they listened to the Sox on AM radio back in those pre-TV days.

Randy's response sort of jolted me. The only other people I knew who liked the Bruins were my parents' friends and their kids, whom we called "cousins." We saw them twice a year, once when they came up to Montréal, and once when we went to Massachusetts to visit them. The last time we'd been there, they'd played street hockey with me. I had pretended to be Ken Dryden when I was in net, though their preference was for Gerry Cheevers. I briefly wondered how I could relate to Randy if the Bruins were his team, too.

Thinking about street hockey brought me back to the present. *That was it. I would connect with Randy that way.* "Do you want to go outside and take shots?" I asked. It was something I did with my friends in the neighborhood almost every day of my life.

"Sure. I don't know how to play in goal, though," he replied.

Although I was the younger cousin, I immediately felt the power of my position. "I'll show you," I said over my shoulder as I started out the door. "I have the pads and everything." I had recently convinced my dad to buy me a set of goalie pads. After that came my goalie mask. Then my mom brought me some gloves home as a present from a business trip.

Out we went to the driveway, and I told Randy to lie on the grass while I strapped the pads on him. They were a little short on his legs when he stood up, but I figured they'd be OK. I gave him my standard lecture about taking care of the pads, not going down and sliding on the driveway, because I wanted to keep them in unscuffed perfection. He nodded his assent to my demands.

We spent a couple of hours that afternoon taking shots on goal, each of us having a few turns in net. At first Randy was awkward with the goalkeeping duties. But once he got used to the pads he was pretty good. His height was actually an advantage once he learned to come out of the net to cut down the angles. By the time my mom called us in for supper, I thought I'd created a pretty good protégé, and it occurred to me that while we were playing, the word "seizure" hadn't entered my mind at all.

Over the next few days I saw very little of Randy as he went back and forth to The Montréal Children's Hospital for tests and evaluation of his condition. But when the weekend came and he had a break, we were back in the driveway. It was more than just two kids playing hockey. It was me bonding with a side of my family I had never really known. Although my mom was one of 16 children, and I have about 50 first cousins on her side, we had always lived far away from them.

Toward the end of the next week, the visit ended, and Randy and Aunt Joan prepared to go. Before my dad took them to the airport, my aunt gave me a new blue-faced Timex watch, which I still have, and my dad gave a present to Randy. Dad had gone to the pro shop where he'd bought my goalie pads and gotten my cousin a pair exactly like them. Randy and I were amazed when Dad unveiled them in the vestibule of our house, and although I had a fleeting thought that Randy hadn't had to undergo the same tortured negotiations I had had to go through to get my pads, I was still happy for him. They left, and I didn't see Randy, or hear much from him or Aunt Joan, for years.

Three decades later, when we were both reaching the age when players retire from the NHL, I saw Randy again on a trip to the Maritimes to visit my mom's family. He stopped by my Aunt Ev's house on the Friday night my dad, my wife, Gaby, and I arrived. The first thing Randy said was, "I've still got those goalie pads, you know." I keep a lot of old stuff, too, but I had to admit that mine were long gone. I was dying to have a look at his, though, and I told him so.

We chatted about life and the past. We now lived farther apart than ever, with me in California, but Randy seemed to be a cool guy, someone I'd enjoy hanging out with. The last thing he said before he left was, "Hey, you know, we should strap on those pads one more time. Maybe Sunday."

The next day, my Uncle Millett's 80th birthday, I spent much of the time at the party talking to Randy again. And again he renewed his offer. "Let's strap on the pads one more time," he said at one point.

"Tomorrow," I replied in echo of what he'd suggested.

The next day it rained, and we never got to play. Maybe we wouldn't have, anyway—the equipment by now was far too small for two middle-aged men. But the point is, we could have, and I believe the possibility bound us together more than being first cousins did. I left the Maritimes feeling as if I'd gained a friend.

A year later, at 45, Randy died suddenly at work. My dad called me with the news. I was sad for his wife and my extended family. But I also grieved the new relationship that we had built. As I absorbed the news, I realized that we would never have a chance to strap on those pads one more time. Even had it been silly to do so, or perhaps impossible, the thought that we could have gone out there and played, using the same equipment that had made us friends 30 years earlier, had been comforting, kind of like the past wasn't so far behind us.

By coincidence, after the visit with Randy the year earlier, I had found a pair of used goalie pads at a sporting goods store near my house. They weren't quite as old as the ones Randy had, but they were at least 20 years outdated, so they came pretty close to the design of the old-school ones I missed. I bought them, at Gaby's encouragement, to use on my driveway with the kids of some friends who were spending a day with us. That afternoon, we played the same way I'd done all of my childhood, taking shots at one another and making spectacular moves in goal. The game had ended only when Bryan, the smaller of the boys, had made a huge backswing with his stick and clipped his brother, Jonathan, in the face.

Now, a year later, with the news of Randy's death fresh in my mind, I went out to my garage and got out the pads. I strapped them on, alone, and stood in the backyard, looking at the moon. As I did so, I had a chat with Randy, the conversation I was wishing I could have for real. I told him that I was sorry for what had happened to him, and sorry that we had blown our chance to be kids again, if only for an afternoon. I made a promise that I'd never pass up the chance to strap on the pads again, and that whenever I did, no matter whom I was with, I'd think of him.

chapter twenty

Band of Brothers

Eric Staal

K ids these days have everything, or at least it seems that many do. Let's say a kid wants walkie-talkies, a scale-model racetrack and a train set for Christmas. No problem. All he has to do is use the logic my nephew uses— ask Santa for one, his parents for another and Uncle Bean (me) in California for the third. Chances are he'll do pretty well. (And in truth, that kid gets his wily ways from me, according to my dad.) But some parents are still doing things the old-fashioned way, making their kids earn most of what they want themselves. And in the case of Henry and Linda Staal, encouraging their boys to strive for what they desire is why they have four sons in or poised to be in the NHL.

Today, the oldest of the Staals' sons, Eric, is already a Stanley Cup champion, with Carolina in 2006. From the time he was young, he worked in the family business, a sod farm. Eric says that doing so helped him to appreciate what it takes to make a living, to support a family. "We earned what we got, we worked, and we knew if we worked hard we would get rewarded for it with money," he says.

Staal shares a vivid example of one of the lessons his parents taught him. "I bought a go-kart when I was 10, for 400 bucks, and I continued to work. I ended up selling the go-kart, and I bought a dirt bike. We worked hard, and when we got paid, on the farm, we got to treat ourselves with things like that and use them for enjoyment. It definitely makes you more responsible and helps you appreciate what it takes to work in life."

Acquiring hockey equipment was a different story, though. "We always wanted a lot of things. Like any kid, you want the new aluminum Easton or the new skates. We didn't always get them, but we got what we needed. Our parents were pretty good, and we'd hit the Play It Again Sports and get some of the used equipment and stuff like that. For me, I was a little more fortunate because I got the new skates, and they got passed down."

Of course, having the proper gear and a strong work ethic alone doesn't translate into hockey greatness. For that, you've got to add in the magic ingredient of a backyard rink, and that's just what Eric's father did. The first iteration of the rink was built when Eric was a little boy. "I was pretty young, but I remember being there. I don't know if I was helping, but I was right there with him as he was putting up the boards. I remember we had the mesh on the back, which he set up. I don't think I specifically hammered any nails—I was probably too young to do that—but I remember being there when he was building it."

The rink itself has now become the stuff of legend, almost the same way that Gretzky's has, though Staal doesn't see it in quite those terms. "I don't think that there was a mythology built around it. It was just being able to be on the ice and play the game and work on your skills that made us good. I think having an outdoor rink definitely made me a better player. It improved my game. That's not to say that if you don't have an outdoor rink you're not going to be a good player, but I think it helps. It was something that we all liked to do, being outside and playing outside and playing against each other, just having fun and enjoying the game."

You might think that, with his kids growing up in the aftermath of the Gretzky era and the sense from early on that they might have some hockey talent, Mr. Staal would try to emulate the type of precision drills that most people think of when they recall the suburban Brantford backyard rink that Gretzky played on as a kid. That whole, "Go where the puck's going to be" deal. Eric doesn't recall it being that way.

"I think it was more scrimmaging," he remembers. "Dad would come out once in a while. When we were younger, he had the pylons out there, and he'd kind of show us something that we could do. You get looking for things to do, and my dad, obviously playing the game, would know certain drills. Then we would make up our own, and we'd have the pylons, weaving in and out, and doing different things. A lot of it was made up on our own. We did our own thing and just kept doing it."

Like all boys who love the NHL, the Staal brothers also had their fantasies, and they played them out on the rink. "We played for the Stanley Cup all the time. We were Wayne Gretzky, we were Ed Belfour in the net, Doug Gilmour and those guys, Joe Sakic out on the rink. You always named one of your favorite players, and you had to call them before someone else did. Gretzky was always the first name pulled out, so you always had to call that one quickly," he recalls.

The fun ended when the rink's lights were shut off, the family signal that it was time to come in for dinner or to do homework. The Staal boys then took the game, and their gamesmanship with each other, inside. Among four brothers, there's bound to be some shenanigans in the house. There's a story floating around about an incident with a glass-topped table, but it's not something that comes first to mind when Eric recalls his younger days with his three brothers.

Instead, he says, "Having four boys in the family, all playing sports and having that desire and fight to win everything, or try and win everything, there were always little fisticuffs, or things like that. I remember on the outdoor rink,

I think it was Jared, my youngest brother, who slashed Marc in the back of the legs, and Marc grabbed Jared's stick and threw it as far as he could over the boards into the snowbank, so he had to go crawling through the snow to get his stick back. There were a lot of instances like that, but in the end, we all enjoyed being out there and enjoying each others' company."

Despite an early promise of future success, Staal has childhood hockey memories that sound similar to those of most kids. "I believe my first year ever playing, I got an Esso medal, 'Most Improved Player.' I was five years old. The next year, I think they gave me…there's three medals, there's 'Most Dedicated,' 'Most Improved' and 'Most Sportsmanlike.' I think the second year I got 'Most Sportsmanlike,' and then when I was seven, I got 'Most Dedicated.' Then I won the Top Scorer trophy and MVP of the team."

When Eric brought the awards home, he kept them with him in his bed the first night. "It was awesome. I was really excited. I was seven years old when I first got a trophy. The medal was cool, to show the grandparents, to show the friends, but when you get the actual trophy, that's something a little bit different. They were in my bedroom. I had a little mantel thing set up, and I had them up in the room. I'd shine them up, and we were definitely very proud of them."

Eric shared a bedroom with Marc for a long, long time, until their parents finished the basement, and then each boy got his own room downstairs. "I don't think that was until probably in high school, grade nine or ten," he indicates. Shortly after that, he had to move out anyway.

He left home when he was 15 to play Junior hockey in Peterborough. He still remembers the struggle. "I was really rattled the first month, two months, until I got into the routine of being in school and in class, and in practice." But there were other costs as well. "Jared was probably eight, nine years old when I left, and that's not very long being in the same house together and moving away from home. It was difficult, having four kids who have something to do with each other all the time, playing with each other and then me having to go somewhere where they're no longer around. It was definitely tough. But hockey was all I wanted to do, and that was the sacrifice I wanted to make."

Now that the brothers are all grown up, they relate to each other as adults, but Eric still realizes his responsibility as the eldest. "I talk to all of them, you know, try to talk to them every week, every two weeks. For me, I'm the oldest, I'm the one who goes through most things first, so if they have any questions, I try to be the guy to let them know what to expect maybe, or what it was like for me in a certain situation. We all get along great now, and it's neat for me to see them growing as people, and as players, in the NHL and in the OHL, too." At the time he says this, Marc is playing for the Rangers, Jordan for the Penguins, and Jared is a Phoenix draftee who is in his third season with the Sudbury Wolves of the Ontario Hockey League.

And as for the superstition that goes with being a Stanley Cup hopeful, that, too, reflects life among four brothers. The day Eric had the Cup after he'd won it with the Hurricanes, the family took turns drinking champagne and beer out of it, and they took a family picture. But he says, "My mom, my dad and I touched the Cup, but not the other three." Then he says something that sums up his role as the pathfinding brother. "The other three will get their chance and the opportunity to hopefully hoist it one day." Jordan's day with the Cup came in 2009, after his Pittsburgh Penguins defeated the Detroit Red Wings.

Eric recognizes that the success he and his brothers have is not the result of magic but a product of where they come from. "There's a combination of skill and talent, but it also takes a lot of determination, it takes a lot of work and drive. We all had the passion to want to play in the NHL since we were really little, and we worked extremely hard. Any professional sport is an elite company of players, and all of us worked hard as far as working out and being on the ice. We really pushed ourselves to be there. We obviously had some talent and skill, but before that comes a lot of work ethic, and that's what we pride ourselves on."

He plans to replicate the kind of upbringing he had when he has a family of his own, saying that despite the brothers' competitive nature, he doesn't remember fighting at the dinner table. "We'd talk a lot about school, talk about our days. I remember growing up, and I don't know if it's as much like that now, though it should be, that we had family dinners every night. That was our family time, just engaging with each other, and that was really good. I think people should do that more now, and when my wife and I start a family, I'm going to focus on doing that."

chapter twenty-one

Repeat Performance

Ray Ferraro

When Ray Ferraro was a toddler, his dad built a rink in their backyard. The other kids in the family weren't so keen on being out there, so Ray played alone, and the games always started the same way. He stood at the side of the ice sheet and sang the national anthem. Then, he jumped onto the ice for a simulated game, passing the puck to himself and going in to score.

When summer came, Ray fired shots at a net under the carport hour after hour. "My mom's friends would see me and ask, 'Why doesn't Raymond do something fun?'" he says now. "She'd tell them, 'To him, that is fun.' I'd be out there all day, all summer."

His room was carpeted in fake Astroturf, and he took the little plastic hockey players he had collected from Sugar Crisp cereal and played with them, always taking on the role of Bobby Orr. While he played, the great defenseman looked down on him from a poster on his wall. The bed sheets, too, bore the mark of the game—the NHLPA logo. In those respects, the room was no different from a lot of kids' bedrooms at the time, except for one thing: Ferraro really believed the NHL was in his future.

Ferraro's mom kept a scrapbook of the young lives of each of her four boys. The format was the same for all of them—class pictures, teachers' names, best friend, and each year, an indication of what each kid wanted to be. There was a list with the common career goals on it, including firefighter, coach and doctor. The idea was that each boy would check off the career that suited him. When Ferraro was in the first grade, instead of picking any of the choices offered, he had his mom write one in at the bottom of the page: NHL player. "I never assumed I was going to do anything else," he explains.

"I assumed I was going to get there, but as I progressed through minor hockey, everywhere I went, there was another doubter to be silenced. I was too small, too slow, not tough enough. I was in Junior B at 16, and I scored 80 goals. I was in Penticton the next year at 150 pounds, and I got 65 goals. I was the third center when we won the Memorial Cup in Portland, and I got traded that summer to Brandon and scored 108 goals. I went to Hartford's training camp and was sent to the minors in four days to play for Binghamton." But during that same 1984–85 season, Ray made the NHL, and he stayed nearly two decades and scored more than 400 goals.

This might be the story of a player whose persistence paid off in unlikely success, and it is. But all those numbers and all those years were the product of more than a guy with determination and talent, because Ferraro's dad played a big part by being a steadying influence and a guide, someone who gave the right advice at the right moment. It's a role that Ray himself has embraced with his own boys.

Ray's father, Ed, worked in his own concrete business, leaving the house at 6:00 AM each day. But whenever Ray had a game, Mr. Ferraro was at the rink in Trail, BC, at 4:15 PM sharp. The other days, he'd get home for dinner, which had to be on the table at 5:30 PM. "Not 5:32, not any other time," as Ferraro remembers it. When the meal was finished, Ray's father would leave the table to go watch Walter Cronkite deliver the evening news. Ray would go with him, curling up in the same armchair as his dad. "Finally, when I was about 11, one day he said, 'I think you're too big to share this chair anymore.' I just wanted to be near him."

His father's wisdom in business and life extended to the hockey arena, though he never played himself and had never even skated. At Ray's games, Mr. Ferraro didn't stand with the other parents. He didn't want to get involved in the politics of who got played and who didn't. Instead, he watched from the stands, and after the games, Ed would be quiet. "He would

never start the conversation," Ray says. "But about three [traf-
fic] lights from the arena, I would say something, and I'd ask
him to evaluate my game. If I'd done well, he'd say, 'You had
your legs today,' because he knew so much about how I played,
he could tell me exactly whether my game was working."

Ed was also unafraid of giving his son direct career
advice, and it always paid off. When Ray was 15, he played
Junior B hockey. The next year, he made the Penticton Knights,
but he was slated to be a fourth-line player. "My dad said, 'Why
don't you stay home and master the league you're in?' I did, and
I set a record that still stands today, 80 goals. When I moved to
Penticton in Junior A the following season, I had 65. That might
not have happened had he not given me the advice he did.
I can't ever remember not trusting his judgment."

As Ray's hockey career progressed, his father followed
him. When he was in Penticton, which was three and a half
hours from the family's home in Trail, his dad drove down
after work. "He'd get there about midway through the first
period, and I'd see him. I took great comfort in the fact that
he was there. 'He's here, he's safe,' I'd say to myself. I just knew
where he was in the arena."

Ferraro's career in the NHL eventually took him to six
different cities, and into the role of parent himself, and it is
here even more than in his own career where Ed's lessons are
paying off. Ray's first two boys, Matthew and Landon, were
born in 1988 and 1991, respectively, and each has pursued

a hockey dream. Ferraro and his second wife, Cammi Granato, recently welcomed their first child together, son Riley, who is setting out on his hockey future at this very moment.

What Riley becomes, whether in hockey or in another pursuit, will owe much to Cammi's steadying hand. "Obviously, she's made a considerable name for herself in hockey, and our house revolves around the game. But it's well-rounded because of her way of keeping things balanced. I'm amazingly lucky to have met her," Ray remarks. (For Cammi's story, please see the chapter entitled, "The Single Word, 'Player.'")

Kids tend to do what their fathers do, but the lives of Ray's first two sons were unlike most, because they had the privilege of NHL locker rooms as their playground. "When I was with the Islanders [1990–95], the two boys would hang out in the dressing room after the games. Each of the guys would give them some candy or gum and tell them, 'It's OK. Your dad won't mind.'" Matthew and Landon would smile as they exited the room, their mouths stuffed with several pieces of gum, candy crammed in every pocket, and the conviction that a hockey life was pretty cool burning itself into their minds.

On the ice, Matthew Ferraro's hockey path took a slightly different route than his dad's. He played three years of Junior B in British Columbia, in the nets, and eventually progressed to Junior A with the Cowichan Valley Capitals of the British Columbia Hockey League before adopting his adult pathway as an apprentice electrician.

Landon Ferraro has always had an NHL dream, just like his dad. When he was in third grade, at which time Ray played for Atlanta, Landon had a school assignment to write a speech similar to Martin Luther King Jr.'s "I Have a Dream." Landon's dream, of course, was to play in the NHL. And surprisingly, he knew even back then when his draft year would be—2009—and he talked about it in the essay.

When the family moved to Vancouver a couple of years later, Ferraro casually asked his son one day, "If you were going to score on a penalty shot, who would you score on?"

The answer came back, "'Martin Brodeur,' because Landon thinks he's the best," Ferraro explains. Ray already knew which team his son would be playing for—the Maple Leafs—so he had an artist paint a replica of the Air Canada Centre on Landon's bedroom ceiling. In the picture, Landon has his arms raised in celebration because he's just scored on the great New Jersey netminder.

As Landon's childhood progressed, it seemed more and more likely that he would get to play against Brodeur one day. Landon was drafted by the Red Deer Rebels of the WHL in 2005 as the second overall pick, and he had played 126 games with the team by the time of the 2009 NHL draft, in which he was taken 32nd overall by the Detroit Red Wings.

It was just into the start of the second round, and it was the Wings' first pick of the draft that year.

Parents might wonder what formula Ferraro used to move both of his older boys along in the hockey world, but what they will find if they examine his method is that, unlike a lot of parents these days who are desperate to get their sons to the level where the NHL dream might happen, Ferraro never pushed his sons. He's never coached them in-season, saying instead, "I leave that to other people, and we've been fortunate to have some good people in that role over the years."

On the matter of achieving a hockey dream, Ferraro says, "If it's in you, that's just what you do." But when it comes to his sons and hockey, he adds, "You just want your son to be OK. I just want them to do well. Be happy. Jump in with both feet like my dad taught me. How could you want anything else?"

There's also a downside to having a hockey dad who is an NHL veteran. Ferraro understands that his sons carry around a famous name. Matthew circumvented comparisons with his father by becoming a goalie during his career. Landon is a center, like his dad, but as Ferraro says, "Just because he's my son doesn't mean that he'll play like me. Put it this way—I hope he's a better player than me." Ray wants to help his boy, as any dad might, but he refuses to let himself nit-pick, though he admits that at times he has to bite his tongue. His attitude is simple. "Who wants to be criticized every night? I know I didn't, so why would it be any different for him?"

When Landon plays, Ray will talk to him about the game, but he takes it easy, as his dad did with him. "After I saw Landon play in Red Deer recently," he says, "I greeted him. I hadn't seen him for a few weeks. Then we got to the game. I told him, 'There are two plays I want to talk to you about.' He appreciates the advice, and he will ask as much as I offer. It was the same for Matt when he played—they both want to do it on their own terms." When asked about evaluating Landon's play in public, in Ray's role as hockey commentator on TV, he responds, "I'm not going to say anything. I know that lots of other people will be evaluating [him]."

Unlike parents who haven't made it to the NHL themselves, Ferraro says he has an easier time of dealing with the boys' dreams. "I'm far more realistic than most. I know what is required because I had to do it. Some parents have unrealistic expectations. The gift of ability matched with desire is what it takes to make the dream come true, and all of that requires good fortune." Then he adds, "Watching your son play is a powerful thing."

But it's not the only thing that matters. Growing up, despite the boys trailing around after an NHL dad who later became a hockey broadcaster, their lives weren't all hockey. When Ferraro spent a weekend in LA recently for a fantasy camp, Matt accompanied him. As they were driving around, the young man reminisced about their time there, when his dad was with the Kings (between 1996 and 1999, when Matt was 7 through 11 years old). "Hey, that's where we would hit baseballs," Matt said as they passed a park. It was a reminder not only of what they'd done but also that dad Ray had been willing to take the time from his life as a professional hockey player to interact with his kids through other sports. It is a legacy he continues with his youngest boy, Riley, born in 2006.

Ferraro sums up his feelings about family with this concise thought: "I only hope my kids love me and respect me as much as I did my dad." It's obvious that the care with which Ed raised him has been passed to the younger Ferraros. And in the end, it is this outlook that will transcend any hockey dreams that might come true.

chapter twenty-two

Growing Up the Son of Mr. Hockey

Mark Howe

Mark Howe ended up playing 22 years of professional hockey, from 1973 to 1995, and amassing nearly 1250 points, many as a defenseman. But his accomplishments always come with a footnote, one that he doesn't regret at all—he will forever be known as one of Gordie Howe's kids. So the natural question when you meet him is, "What's it like to grow up the son of Mr. Hockey, anyway?"

"I always knew who he was, but we just looked at him as our dad, even though everywhere we went people flocked to him," Mark claims. Of the four Howe children (Mark; hockey-playing brother Marty; Murray, a doctor; and a sister, Cathy), Mark might have been the most keen on following his father's accomplishments on the ice. "As a kid, I went to more games than Marty, Murray or Cathy did, I'm sure," he says. "I tried to go to every game I could."

And that's why he was in the arena for two of his father's most important goals, the ones that tied and broke Maurice Richard's record for all-time goals (544). Mark was lucky, because both happened at the Olympia in his hometown of Detroit, exactly two weeks apart.

It was the fall of 1963, and Mark was eight. "I remember being in the car, a Pontiac Le Mans, going to the rink. My mom might have been there, too, I don't know. But I do know that there was more than the usual anticipation and excitement. With the record tied, we knew what could happen," he says.

Like always, the family sat in section seven, in the corner where the visiting team came onto the ice. Looking around, Mark felt at home. Back then, there weren't all the corporate tickets, so it was always the same people in the section. "I think everyone there, and every usher in that building, knew who I was."

Mark watched and waited, tense, with the rest of the Red Wings fans. The goals were both scored at the far end of the ice from where he sat, and he vividly remembers the second goal, which made his dad the all-time leading goal scorer in the NHL. "Charlie Hodge was in net, and he was playing deep. The shot went high to his glove side. I looked around at the crowd, and of course, since it was at home, everyone was going nuts. And I thought to myself, 'I'm the only one in here who can say that that's my dad.'" This regard for his father's greatness lasted until the end of Gordie's playing days, by which time Mark was not only Gordie's fan but also his teammate.

But future events weren't in view on that momentous day, only the goal. As on every game day, Mark performed his usual post-game routine. "I'd go to the locker room door. An usher would let me peek around to catch my dad's eye, and he would give me a hand gesture, either to say 'come in,' 'wait five minutes' or, when things had gone bad, 'no, not today.' If I had to stay outside, I'd roll up a ball of tape and find some-one else to play hockey with. We'd use broken sticks, or this little stick that I had and took to the games." The day of the record-breaking goal, Mark went to the door of the locker room early so that he would be there when the game ended. As Gordie was walking toward the dressing room, he noticed him and offered his hand. They walked into the dressing room together.

For many kids, the thrill of proximity to the NHL and having a father in the league might have been enough, but Mark wasn't satisfied with that. He wanted to play the game himself. His first great achievement in hockey was being on the team that won the silver medal at the 1972 Olympics, for the U.S. He showed his medal to his dad as they passed through the Chicago airport at the same time. "I had it in a little carry-on suitcase, and I took it out for him. It wasn't until I got home that I had a chance to really show it off, though. I went around in the car to everyone I knew," he says.

The next season saw Mark win the Memorial Cup with the Toronto Marlies, a team that brother Marty also played on. At the time, Mark was 18, too young for the NHL draft, which back then didn't pick up players until they were 20. But that didn't mean his professional ambitions had to wait. The World Hockey Association decided to sign players who were younger than 20 and playing Junior hockey, because they were considered professionals by NCAA rules and were not eligible to play college hockey.

"Houston wanted both of us, Marty and I. At the time, our dad was retired." Mark says this with a laugh, knowing the history—Gordie had been retired for two seasons but would come out of it and play pro hockey (WHA and NHL) for another seven years and 189 goals.

"Bill Dineen, the Aeros' coach, was an old teammate of Gordie's. Doug Harvey was also with the team. Bill called my parents to tell them that they would draft both of us boys in the first round of the WHA's professional player draft. At that time, we were the first two players under 20 to play at that level since Bobby Orr had come up," says Mark.

After flying up from Texas, Dineen and Harvey showed up at the Howes' Detroit home. They were considered friends, and the men played it cool with the paperwork while everyone got caught up on each others' lives. Then in a pause in the conversation, Mrs. Howe said to them, "Hey, why are you signing these two? What if Gordie wanted to come back and play?"

Mark recalls that Dineen's and Harvey's eyes widened, and one of the men said, "OK, let's start over again. We'll sign Gordie, and then get these two done," indicating the boys with a nod. And that's what they did.

The family still has warm memories from that time. The season began with a game against the Cleveland Crusaders, and the three Howes went through warm-ups on the ice and were coming off when Marty noticed something unusual. Because there were now three Howes, each had his full name on his jersey, but Gordie's was misspelled. "It said 'Goride,'" Mark says. "Boy, did we get a laugh out of that. We still call him Goride sometimes."

The Howes' time in Houston included two AVCO Cups as league champions, and when their four-year contracts expired, the trio went to Hartford as free agents. They played as a group for three more seasons before Gordie retired once more, in 1980.

However, Mark says that his father could probably have played another year, "They [the team] asked him to move on, though he wanted to play another season. I think he was better than some of the guys we had, honestly." He elaborates by saying, "He was just so smart and so strong. He didn't have the speed he used to, but we had such great chemistry. You can put two players together sometimes, and they don't play worth a lick, but we had a special connection."

With his father now retired, Mark played in Hartford for two more years, but the relations between Mark and the team started to fall apart. "I had suffered a serious injury that greatly affected my play for a long period of time. Neither I nor the team was very happy. I asked them to trade me." It was after the trade that Mark proved that he was more than the son of a famous player. He was a player in his own right.

"I'll always be Gordie Howe's son, but when I went to Philadelphia, the trainer shook my hand first thing and said, 'I'm glad to meet Travis' father,' and I knew I'd do well there. It was the first time I'd played on a team that my dad wasn't associated with. Even in Hartford after he retired, Gordie was in the front office. I had played on a line with him for six years, and he had a lot to do with my success, but in Philly it was the first time I started to get credit for myself."

Being out of his father's shadow allowed Mark to blossom into the defenseman he became. His NHL career eventually included 197 goals and 545 assists in 929 games, as well as three Norris Trophy nominations.

"I loved the philosophy of how the game was played in Philadelphia. It was how I'd been brought up—winning was everything. Everything I had been brought up with was practiced. It was a good fit for me," says Mark.

He eventually retired, far short of his dad's retirement age of 52. "I think about that sometimes and am amazed at how my father did it," he comments when asked about his father's longevity in the game. "To this day, my dad is impossible to tire out. We were fishing in Alaska. It took four planes to get there. We went out the first day, then the second, and by the afternoon of the third day, Marty and I were done. But Gordie was still out there. It's no wonder he played hockey for so long."

Before he was done, Mark played three seasons with Detroit, the last one in 1994–95. He then went to work for the Red Wings as a pro scout, garnering four Stanley Cup rings for his troubles. "I gave the first three to my kids, one each," he says. "The last one's for me, though I'm not the kind of guy who wears flashy stuff like that." Nor is he the type who holds onto memorabilia from his playing days. He has given away much of it to various charitable causes, for auctions.

And that gesture might be one more way that he is Mr. Hockey's son. "Everyone Gordie meets has this feeling of connection to him, and he reciprocates it, sincerely. It's his most special gift," Mark says.

Mark has inherited that way of touching those around him. Although he doesn't have the same dominating physical presence as his father, if you take one look at his hockey success and at how he lives now, it's easy to see that Mark Howe patterns his life in a special way. "My parents taught me to always say 'please' and 'thank you' and always be respectful of others," he comments. A simple lesson, but one that shows that he's Mr. Hockey's son, both on and off the ice.

chapter twenty-three

From Father to Son
Kevin Lowe

Nearly 40 years after it happened, Kevin Lowe remembers something his dad told him on the way home from a hockey game one afternoon. Mr. Lowe said, "You know, you could play in the NHL some day if you keep applying yourself." And only a handful of years after his father uttered those words, Lowe did precisely that. Sadly, his dad died when Kevin was 13, before he could witness any of his son's NHL accomplishments. But the foundation that he built into young Kevin's life undoubtedly made Lowe the player, and the person, he became.

Kevin started skating early, at age three. Unlike most kids, though, he had the luxury of an indoor ice rink all to himself in the glorious free days before he was old enough to be in school. His father, along with some of his siblings, owned a dairy company that packaged milk products and delivered them to homes and stores over a broad swath of Québec. Lowe Brothers Dairy of Lachute sat on a large piece of property, and one year the men decided to build what would be the first public artificial skating rink in the area on the company's land. It would allow kids to play hockey and skate in the winter, and in summer the dairy benefited from the ice-making equipment that did double duty in manufacturing ice cream.

None of that mattered to little Kevin. He was concerned with playing hockey. Each winter day, his father took him to work with him, put him on the rink and shut the doors, leaving him to skate and play all he wanted. From time to time, Mr. Lowe would send one of his staff to check in on the kid. No one ever found Kevin sitting on the bench.

Kevin's love of hockey was also fostered by his dad's effort to expose him to the game at all levels. The year Lowe was five, his father took him to an exhibition game being played by the Detroit Red Wings that had an affiliation with the Junior team in St. Jerome. They sat close to the players' bench, and Kevin was free to wander around during the game.

At one point Kevin walked up behind the bench and tugged on the sleeve of Gordie Howe's sweater. Howe turned around to see the little boy standing there, pen and paper in hand. He took off his gloves, put them down and gave Kevin his autograph while play went on in front of them. Lowe was a Red Wings fan from that moment on.

A year later, in 1965, Kevin was old enough to play organized hockey. Mr. Lowe and his brothers were involved in coaching the local teams, and his father was, in Lowe's words, "very instrumental in my younger years," with respect to developing the boy's hockey skills, but even more, his leadership abilities. "At a very young age, I was made captain of teams, and my dad felt it was really important for me to reach out to kids. For instance, he used a little thing like letting kids know when practice was. The coach has to phone to tell the kids what time it is, but my dad used to give me that responsibility. I didn't speak very good French at the time, but he would make me do it, to get over that shyness of having to step out of your comfort zone. That was my early leadership experience," Lowe says. His career started in goal. He then moved to forward until he was about 10 or 12, at which time he moved to defense. His father made this decision for him to change positions, figuring his son would get more ice time that way.

At the time, Lowe was beginning to display an ability that might take him somewhere in hockey, but he says that he was not a superstar early on. "I was always one of the better kids, but not necessarily the best," he says. "Maybe one year I'd be the best, and the next year I'd be second or third, sort of always in that range. I think, now that I know how to scout kids—know how you describe a player—I'd say that I probably had above-average hockey sense and above-average desire.

I think probably talent-wise, I was not elite talent, but above average."

Off the ice, Kevin worked in the family dairy business from a young age, as did his siblings and many of his 35 first cousins. At five, he was picking up garbage and cleaning up the grounds. Around age seven, he made runs on the dairy trucks, which, back in those days, took milk directly to people's doorsteps. Later still, he worked cutting the lawns. "We were always given lots of responsibility," he says, "and the work ethic thing was important for all of us."

His upward path might have all changed when Kevin lost his dad just as he was entering his teenage years, but the family structure was too solid to allow the boy to fail. His older brother and a couple of cousins who were heavily involved in hockey stepped in to provide mentoring. "One of them was my coach, and they all kept an eye out for me, assuming the father role. We had a really close-knit family, so it was never a question that I'd have a proper upbringing," he recalls.

Lowe's hockey life took off when he joined the Québec Remparts for the 1976–77 season. He played there for three years, becoming their first non-native French speaker to serve as captain. Around this time, he got his first sense that perhaps the NHL would be his future. "When I was 17 or 18, I saw in the paper that a couple of WHA teams were thinking about signing me. That's when the light went on. In those days, the NHL draft age was 20, but those reports gave me the taste that maybe the next level was possible." Before that time, he hadn't thought so far ahead. "For me, each year it was just that hockey moved on. I wasn't thinking about playing in the NHL. I was just thinking, 'Next year, I'll play in this league,' then the next year, 'I'll play in this one.'" When he was in Junior, though, he started hearing from scouts that NHL teams might be interested in him. The Oilers eventually drafted him with their first-round pick, 21st overall, in 1979.

He thus began an NHL career that spanned 1254 games over 19 years. Had his dad been around, they would have shared six Stanley Cup celebrations together. The first win happened in the afternoon, and when Kevin came out of the arena, despite having spent a couple of hours in the dressing room with his teammates, he remembers that it was still daylight. "It was an early game in Edmonton, and because we're so far north, we get a lot of sunlight. I thought to myself, 'Man, we've got a lot of time to party.' We had a celebration across the way with the team, and then we went out to a bunch of different bars."

At the time, Lowe and Mark Messier lived together, so everybody ended up going to their house. In the middle of the living room sat a big bottle of champagne that Lowe's hometown had given him some years before. He had always saved it for an occasion such as this, so they decided to open it. What they didn't know was that somebody had given it a good shake, so when the cork popped, the contents ended up spraying everybody and making a mess of the house.

Later that summer, he had his one day with the Cup; at the time, what the players did with the trophy was less scrutinized than it is now. "Now, when you get the Cup, it's a little more organized. The league sends their guy, basically because of our era of having the Cup. It ended up getting dented one time, though not with me. But a funny story about the Cup was, I'd just bought a new Mercedes that spring. Mark Messier and I were taking the Cup to a little spot in his hometown, so I had it in the trunk because I didn't want to put it on the nice seats in the Mercedes. After a few stoplights and stops, I realized I could hear it rolling around. So I thought I'd better get it out of there and put it in the back seat of the car," he says.

He also took the Cup to his hometown in Québec a number of times, where he put it on the lawn in front of his mom's house. Whoever was in the house at the time watched as people drove by, did a double take and backed up. Most then came up and knocked on the door to offer their congratulations.

Lowe's last Cup was in 1994, with a New York Rangers team that was made up of a lot of the guys from Edmonton. The Cup win was special for what it did for the franchise and also because of how it made him feel. "It came at a time when my body was getting beat up. I had to play through a lot just to get there, so I have a lot of personal gratitude." He retired a few seasons later, in 1998, after another couple of campaigns with the Oilers, the last of which saw him appear in just seven games. Then he moved on to coaching and team management.

Why didn't Lowe just retire? The reason he gives can be traced back to his dad's legacy. "I've always worked. I've never not worked, evidenced by starting to work very young, so that part comes naturally," he explains. "Having the opportunity presented to you, you can't turn it down. I retired [as a player] mostly because I had to because of my inner ear problem. When I went back to Edmonton, I had a verbal agreement with Glen Sather that I would get into coaching. I thought I'd be an assistant coach for a while, but he wanted to make a coaching change and wanted me to go into that afterwards. Then when Glen left to go to New York, I really didn't want to work for anyone else, so I transitioned into management."

Lowe turned 50 in 2009, and he finds himself busy raising four kids with wife Karen Percy, an Olympic medalist in skiing. He imparts the lessons he learned as a kid, a favorite being to tell his children that he got his first job at five years old. But his way of being a dad goes beyond offering guiding principles. He and Karen both left home early to pursue their sporting ambitions, so when it came time to decide whether their son, Keegan, should move away to play hockey, they had to consider the emotional costs carefully. The way Lowe reflects upon this decision reveals the type of father he is.

"You know," he begins, "I was thinking about this the other day, visiting my son, who is 15 and goes to Shattuck-St. Mary's. I thought to myself, 'I've already had two years longer with him than I did with my dad.'"

The words portray a legacy that began a generation ago when a father put his young son on the ice to enjoy himself day after day and culminated in that boy becoming one of the NHL's great defensemen—and an even better man.

chapter twenty-four

Golden Jet Jr.
Bobby Hull Jr.

S treet hockey games. A family meeting. A bucket of hockey sticks down in the basement. None of that sounds all that unusual. But what if those sticks were ones your dad had used to score his 30th or 50th NHL goal? What if those street hockey games were played while busloads of tourists gawked at you? And what if that family meeting had included a declaration from your dad that went something like this: "Pack your bags. We're moving to Winnipeg"?

In that case, you wouldn't be just any family growing up in hockey country. You'd be the Hulls, and the dad in question would be Bobby, who in 1972 became the most sought-after and richest player in the history of the game. You, in turn, would be Bobby Jr., but it would take you a while to figure out why your life was so different from the lives of other kids your age.

Such were the thoughts of Bobby Hull Jr., currently working as director of player development for the Tampa Bay Lightning. His recollections of his childhood in Chicago suggest a fairly normal life. Sure, his dad was a hockey superstar, but Bobby's concerns, and those of his four siblings, were similar to those of any other kid. The big question of his early days revolved around his hopes to someday live in a house where he could have his own bedroom.

Then the summer of 1972 came along, and Bobby Jr. and the rest of the family knew something was up. "It started when a *Sports Illustrated* guy came by, and he did a photo shoot in our backyard," Hull recalls. "He wanted a bunch of pictures of my dad with his Blackhawks jersey on. We asked him what was going on, and he just said, 'Ah, some guys want my picture for their magazine,' and left it at that." But things didn't settle down, and the phone rang all summer, something that wasn't the usual routine.

Just prior to this change of pace, the family had made the move to Glen Ellyn, a suburb of Chicago, and they were settling into their house. The big attraction of the new place was that each kid finally had his or her own bedroom. And then the big moment happened. "My dad came in one day and said to get downstairs; we were having a family meeting. 'What in the heck is a family meeting?' I asked myself. We'd never done that before."

So, with the family all gathered, Bobby Sr. told them they were moving to Winnipeg, and he walked out. None of them could grasp the changes that this announcement would bring to their family.

"Where's Winnipeg?" was the only thing Bobby Jr. could think to say. Then he looked over at his mom and noticed that she was crying.

But as anyone who reads hockey history knows, no amount of tears would change the course of events that took the Golden Jet to his new home with the World Hockey Association's Winnipeg Jets. The way things happened was just short of surreal for the surprised Hull children.

"We got on a plane in Chicago and got off in Winnipeg, where they put us right in cars and took us to the corner of Portage and Main streets downtown. We got out, and there were 50,000 people there. They had a stage built across the corner of the intersection, and we were all introduced to our new neighbors," Hull Jr. says.

Their dad was there to play hockey, but 11-year-old Bobby Jr. and his siblings had to go to school, so a few days later he found himself in his new classroom.

"I walked in with the teacher, and she said, 'Kids, we've got a new student. His name is Bobby Hull Jr.' Those who had no idea who I was until that moment suddenly snapped their heads around to see me. The rest of the class was already staring at me."

The scrutiny didn't stop there. The teacher did a quick assessment of where young Hull was in relation to what they were studying in her class, and he remembers being handed a math book. "That looks familiar," he stated.

Immediately, the whole class broke out in a long "Oooooh."

"The problem was, it was the book that this class had used the prior year, so I was a year behind right out of the gate," Hull says. He sums up those early days in his new school by saying, "It was like you had two heads."

At home on their street, life was just as taxing. The Hulls and their neighbors had a street hockey game going, an all-comers challenge. Kids from neighborhoods across the city showed up to play. Why not, when a touch of fame could be had along with the game? A kid never knew, if he came to give it a go, whether he might get to use an old Bobby Hull stick in the bargain. "I shoot right, but my brother Blake is a lefty like my dad, so he'd just grab whatever he could out of the house. Some 50 goal sticks got destroyed in the process, but my dad didn't care," Hull says.

The games got to be so well known that, once a week, a double-decker bus filled with tourists on Winnipeg's version of a "tour of the stars' homes" took to stopping by to watch.

The Hull kids hated to be put on display, so they started shooting tennis balls at the bus whenever it stopped. When that didn't deter the bus, they switched to pucks. Pretty soon, Bobby Sr. found out about the situation.

"He got us together one afternoon and said, 'I got a phone call the other day. Is it true that you guys are doing it? They say you've damaged their bus.'" The great man is one of few words.

"We told him yes, it was, but that they would always stop and gawk at us. When they kept coming, we lined the pucks up all ready, and when they stopped that week, we took aim and let go," says Bobby Jr.

The Hulls' dad considered the matter for about five seconds. "'OK,' he said, then he smirked and mumbled something about 'it serves them right,' and that was the last we heard about it," says Bobby Jr. The tour bus wasn't seen again.

Fortunately for the siblings, there was one refuge: the Winnipeg arena. They had the run of the place, including game days, when they arrived two hours before the Jets played and got an hour on the ice. And after the WHA games, they were back out there. It was good practice, because Bobby Jr. was starting to work on his hockey skills, with the eye to repeating his father's success. Winnipeg's local league didn't have space for him at his age level when he arrived, so he ended up playing one age group up, and the development was good for him.

A few years later he was drafted by the Lethbridge Broncos of the WHL, and his days at home were over. "My dad put me on a bus to Lethbridge, and as I was leaving, he said, 'If you're back here, you've failed—so don't come back!'" He meant it in a way that would encourage the youngster to do his best in the game.

But Bobby didn't have to go back, because he went on to a respectable Junior career with Lethbridge, then the Cornwall Royals of the Québec league, where he won the Memorial Cup in 1980. By the time he did return to Winnipeg, as a member of the WHL's Winnipeg Warriors, his parents had broken up, and his mom had relocated to the West Coast.

Meanwhile, his hockey dreams were taking a different tack. Playing Portland one night, one of only 10 skaters on a team ravaged by the flu, Hull threw a puck into the corner and turned to skate back to his Winnipeg bench. It was an important game for him because Bill Lesuk, a professional scout, was traveling with the team. As he cruised back to his bench, Hull was intercepted by a Portland player who checked him, blowing out Hull's shoulder. "That was the end of me," he says. "As it happened, I'm thinking to myself, 'Great, now the whole NHL will know that I got hurt really bad.'" Lesuk returned to Winnipeg, where word of Hull's injury spread, fast.

Hull did manage to get invited to the Maple Leafs' training camp in the season following the injury, and although he wasn't quite at the same level as the guys there, he wasn't far behind. The team offered to send him to St. Catharines to play, without a contract, but prudence told him that this wasn't what was best for him. "I decided that I wasn't going to go down there and have six or seven guys running me every night just to make a name for themselves."

He changed his course in life at that point, attending the University of Manitoba and earning a BA degree in economics in 1984. Then, realizing that he could still play, and that he had college eligibility remaining, he went west and joined his mother in Vancouver, where he spent a year with the UBC squad, netting about a point a game over a 22-game schedule in 1984–85.

His decision to move to BC almost cost him his life. One morning as he lay still asleep, he dreamt about a big bonfire. When he awoke, he smelled smoke. Upon jumping out of bed, he realized that the whole back half of the house was ablaze. "If I had slept five more minutes, I would have been lost, along with a bunch of my dad's stuff that I had become the unofficial historian of. We had a number of jerseys in the house, game-used ones from the Blackhawks, the WHA, ones he had worn in All-Star games. All of them burned. For months afterwards, I was sick when I even thought about it.

"I showed up to the arena that morning wearing shorts, which was a no-no. But I was a jokester, and the coach came up to me and asked why I wasn't dressed, assuming I was pulling some kind of prank. I told him what had happened, but he didn't believe me. So I said, 'Hey, smell these clothes.' He did, and he immediately said, 'Holy Moly, Hully—what are you doing here?'" Hull headed home to deal with the tragedy.

Degree in hand and his hockey-playing days over, Hull went about the business of forming an adult life of his own. "I've never felt normal my whole life," he admits. "I don't like being referred to as Bobby Hull's son. But ironically, I went from being Bobby Hull's son to Brett Hull's brother in a few short seasons."

As people do, though, Hull forged his own path, ending up in California. He wasn't a newcomer to the Golden State. He was born there. Now, aside from making a living in professional hockey, he lives an otherwise-normal life, with two kids, a girl and a boy.

His daughter, Brandi, is a great golfer, rookie of the year in her freshman year in high school and MVP as a senior. His son, Blake, he reports, is "a big kid with a mean streak in him," and he plays hockey, too. He's in the Ventura, CA, city league, a long way from the spotlight of a Canadian city.

Asked whether there's any chance that Blake might be the one who takes up the family legacy on the ice, Hull replies, "Who knows? All the Hulls are late bloomers. The next year or two will tell if he's going anywhere in the game."

And as for Bobby Jr. himself, if you meet him, you'll be hard-pressed not to think of the pictures of his father in his prime, because the son has the same build, the same handsome blond looks and a hand that engulfs yours when you reach out to shake it.

Bobby Jr. is also a guy with a compelling ability to tell a story, a natural conversationalist whose memories of his growing up give fans an enjoyable glimpse into the life and times of a family who took a wild ride from Chicago to Winnipeg and beyond.

chapter twenty-five

A Short Time But a Good Time

Ian Turnbull

When Ian Turnbull was little, his mother would hook a harness up to the clothesline in their Montréal-area backyard and tether him to it. "I had just enough room to roam the whole yard but not get out," he says with a laugh. "I was a handful as a kid, no doubt about it. My mom was always worried about me getting away."

At age four, Ian loved to observe the construction work that went on near his street. "I'd be down there, standing right behind the guys who were working, like a little foreman," he reports. "One time I parked my tricycle just like a truck, behind one of the work trucks, and when it backed up, my trike got run over. I was heartbroken, and I took it home in pieces. My old man just looked at it and said we'd get it welded up. That's what we did. No big deal."

These differences in parental reactions say a lot about the future Toronto Maple Leafs defenseman and his life. Ian's dad was an old-school kind of guy, all hard knocks. His mom spent her time worrying about her boy and the trouble he was more than capable of getting into. Her interest was in seeing him go into the arts, maybe acting. Ian's dad coached him in hockey and could see the boy's potential early on.

Mr. Turnbull came by his grit honestly, having played as a goaltender. "In those days, goaltenders wore basically the same kind of stuff as the forwards, and no mask. And he had bad vision, so he wore his glasses. He was one of the only goaltenders out there to do that. He reached Junior level, playing like that," says Ian.

The goaltending gene almost rubbed off. "I was the all-time best ball hockey goalkeeper in the world," Turnbull jokes. And when he played in net, he emulated one of two guys—Glenn Hall or Roger Crozier. "Crozier was a southpaw goalkeeper, and he always had his glove up on the crossbar. He was very spectacular, so that's who I was." Ian played the position with some unlikely equipment. "There was this pair of goalie pads around our house that had been my dad's. They were from the late 1930s, early 1940s era. They were the old 'bar pads'—there were four bars running up and down and three parallel ones across the knees. They buckled around the legs, and they offered hardly any protection. But I inherited those pads, and I'd use them in our games, but only in the wintertime in the backyard."

Something probably nobody knows about his NHL career is that Turnbull was the backup practice goalie for the Leafs and that he was on the scoresheet as the extra goaltender one night for a game in Minnesota in the late 1970s. He played the game at his usual spot on defense, but had Mike Palmateer been hurt that night, he would have gone in, fulfilling his childhood dreams—"Everyone wants to play that position; it's where the glory is," he says. His role, however, was to be elsewhere on the ice, and his days in the NHL were still a long way off when he was playing net on his schoolyard.

Another story finely illustrates the way Ian's father shaped him. One year, when Ian was 12, a kid interrupted an afternoon street hockey game with this stunner: "I know where we can get a lot of candy, for free." Naturally, the ears of every boy playing perked up. Nearby, a candy store had gone out of business, and the leftovers had been stored in a locker. Several of the kids had been taking from it.

Amazed at their luck, the group of them headed over to partake, but before long, the police arrived. "They knew what was going on by this time, since other kids had been going in there," Turnbull says with a chuckle.

Seeing the police cars pull up, the boys scattered. It took only a few minutes for the cops to round them up.

Off they went to jail, to be held in a big room awaiting the arrival of their parents. The afternoon wore on, and one by one, each kid disappeared with his angry dad. Young Ian still sat there.

After about two hours, the police officer walked in. "I called your father," he said. "He told me just to leave you there," and the officer walked out of the room. It was hours before Mr. Turnbull came to get his boy, long after the others had found their release.

Ian tentatively accompanied his dad to the car, wondering what fate awaited him at home. "When I got in the car, he asked me if I'd learned my lesson. I said I had. He asked me if it was going to happen again. I said 'Nope,' and that was the end of it," Turnbull says.

About this time, his hockey career was taking off. "Actually, I'd known since I was about eight that I was good at the game. People started coming around, asking me to play in this or that tournament. My dad would greet them at the door and hear them out, then turn to me and go, 'We've got these folks here who want to know if you want to go play in a tournament.' You start getting an inkling that you might be doing something right on the ice. But when I got to 13 or 14, scouts began to turn up, because I was a prospect for Junior hockey."

His dad, meanwhile, used his role as coach to shape the boy into a quality defenseman. "Looking back, he pushed me pretty good. He was a father-coach, and he never cut me any slack. He didn't want anyone to say anything about him being my father. If he was going to take it out on anyone, he'd take it out on me. I used to say I played the game twice— I played the actual game, and then we'd play it again in the car on the way home. We'd go over every play. But if you're going to become a pro athlete in any sport, you're going to have to grow some tough skin."

Turnbull knew his dad's intentions for him when he got a new pair of skates at age 13 or 14. They were the CCM Tackaberry (later Tacks) model, lined with kangaroo leather. Shortly after Christmas, with Ian still growing, the skates started to feel small. The young Turnbull inquired as to when he might be furnished with a new pair. "My dad told me, 'You know what? Play better.' I said, 'What?' And he repeated, 'Play better.' What he meant was that someone else would buy me a new pair of skates if I played at a higher level."

Ian's mom, on the other hand, had no use for hockey, or the idea of a hockey career. "My mom absolutely hated the fact that I was a hockey player. She'd bring a book to tournaments and read when I was younger, if she would come at all," he claims. "She wanted me to go to church, play an instrument. Her side of the family, my grandparents, were into the arts. They took me to hear the Montréal Philharmonic, and I loved that. But there was a clash—if you were going to take ballet and play hockey, you'd better be a pretty tough kid.

Of course, it was pretty cool later when you could play Jimmy Hendrix on the guitar."

One of the only things that kept "Hawk" (as he later came to be called) interested in school after a rough year in grade six was participation in the staging of *A Midsummer Night's Dream*. His role was Bottom, the weaver, and Ian states, "It was appropriate, since I had to wear a jackass' head." But it was not his fate to carry on with acting, and at some point in his growing up, Turnbull's mother finally gave in to the hockey idea. Still, her hopes for him were not dead. "That grade six year was where I realized that I really enjoyed the arts, and I carried on with it," he says. "When I was playing for Toronto in the late 1970s, I would go to the Royal Alexander Theatre all the time, and I could see people looking around at me going, 'What's he doing here?' like you had grown 10 heads. But I happened to like the theater. I could play hockey and enjoy the theater. 'What are *you* doing here?' I felt like asking back. I could ask the same question," he says with a laugh.

He signed with the Montréal Junior Canadiens in 1969, at 16, and played part of the 1969–70 season and also the playoffs with them. He was with the team for the whole of the next season, when they won the Memorial Cup. "It was around this time that I had a bit of a showdown with my dad," he says. "I'd play the game and hear from the coach what I'd done right and wrong. Then I'd get home, and my dad would want to go over it all again. I told him it was enough, that

I knew what I'd done wrong. I felt like I'd outgrown what he had to tell me, since I was already playing at a higher level." The elder Turnbull backed off, leaving it to the young man to find his own way in the game.

As it turned out, Ian fulfilled both of his parents' wishes as an adult. He played in the NHL for 10 years, many as the partner to Borje Salming, forming one of the most productive and effective defensive pairings in Maple Leafs history. Among his career highlights were 79 points in his fourth season (1976–77) and five goals in a game in 1977, making him the only defenseman ever to do that. Unfortunately, his father died of a heart attack at age 52, midway through Turnbull's time in the NHL, so he did not share in all of his son's accomplishments in a career that stretched from 1973 to 1983.

After he retired, Turnbull became more the man his mom might have imagined him being. "I'm a Renaissance man," he says proudly. "I'm into the arts." He plays guitar, he paints, he works with pottery, and he was a partner for a number of years in a gallery in San Pedro, near his home in Los Angeles. "Some people might call me carefree, but does that mean that I don't care about things? No. It means that I go where things take me. I'd call myself more of a free spirit. I prefer to do things that I'm interested in. We're only here for a short time."

chapter twenty-six

Claiming Her Place in the Game
Chris Simpson

From the time Chris Simpson was five or six, she was familiar with a ritual that hockey people everywhere will recognize. Standing in her family's Ontario kitchen, she would watch as one of her brothers sat at the top of the stairs while her mom laced up his skates. Then, as her mother affixed skate guards to protect the blades, Chris would pull on her hat and mittens in preparation for piling into the family station wagon to head to the rink. It wasn't something she questioned; it was a part of who she was. What neither she nor anyone else in her family could have predicted was that as adults, three of the four Simpson kids—oldest brother Dave, Chris and baby-of-the-family Craig—would make their mark in the game. (Jan, the eldest Simpson sibling, didn't follow the hockey path but instead earned a PhD and now works as a consultant.)

By the time the family arrived at the rink, the car often contained another kid or two, picked up from one of the west London neighborhoods in the path between the Simpson house and Oakridge Arena. With the front and back seats filled with boys, it might seem as though the one tiny girl sitting among them would find the atmosphere overwhelming. Chris, though, suggests that it was nothing of the sort. "I enjoyed it. The games, but also the camaraderie. Half our social life was hockey. It was our community," she explains.

When they got to the arena, Chris was all business. No taking along a case of Barbie dolls to play with while the game went on around her. "I would have a hot chocolate, and I'd sit beside my mom and watch the game," she reports. Often, dad Don would be there as well, having rushed home from a business trip to some far-flung spot in the world to take in one of his boys' contests. When the game ended, they'd all pile back into the car and reverse the journey. If it was dinnertime when they got home, they would discuss the details of what had happened on the ice.

Although hockey obviously meant a great deal to the Simpson family, Chris notes, "I don't remember it dawning on me that either boy could make hockey a living—let alone that I would. It was never a topic of conversation in our family. It probably wasn't for anybody back then." "Back then" was the 1970s, when kids didn't have such grand hopes of future hockey riches as many do today.

Yet as the two boys grew up, both showed promise in the game. They moved to playing at a rep level, and then Dave went to Junior A with the London Knights. Meanwhile, Chris competed in high school track and volleyball, but she was also a fixture at her brothers' games. She became so familiar a face that one night when she wasn't in her usual spot in the London Gardens, a press guy happened to notice her absence. He approached Dave, the team captain, after the game. Instead of asking him what had happened on the ice, the reporter blurted, "Do you know where your sister is?"

Dave looked at him with a puzzled grin. Surely this was going outside the boundaries that separated the personal from the professional? And anyway, he hadn't noticed that Chris was missing. He shook his head, looked around as if the answer was in the dressing room somewhere, then stared back at the writer. "No, I didn't notice," he said.

"She was competing in and winning the Miss Teen London contest," the bemused press guy responded.

Miss Teen London? And at the cost of a Knights game? The guy might as well have said that she'd been named head cheerleader of the Dallas Cowboys (hey—this was the 1970s, man). Brother Dave didn't know what to say. Nothing about a beauty contest had been mentioned at home that day, and entering a pageant hardly seemed like something Chris would do. Of the four Simpson kids, she was the retiring one, a person not likely to seek the spotlight.

To shed a little light on Chris' character, consider the story that her dad tells about watching her play softball one afternoon. As she was about to go to the plate, he yelled out at her. Before taking her turn at bat, she turned, found him in the crowd and glared. No words came out of her mouth, then or after, but he got the message. "She was telling me loud and clear that she wasn't an athlete who appreciated that kind of attention," Don says with a laugh.

Chris herself explains: "In sports, I wanted to do my thing, and do it well, but I didn't want to be recognized for it in that way. To hear my name shouted out loud, my first thought would be—no, don't single me out!"

So why compete for Miss Teen London? It was a chance to put herself out there, to be brave. And although it doesn't seem at first to have much to do with her love for and eventual place in hockey, the pageant was a crucial first step in becoming the adult she turned out to be.

Winning the contest gave her incentive to carry on with modeling, and she moved to Toronto, away from her small-town upbringing and into her first post-university jobs. Rather than being a complete departure from her hockey roots, her time in the public eye prepared her for the career that introduced her to millions of hockey fans as a hockey features reporter for Rogers Sportsnet in Canada and a rinkside reporter for Versus in the U.S.

Meanwhile, the boys in the family were forging ahead with their hockey careers. Dave had the greatest season in the history of the OHL with the London Knights in 1981–82, with 155 points (67-88-155), and was drafted by the New York Islanders. Craig spent 1985 to 1995 in the NHL and later coached with Edmonton. He won Stanley Cups with the Oilers in 1988 and 1990 and recently became a part of the *Hockey Night in Canada* broadcast team.

For her part, Chris got a job as marketing manager with the Hockey Hall of Fame in 1992, and at the same time started to work as the in-arena host at Toronto Maple Leafs games, thus combining her ability to be in the spotlight with her knowledge of the game she'd grown up on. It was as if all she'd done from the time she was little suddenly added up to what she ought to be doing as a calling. She explains, "As a kid, I was just going to my brothers' games. But without even knowing it, that's where my initial training came from. Of course, I had no idea back then where I'd end up professionally.

"Even though I was there for the games, hockey was my brothers' world. I came to it, professionally speaking, later. Earlier in my life, I was known as Dave Simpson's sister. Then Craig's sister. But now I see that my job grew from that early experience I had, as a byproduct of growing up in a hockey family. The reason I'm working in hockey is that my training began when I was five years old. I got the love of hockey from my family, and I learned by watching my brothers," she says.

She believes that growing up the way she did gives her an advantage that some other reporters, of either gender, might not have. "I understand, when I'm talking to a player, what he's going through, what he's thinking on the day of a game. I don't think you can get that without being really close to the game," she explains.

Her duties with Sportsnet, where she worked until 2008, included gathering feature stories from all aspects of the hockey world. Some notable interviews from that time included several with the Flyers' Bob (Bobby to hockey fans) Clarke and the first broadcast interview given by Bob Gainey and his two daughters after the loss of the third Gainey sibling, Laura, in a boating accident. Her approach in encounters like these builds on the sense of trust people in the game have developed for her. "People in hockey know that I respect them. I won't approach them for an interview unless I think the timing is right. And when I do the interview, they know I'm not there to ambush them. Especially in a difficult situation, I try to be sensitive to what they're going through. It's important to me that they go away feeling better for having told their story to me," she says.

After leaving Sportsnet, Simpson continued her work as a Versus rinkside reporter as well as hosting an original show for the NHL network. *Captains Driven by Bridgestone* profiles great leaders in hockey in one-on-one sit-downs with Simpson. The 20-part series features the stories of how these NHL captains developed into the players they became.

Fifteen years into her career in hockey, Simpson now laughingly says that her network of contacts in the game is probably bigger than Craig's. It's an irony that's not lost on her. She knew that she had truly succeeded on her own the summer she was invited to his charity golf tournament in support of people with spinal cord injuries and was introduced as a celebrity along with other distinguished guests. "I was thinking I'd been invited as Craig's sister, so when I was introduced along with the other celebrity guests, it took me by surprise. But it's kind of neat for me to know that both boys are saying, 'Hey—look what she's doing now!'"

Simpson summarizes, "For as long as I can remember, hockey was a major theme in our family." And whereas nobody could have predicted the future of the little girl patiently waiting while her mom's lace-calloused hands did up yet another pair of skates for one of the boys, Chris Simpson has claimed her place in the game as fully as either of her hockey-playing brothers.

chapter twenty-seven

When the 60 Minutes End

Mike Weaver

If you work for a large company, you probably have an employee handbook that tells you the rules and bene-fits of your position. How many days you get off, what to do when you're sick, whether there's a maternity or paternity leave benefit, that kind of thing.

But what if you played in the NHL? That sort of stuff wouldn't matter anymore, right? The amount of money you'd make, the glory of playing in the league, not having a regular day job like the rest of us—all of that would make personal considerations, or the things that plague the rest of us mortals, unimportant, right?

That's what you and I might think, but then again, players are not commodities—they're people, and for many of them, life in the league is much less certain than it might appear to outsiders. Forget the superstars, the guys who can write their own ticket, and think about the core guys—the third- and fourth-line forwards, the defensemen other than the first two pair—who make up a team. It is those players who largely live on a delicate edge between glory and uncertainty, sometimes almost daily.

Mike Weaver, who has played on the blue line for Atlanta, Los Angeles, Vancouver and St. Louis, gives an illustration of what it's like for those guys. "When I was in LA, one time, I looked at the depth chart the team had posted online. I wasn't even listed, though I was playing. I went to the Information Technology guy and asked him what was going on."

In his early years as a pro, with Atlanta, he learned that an important part of his game needed to be consistency. But being consistent in his play hasn't always meant that the course of his career was steady, and he has had to deal with doubts about his future almost on a yearly basis.

Weaver is one of those defensemen who isn't top-four, nor even top-six in most of the lineups he plays with. He's the seventh guy, or the eighth, the one who shows up to games in a suit and tie, and might stay dressed that way on any given night. The guy who finds out after the warm-up whether he will be on the lineup card. But he's no less eager to perform, and it's his can-do attitude that has kept him in the game for closing in on 10 years.

He's listed at 5 feet 9 inches (or as he says it, "I'm 5 feet 8¼ inches, but I round up"), and he's always been told he's too small. "All the coaches growing up said to me, 'Why don't you play forward?' but I came to a point in my career where I was able to tell myself that I'm able to play on the blue line. I just have to be that much stronger, that much quicker, that much smarter."

About his career, he says, "Every year it seems like I out-play most of the defensemen. I'm top-six, but then somehow, I get left out on the depth charts. I've gotten the reputation of being the seventh man who doesn't complain about sitting out a game. I don't quite know how. I'm very critical of myself. I look back at every single game video. I try to keep my game simple. My specialization is that first pass out of the zone, the little things that really matter. I'm the kind of player who, when he stays out of the papers, knows he's doing his job right."

Weaver values his career, every game of it, and he cares about what people think of him on the ice, keeping tabs on what fans are saying about him online. "I noticed when the Blues picked me up [in 2008] that Kings fans talked about it on their discussion boards. That made me happy," he says.

That feeling may have made up for the year he had just finished, in which career uncertainty had combined with the challenges of first-time fatherhood. It was a topsy-turvy ride that sometimes had Mike and his wife Rhianna holding on for dear life.

After his two-year stint with the Kings was up, in the summer of 2007, Weaver found himself out of a job. He was looking for a one-way contract—one that wouldn't put him on waivers if he went back and forth from NHL to AHL. Both Pittsburgh and the Canucks expressed interest, and his agent assured him that something would get done.

In the meantime, Rhianna was pregnant, due a few weeks before Christmas. The couple was hoping as the summer went on that Mike could play somewhere that would be close to family, most of whom were in Ontario, and friends, mostly in Michigan, where he had played university hockey (and graduated with a BS in Computer Science). Fortunately, the Pittsburgh Penguins spoke for him. Thinking that it would be good to be five hours from Michigan and five from Toronto and family, he packed up his trailer and left for camp early, ready to ride out the tryout process and make the squad.

"I talked with GM Ray Shero, and he said, 'You have a chance to make this team,' and I told myself, 'I'm not worried about making it, I've done this time and time again.'" He thrives on situations where three guys are going for one spot, and it's a good thing, or he would have gone mad long before now as he worked to extend his career, which now stretches close to 300 NHL games.

"Talking to Shero, I wanted to make sure that I was not there just to be sent to the minors. I wanted to know that

I was at least penciled in on the NHL roster. You don't want to get pegged as a minor-league guy," Weaver says.

His goals were not only professional but also personal. He wanted to get set up in a place at the start of the season so that Rhianna and the new baby would have a home. The baby was due December 6.

Things didn't work out with the Penguins, though, and in short order, Weaver found himself being picked up by Vancouver, far away from Rhianna. "I was happy," he says, "but at the same time, it's a million miles away, especially with her pregnant."

What to do? Suck it up and go, and Weaver did.

NHL contract rules say that when a player lands in a new city, the team is responsible for his housing for the first month, and that if he survives the first 28 days, he's eligible for permanent housing. But it didn't pan out that way in Vancouver, and Weaver lived in a hotel as the time for the baby's birth was approaching. "It was still unknown whether I would go on waivers, be sent down, or what, so we decided that Rhianna should have the baby in Michigan—that way, she wouldn't end up stuck out there so far from everyone, with me gone." Of course, Weaver notified the team that he would need the requisite leave time when the baby was born.

The problem was, Owen Weaver didn't have his parents' time schedule in mind, and he was born early, on

November 30. So instead of being there for the event, Mike was playing hockey, in Chicago. "She had the baby at 10 in the morning, and I didn't get there until 6," he reports.

At least he had some days off to spend with his new family. Although the typical paternity leave is three days, Weaver was given five, but then it was back to work, and Rhianna once again found herself alone. Fortunately, her mom was able to take a couple of months off work to help out.

Finally, a month later, the family was reunited in Vancouver, on January 1. "I did get to Michigan for two days at Christmas," Mike recounts, "but I missed the whole first month, all the stuff dads normally go through."

Now that the family was together in Vancouver, another obstacle presented itself regarding their housing situation. It was too late to buy something for that season and too late to rent and uproot everyone again, so Mike, Rhianna and Owen lived in the team hotel, albeit in a nice apartment with two bedrooms. And he doesn't begrudge that move, nor the way the Canucks handled the situation.

"The team did everything for us, had us a nice baby shower," he says. "The owner gave us a Tiffany baby rattle with Owen's name and his birth weight engraved on it." Mike also cites the friendship of fellow Canuck Jeff Cowan's wife, Leigh Ann, who did a lot to help Rhianna in the early days.

He sums up the year by saying, "I was living the dream, but family clashing with hockey made it the hardest year of my life."

Dealing with life's challenges is not something that fans think about when they either admire their NHL heroes or scorn a player for making a mistake, but Mike Weaver's experience shows that while the benefits of the NHL life can't be denied, there's more to hockey than what takes place during the 60 minutes when the clock is running.

chapter twenty-eight

Skate the Puck Just Once

My nephew, Daniel Reimer, watched his team win the Stanley Cup when he was nine or ten weeks old. It's not that he had a lot of choice in the matter, but I held him while he wore his Detroit Red Wings hockey sweater and saw them hoist their 2002 Stanley Cup. This was not my doing alone. His dad is a genuine Wings fan from way back. His aunt, Barbara, actually a surrogate aunt, lives in Detroit and sent Daniel the official Wings jersey. And I was in Oshawa, Ontario, just by coincidence, but no way was I going to be doing anything else when the finals were on but watching them.

What Daniel doesn't yet know is that I taped that game, because it's unlikely he'll remember it. I've still got the VHS, in the special cupboard in the hallway of my California home where we stash Christmas presents. I figure that when he's about 10 or 12, he'll be old enough to safeguard it, making sure that nobody accidentally records a sitcom episode over it. When that moment arrives, I'll hand the tape over to him.

This will be my attempt to rekindle what I hope will be his most vivid early memory. Why? Because I, like other people connected to any kid born in hockey country, believe that unless Daniel falls in love with the game, his upbringing will be incomplete.

In truth, I have nothing to worry about on that score. Looking at Daniel in the years since that first Cup, you'd almost think that the love of hockey was genetic. When he was four, he asked Santa Claus for a net—an official, regulation-sized one. The crossbar was six or more inches above his head, but he didn't care. He and I—and his little sister, Sarah, who was two at the time—spent the better part of that Christmas holiday in the driveway at my dad's house trying to score goals on each other. As we played, I saw his skills develop. He went from holding his stick like a golf club to being able to take a pretty decent shot, both forehand and backhand. I thought that maybe he had some innate ability.

Then he played his first season of soccer. Not that it's the same game, but while watching him on the pitch, all I could think was, *Why doesn't this kid go after the ball?* It was obvious to me that if he was a tiny bit better than the other kids out there, he could score all the goals. I talked to him about it, telling him that he shouldn't hang back. I worked with him, teaching him how to handle the ball, how to shoot.

Nothing changed. He still went out and played in the beehive, kicking the ball away every time it got within his range.

Applying the same principle to hockey, I realized that whatever talent Daniel might have with the puck might be undone by his unwillingness to go out and take charge of the play. In my head, I had killed his NHL career before it even began, in other words. But then he played ice hockey that fall, and in an odd reversal of what everyone in the family had come to expect, he played with aggression. He even hit a few kids, in defiance of his league's rules, though admittedly, completely by accident. But rather than being shaken up about it, he just got up and resumed play. "This," I said to myself, "could be the start of something."

I took further hope in knowing that Daniel was growing up in a hockey home, mainly because his dad is a huge fan and a hockey historian with an amazing ability to recall facts and events from games in the 1960s and 1970s, including the ones he played in the Oshawa N.A.S.C. Hockey league when he was younger. Taking after his father, Daniel, at five, could name the starting goaltender of any NHL team you picked, and he could also answer the question the other way, as in, "Hey, Daniel, who does Marc-Andre Fleury play for?"

"The Pittsburgh Penguins," he would shoot back, with a look on his face that told you the question was no test at all.

So when Daniel was six and I made my annual Christmas pilgrimage to Oshawa with the promise of seeing him play four games in a weekend tournament, naturally I did so with high hopes. I again thought that maybe this was the start of something. Daniel was a Timbit, as Sidney Crosby had been once. "Maybe this will be the year when he shows himself to be worthy of the Player of the Year Award," I told myself.

On the second day of the tournament, a Saturday, I walked into the dressing room of the Timbits Light Blues to help him on with his skates. His dad had to work. "Ah, the eternal smell and feel of hockey," I said to myself. After all, my last league game had been more than 25 years earlier, but things seemed not to have changed at all. Then I reminded myself that hockey isn't something that people have been doing forever. The game has been around for 40 or 50 years in the present house-league suburban version of kids' hockey, and maybe 125 years altogether. Hockey seems like it's deeply ingrained in us, but that's really just a trick of memory.

No matter. I had no time for analysis. The goal was to get this kid ready to play and to give me something to brag about when I got home. As I laced up Daniel's skates and got his helmet properly positioned on his head, I went over the speech I'd been planning for three days. What I had to say, I was convinced, would ring with the eternal truths that would make my nephew a more effective defenseman. I realized that the game he was about to play wasn't going to make any difference in terms of hockey history, and that even the idea of giving a boy his age a pep talk was a bit too movie-melodramatic, but I couldn't help myself.

"Remember what we talked about," I said. I had been preparing him for this since the day I'd arrived in Oshawa. "You skate that puck. Don't just swat at it." He nodded. I believed I was making progress, and so I continued. "You don't just skate back with the guy when he has the puck and is coming into your zone. You get in his way, get the puck from him, and then you take it back the other way. If you make it all the way to their end, try to score." I was priming him to be a combination of Ray Bourque and Bobby Orr, unbeatable in any zone. I looked at him, and he nodded. My advice had gotten through.

It wasn't quite game time, but having said my bit, I didn't know what else to do, so I fixed him a good hard stare to reinforce the message, and then I smacked him on the side of his helmet. I quickly realized that this wasn't football, and that at six, he might be a little young for my enthusiastic display, but it was too late. Anyway, he didn't seem to mind. He appeared to be into this fantasy as much as I was, though he would have no idea who Bourque or Orr was if asked. I realized too late that I should have mentioned Nick Lidstrom, familiar to him from watching the Red Wings on TV.

I made a quick sideward glance and saw that all the parents were still sitting next to their kids. Shortly, it would be "parents out." The coach insisted on having 10 minutes before the game to talk to his players without distractions. But having made my grand gesture, I grew fearful that if I waited another few seconds, I'd have to say something else to Daniel.

I worried that doing so would surely ruin the power of my speech, and so I stood up, turned around and found the door.

The game began with Daniel on the bench, but on the second shift, played between minutes twelve and nine on the stop-time clock, he came out and took up his position at right defense. I had already gotten the measure of his opposition, and it was obvious that his team had the upper hand on this bunch. Nobody on the other side skated particularly well, and Daniel's team was already up 1–0 on a goal by the kid who generally got four or five a game.

The play soon came to Daniel, off to his right near the right faceoff circle in his end. The puck squirted free from the three or four little bodies swinging at it and went directly to him. "His first chance," I said to my sister, his mom, who stood next to me. "Watch him skate the puck back up the ice." We both kept our eyes peeled for the big moment. Daniel went for the puck and took a whack at it, sending it back into the scrum it came from.

I wanted to yell, "Skate the puck!" and I almost did, but then I realized that the glass surrounding the rink would prevent him from hearing me. I tried to catch his eye when a faceoff came soon after, planning to motion to him to do what we had talked about, but I considered the impossibility of the gesture. How would I signal to play like Bobby Orr to someone with no idea who he even is?

Instead, I followed Daniel with my tiny video camera, and, once again, he approached a puck that he could have easily scooped up and taken around behind his net and out the other side. But again, he whacked it. "We're going to have a video session when we get home," I told my sister, who just looked at me, bemused.

"Don't tell him he played a bad game," she said. "He's having fun."

Of course, I wanted to say that he'd be having a lot more fun if he were flying down the ice with the puck, scoring a few goals a game and getting the congratulations of all of his teammates. But I realized what I really meant was that I'd be having more fun. More accurately, he'd be doing what I never could or would do during my own hockey-playing youth. In making up for my past failures, Daniel would give me something to talk about the next time I was around my hockey friends.

So I didn't say anything, and when the game ended and Daniel emerged from the dressing room, I said simply, "You did a nice job intercepting that guy coming down on you in the second period." When I got no response, I continued, "You do remember that, don't you?"

Daniel looked at me as if he knew there was more to my question than what I had stated, then he said, "Uncle Bean, when we get home, do you want to play with my walkie-talkies?"

Hockey Friends and Enemies

Most of us who didn't play hockey at any serious level don't know what real hatred of an opposing player feels like. We don't understand the kinds of payback that swim in the minds of those who have taken elbows to the head or butt-ends right in the gut.

Think of the old stories of Lindsay, Howe and others of the 1950s and '60s. Elbows flew, teeth were loosened, and the next night or the next weekend it all happened again. Having only five other teams to play meant that guys saw the opposition's villains with a great degree of frequency and that the animosity could grow to ferocious heights over time. Today, it's not so much that way, of course. So many teams are in the NHL that the encounters between players are less frequent than they used to be. That doesn't stop certain players from being feared villains or super-pests, though.

On the other hand, if the enmity can be ferocious between players, the friendships formed in and around the game can be equally strong. Hockey's intensely up-close and personal nature, both on the ice and on the road, creates bonds that never die. Years later, according to those who really know, the sense of identity and loyalty to chums who saw you through a difficult playoff run are the same as on the day the trophy was hoisted.

Perhaps something about the game itself creates this sense of commitment to one's fellow players. Luckily for fans, that loyalty extends off the ice as well, with the rising and falling hopes of the long-suffering tying them to one another and allowing them to say things such as "we won" and "our Stanley Cup," with the full assurance that what they did 15, 50 or 100 rows from the ice was as important as what their heroes did on the ice. In the end, it doesn't seem to matter to those off the ice how big or small their role was. They still pride themselves on every win and feel each loss with a pain that sometimes even time can't erase.

chapter twenty-nine

Guys You Can't Outgive

There are people in the world you can't outgive. No matter what you try to do for them, they'll do more for you, without ever noticing the discrepancy. They're just good to the core. Serge Gagne is a person like that. He's also a hockey guy who grew up in Montréal, relocated to Southern California and now wears a Stanley Cup championship ring.

It's not that he made the NHL. Not as a player, anyway. Rather, he serves as an NHL off-ice official, holding the position of official scorer on the crew covering the Anaheim Ducks. It's a job he has held since the team first formed, and it's a long way from his home on the outskirts of Montréal.

His dad was a house painter and often worked away from home. His mom was a nurse. The family lived modestly, and what mattered most to Serge and his brother was hockey.

The arena near their house had one staff member, a municipal employee in the old tradition. "Let's say it this way," Gagne comments, "if there was a Montréal Canadiens game on TV, he'd put us on the ice, tell us to lock up when we were done and disappear. If we weren't the last game of the evening, who do you think ran the tractor to clean the ice? Nobody!"

Gagne's hockey memories were forged during the time when the Canadiens were surging to all those Stanley Cups in the 1970s, so when he moved to Southern California as an adult, he thought the game was lost to him. But when he saw that the then-Mighty Ducks of Anaheim were coming into existence, he decided to fire off a resumé. "I knew more about hockey than most people out here, I figured," he says, "so I said to myself, 'Why not? They could use a French Canadian on that crew.'" He was right, and 16 years later, he's still at it, and the ring comes from the Ducks' Stanley Cup championship in 2007.

For many hockey fans, having a part-time job like Serge's would be a dream. You get an official blazer, the NHL crest proudly displayed on the front pocket, and a tie with the logo of the league running down its length. Heck, how many of us would be tempted to wear these fashions around the house so we'd see ourselves in the mirror as we passed by? I know I would. But I doubt Serge does that. He isn't that kind of guy.

In fact, he's the most down-to-earth and generous person you'll ever meet, as I can tell you from my own experience when *Growing Up Hockey* came out.

Early in 2008, I was covering a Ducks game for *Inside Hockey*. Serge had seen me a couple of times in the fall, and he'd asked about the book. Now on this night, he caught me before the opening faceoff, two copies of my book in his hand. "I want you to sign these—one for me, one for my brother back in Montréal," he said. I was flattered and thrilled, and I gladly obliged.

A couple of weeks later, I was back in Anaheim to watch the Kings play the Ducks, and Serge approached me to say that his brother had flown through the book, as had he. I thanked him again for his interest and support, but he waved my words away, and instead held out his hand, which contained a gift bag. "It's a little late Christmas present for you, my friend," he said in a voice enlivened by a hint of the rhythms of his first language. I thanked him and opened the bag.

Inside was something wrapped up and a few other things underneath it. I pulled out the wrapped gift and opened it. It was a tiny figure of Jean Beliveau, who Serge knew was one of my favorite players growing up. "Where did you find such a thing in California?" I asked. Again, he waved his hand as if to say, "Hey, no problem."

I dug deeper into the bag and pulled out a pile of hockey cards. All were Montréal Canadiens players from the recent eras, including Guy Carbonneau and Kirk Muller. I thumbed through them and looked up to say thank you.

"You like those, you should see the others that I've got," he said with a smile. Then Serge reached into the side pocket of his official NHL blazer and placed a tiny pile of cards on the table in front of me. I looked at them, stunned. Right on top was a Jean Beliveau. But it wasn't only the card that surprised me. It was that it was signed, in ink, a signature I knew well from having received an autograph from Beliveau when I was a kid, something that I still have and that I had talked about in my book.

"Wow," I blurted out. "Signed."

"Look what else," Serge urged me. At the bottom of the pile, I found a card identical to one I'd dreamed of having as a kid: Ken Dryden's 1971–72 "rookie" card. I had traded the cream of my collection for one like it in about 1973. Actually, I'd traded away most of my good cards in a fit of panic when the boy I was trading with managed to procure a Dryden—to this day I have no idea where from. The trouble was, it was a Dryden with a large crease down the center, a card that I would have rejected outright had it been that of any other NHL player. But I had gone ahead with the trade anyway because of a combination of want, admiration for Dryden and the peer pressure I felt standing on the steps of my elementary school with every boy in my grade eyeing me to see whether I had the guts to back out.

Now, I stared at the card in my hand. Dryden in perfect form. Dryden as I'd longed for him to be 35 years earlier.

It was almost as if the past had come to life in that moment. I looked at Serge and was about to ask him where in the world he'd come up with this kind of bounty, when he spoke first.

"They're yours," he said.

"What?" Actually, I didn't say this out loud. All I could do was pause, trying to decipher the meaning of his words. It was simple enough, but I couldn't get my head around it. My first thought took me back to the Preville Elementary School playground of my growing up, the words reflexively forming in my head: *You mean I don't have to trade you for them?*

Nobody gave cards away at my school, except this kid called Brad Chambers, and he only did it for attention, and never with cards as valuable as these clearly were. Brad had used cards as a weapon, a currency, a means of control. He had been the one who had raided my collection for the Dryden.

I shook myself out of my silence, which had already stretched the limits of politeness. What could I say? "I mean, this is unbelievable. These cards are my dream. I will treasure them forever," I blurted out. I meant every word, and even as I think about the moment over a year later, I still feel a surge of emotion at the generosity of his gesture.

But Serge didn't want thanks. He's not the kind of person who does things for that. Instead, he pulled a program out of his pocket, an old one from when he had played Midget hockey. "I played for Immaculate Conception, just like the team you guys feared when you were a kid," he said as he smoothed out the paper. We both grinned at the irony that had I been a couple of years older, we might have shared the ice as kids. I marveled at how small the world of hockey can be and commented on his picture on the program, which showed him with wild 1970s hair. As I did, I tucked the cards into my pocket, determined to safeguard them. He glanced at the clock counting down toward game time and pointed a finger in the air to signal that it was time for him to head upstairs to do his job.

I watched the game as usual, but between periods I did what I'd done every day on the playground as a boy. I sidled up to the various people in the press box and pulled the cards from my pocket to show them off.

A few weeks later, when I read from *Growing Up Hockey* at Vroman's bookstore in Pasadena, I had the cards in my breast pocket, like a team of guardian angels. And later still, when I went to England for three months to teach, I did the only sensible thing I could think of—I marched into my bank, rented a large safety deposit box and stored them there.

chapter thirty

Playing it Forward

Rick Kehoe

Every morning before he went to school, Rick Kehoe could be found in the same place—on his driveway with a friend. Each boy took 10 shots on the other one, trying to score as many goals as he could. Kehoe still believes that this was more effective training than taking shots on an empty net. "Anybody can score when there's no one in there. But when you've got to pick the spot, when the guy cuts the angle on you and you have to pick something else, it's different, " he says.

It was a skill that was to net him more than 350 NHL goals, but Kehoe's career—and his life—are about more than scoring points. He embodies a hockey version of the Kevin Spacey and Helen Hunt movie *Pay It Forward*, only in this context it would be called Play It Forward.

Growing up in Windsor, Ontario, Kehoe spent a lot of time with his grandfather, Russ Hillman. According to Kehoe, Hillman was a decent and generous man. "It's just the way he was. I never really thought about it. I just watched him. When you watch somebody, you try to do the same things they do. Because of your upbringing, your nature, you do certain things."

At the same time, Kehoe was keeping an eye on his favorite hockey player. "Everyone had their one player that they idolized, and mine was Dave Keon. He was the type of player that could score goals; he could check; he could do a lot of things, but he was a clean player. That's what I imitated in my playing career. I had the chance to play with him in Toronto, and I even played on the same line a few games with him when I was with the Leafs from 1971 to 1974," Kehoe says. Keon played almost 1300 NHL games and ended with just 117 penalty minutes. He won a couple of Lady Byng trophies, in 1962 and 1963.

Almost two decades later, in 1981, Kehoe was awarded the trophy himself. He had 55 goals that year and six penalty minutes. The same season, his teammates on the Penguins voted him the Players' Player. "I think they were recognizing my play and my personality. If somebody needed help or to work on something, I'd try to help them out. Maybe go out for lunch or whatever, talk to them," he says. "On the ice, if a guy wanted to work on some shooting drills, I would do it, because I remember when I was in Toronto, I got called up, and I asked Bobby Baun, 'Boomer, would you mind passing me some pucks?' So he said, 'Sure, no problem.' He got all the pucks in the corner, and he was passing them to me in the slot, and I was firing away. After it was all done, I said, 'Thanks, Boomer, for passing to me.' He said, 'No, no. Go and get all the pucks again. Now this time put them all in the net.' I never forgot that he took that time to help me."

Kehoe played it forward not only as a player in the NHL but also after, as a coach. "I'd work with players after practice, or if I saw something in a player that I thought could make him better, I'd spend time with him. Not all the players really wanted to spend time after practice, but the ones that did, and there were quite a few of them over the years, I'd work with. It was nice when you saw that they had some success in the areas you worked on. I'd try to give them some pointers. Young guys want to know a little bit about the league, the team we were about to play, and so on."

In his role as assistant coach, a job he held with Pittsburgh from the late 1980s to 2001, his most famous pupil was Jaromir Jagr, though Kehoe hesitates to call Jagr his protégé. "He wasn't my protégé, but Bob Johnson came to me in Jagr's first year and said, 'I want you to teach this guy how to shoot.' I used to work with him after practice all the time, and back then he was intense. Bob would come to me and say, 'Get him off the ice.' We'd have these morning skates on game day, and he just loved to be on the ice. When you have guys that work that hard, you're happy that they do have success. He was the type of guy where he was dedicated to being a top player. I worked with him just on the shooting, but he studied the game, how it was played, the players."

Kehoe's gentlemanly ways also reveal themselves in the pattern of generosity he has shown to others over the years. When he won the Stanley Cup, as an assistant coach with Pittsburgh in 1991 and 1992, he and another Penguins assistant, Rick Patterson, sat with the trophy between them on the plane. They took turns sipping out of the famous bowl. But when Kehoe's day with the trophy came later that summer, he didn't keep it for himself. Instead, he displayed the Cup in a pub he partly owned. He invited about 70 people to come see it, but about 2000 came through, got their picture with the Cup and donated money to several charities. He also had a family gathering so that those close to him could share in the excitement.

Like anyone successful, he had some memorabilia around when he finished playing. And he still has his 300th-goal (scored in Montréal) and 50th-goal (Edmonton) pucks. "I also have my All-Star team sweaters and the ones they gave us when we were coaching the All-Star game," he says. But Kehoe has also given away some of the tokens from his career. One of the trainers in Pittsburgh was a close friend. He requested one of Rick's sweaters for his personal collection. Kehoe gladly obliged.

Perhaps not surprisingly, when Kehoe gets mail from fans, he signs whatever they send and returns it promptly. I ask him about an Internet story that said a guy had sent four cards to Kehoe, who had them signed and returned within the week. Kehoe doesn't blink as he explains. "It must have been back in Canonsburg [Pennsylvania]," he says, almost as though his speedy response to the fan was an accident. "When I'm home, people send things, especially the kids. They take their time out and write you a letter, so when I'm back in Pittsburgh, I try to send things back to them as I get them. They might pile up while I'm on the road, but I eventually get to them."

Kehoe's modesty also comes through when talking about his career accomplishments. "Other people would bring up my success. I didn't think that much about it. My mother kept all the clippings in a book. I didn't look at them. When you start reading everything in the press, you have to be prepared to take the good with the bad. It depends on how you handle it. The main thing to me was where my team was in the standings. I didn't think about the scoring race or how many points I had. I focused on my team."

Of the year he was closing in on 50 goals, he says, "I never thought about it. It was just one of those years when the puck was going in the net. You don't really think about things like that while you're playing. You look back and say, 'Wow, I scored 50.' You try to go out the next year and get better as a player, to help your team win. You go back and play better than you did the year before, because if you're better, the team's better." He remembers the night he got the 50th, but he wasn't the one who dove into the net for the puck. A teammate did that.

Nor was he ever enamored of his own considerable gifts on the ice. "If you're a goal scorer, you always have to work to improve your shooting skills. You practice enough, and you see that puck coming, and you hit that opening. And that's just from practicing, repetition. Shooting and shooting."

According to Kehoe, the key to having a good shot is eye-hand coordination and strengthening the wrists. "There are a lot of things you have to work on. It's almost like a baby walking. You have to start off one step at a time, starting at the beginning. You just can't go to the big slapper right off the bat. Quickness was always the thing. You want to be accurate, but you want to be quick. When it hits your stick—BANG!— it's gone. And you see that spot and know that's where you want to hit. The passes come harder and quicker, and it's all timing in the end."

He describes his post-playing days with a similar lack of ego. "As an assistant coach, I was fortunate to work with some of the best people in the business over the years. I worked with Bob Johnson and Scotty Bowman. Herb Brooks, Ivan Hlinka. Guys that won gold medals, won Cups. They all added something different, and I learned from all of them, but the person that influenced me the most was a former teammate and former coach, Eddie Johnston," he says.

Kehoe's tenure behind the bench as head coach for Pittsburgh from 2001 to 2003 wasn't as successful as he might have hoped, but he holds no grudges. "I was always an organization guy. Whatever they wanted. Craig Patrick was the general manager, and he asked me if I wanted to coach. I thought I had been an assistant long enough, and if I didn't take the shot at it, I didn't want to look back with regret that I didn't take the opportunity to be a head coach. It just so happened that year that they ended up trading Jaromir Jagr in the summertime. We had some injuries and ended up trading some other guys. You have to rebuild sometime, and I just happened to be the coach then."

Perhaps the final play-it-forward moment for Rick Kehoe still lies ahead. He has two Stanley Cup rings that he has not worn lately, but he says that when he gets a little older, he may do so again. "The first ring is one that you can wear all the time. The second one is kind of bigger," he notes. He now has a granddaughter, Lily, and she might get one, though he hasn't spent much time thinking about it. "I'll see what happens down the road," he says.

chapter thirty-one

Hometown Hockey

Jim Fox

For someone who wants to make a living at it, hockey is not about feelings; it's about winning. A player who makes it to the NHL has internalized this notion a long time before he ever suits up for his first professional game. He has to, because at every level only players who marshal their focus and play as hard as they can today get to play tomorrow. There's not a lot of time for sentimentality. But despite the hard-edged nature of the path to success, for most players there's a tipping point between playing the game for fun and playing it for a living, a season in which fun and community spirit still feature highly, but where at the same time, the seriousness of the game becomes evident. The result can be a season that even an NHLer who goes on to much bigger things can look back on with fondness.

For Jim Fox, his first season with North Bay of the Ontario Provincial Junior A Hockey League was that season. He was 15 when he left his hometown of Coniston to play 70 miles away in North Bay in 1975–76. This meant the unfamiliarity of living with a family in a billet situation and being in a new high school. But it also meant that he had a chance to make hockey his life.

The signs that he had stepped up a level were obvious from the first moment he walked into the team's dressing room. "It was closet-sized, but it was ours. That was different from anywhere I'd played before. Walking in there gave me a feeling that I was on the edge of making it, that this is what it would be like as I moved up the ranks in hockey," Fox says.

Also unfamiliar to him was that each player had a specific role. "Before that, I was the best player on the teams I'd played for, and everyone looked to me. Now here I was, and I was just one guy. I learned that year what it was to be a part of a team, that everyone had his place. The games were getting rougher, the competition much better. We even had a tough guy who did the fighting. That was something new to me."

People familiar with Fox's career know that he made the NHL as a right winger and played for the LA Kings from 1980 to 1990, so it might be a surprise that he went to North Bay's training camp a defenseman. It was the natural position for a guy who grew up a Boston Bruins fan and who to this day, if you question Bobby Orr's supremacy, will challenge you with a big smile and the words, "The greatest player in the game. Name one better." As a youngster, Fox even wore number 4 like the great Orr and played in his style—rushing the puck, controlling the game, scoring the goals. But Fox got to North Bay and looked around the room. "I was about 5 feet 7 inches and 170 pounds, practically the size I played at in the NHL [5 feet 7¾ inches and 185 pounds], and I thought, 'Man, these guys are bigger than in the league I came from.'" His new league had players as old as 20.

"I thought about the size of the guys in this league, and I made a decision. I went to the team and said, 'Why don't I try forward?'" He knew that he was as good a skater as anyone, and soon he found himself on right wing. It was a smart move. He ended up potting 30 goals and 45 assists in his rookie year. The following year was even better, at 44-64-108.

The transition to serious hockey was helped some by Fox's parents, who drove over on the weekends to see his games, but some moments still took the young kid by surprise. In the era prior to political correctness, rookie initiation was one such experience.

With the North Bay Trappers, the ritual consisted of having all the hair shaved off your head. This was an era, mind you, when kids wore their hair as long and shaggy as they could get away with, but the experience wasn't traumatic for Fox. Instead, it was the first of a series of events that showed him how hockey can bind a community together and bind the players to the local fans.

The Monday after the initiation, he went back to school to face the consequences. "I walked in there, and no one laughed or kidded. They were as proud as I was. I don't remember being embarrassed at all. It was a sign of acceptance, respect. Even more than that, it was something that you valued, because you got the feeling that the people living there stood behind you. I felt at that moment like I was a part of something," he says.

Meanwhile, the Memorial Gardens, where the Trappers played their home games, was becoming an important site of some of his greatest memories. "It only held 2000 or 2500 people," he remembers, "but every seat was filled. It was just what you did in that town, supporting the team."

Playoff time came, and the Trappers worked their way through to the finals. Most of the teams in the league were in the Toronto area, so it wasn't unusual for the team to travel four or five hours for games. But the loyalty of the hometown fans meant that the faithful always followed. So it was during the finals that year. The series for the league trophy was in a first-team-to-eight-points format, and North Bay dropped the first three games to go down six points to none. They managed to win the next three, however, and they returned to North York hoping to close out the series. The seventh game ended in a tie. That meant the clinching game would be in North Bay—the very next night.

The team trundled through the showers after the tie and got on the bus, all the while not thinking about the local fans who had supported them by making the trek to the big city—in 10 rented buses. Once on their bus, the players tried to sleep through the night, warned by their coach that the opposition would be doing their best to get some rest, anxious to avenge the Trappers' comeback from the most dreaded deficit in sports, 3–0. As dawn approached, the bus pulled into North Bay and swung into the Memorial Gardens parking lot.

As the players disembarked, they looked out the bus windows. There, huddled in the dim light and bitter cold, were their fans. They weren't assembled to cheer their heroes. The job wasn't finished yet, after all. Instead, they were lining up at the ticket windows, which would open later that morning. Fox still remembers it with an incredulous feeling. "There they were, waiting to get a ticket. They had just driven all night, like we had, but what mattered to them was that there was a game, and they had to be there. That, to me, is hockey," he says.

That night, the arena was jammed full in every corner and from every rafter. Fox and his teammates played to a two-goal win, with the last goal being his, into an empty net. After the game, the team's captain, a wiry spitfire of a guy named Ron Fortier, stepped up to claim the Buckland Trophy.

Then he and his teammates filed into the crowded dressing room. Players, coaches, scouts, parents—everyone wanted in.

In celebration, some of the guys who were old enough to drink cracked open some beers. Fox grabbed one and opened it, then looked toward the door. In walked his dad, his heavy overcoat, gloves and boots betraying the truth about the weather outside. Without a word, Mr. Fox squeezed through the crowd and took the beer out of his son's hand. It was a subtle reminder that although Jim was old enough to be away from home, he was still a kid. They celebrated together anyway.

Fox's miracle season didn't end there, because the Sudbury Wolves called him up to replace an injured Randy Pierce. Fox scored a hat trick in his first game, played in Sudbury's home rink. "That was Hollywood," says Fox. "We were playing Sault Ste. Marie," he adds, "and I never realized how big a rivalry it was until I stepped into that dressing room. Guys like Randy Carlyle and Ron Duguay were there. It was big."

That success led to him being selected first overall in the Junior draft in the spring and ultimately playing three seasons with the Ottawa 67s, where he won the scoring title in the last season before he made his NHL debut with the Kings. But when he thinks back to that era of his life, it's not so much the success he was headed for as the closeness of the community in North Bay that sticks in his mind.

"The team and the town—I was in the perfect situation," he sums up. "Everyone in town supported that team. It was their team. You knew that the team mattered. Though it was a feeder league for Major Junior, there was a family feeling there. It was competitive enough so you knew you were in a real league but homey enough so that you knew it was still fun."

Fox has been an NHL broadcaster, working alongside Bob Miller televising Kings games, since the 1990–91 season, but he has not forgotten his roots. As if to drive the point home, when asked if he remembers the guys from North Bay, he reels off names. "Rod Stamler, Lou Boudreau, Pat Mizzi— he was our tough guy. Give me a minute and I'll get them all. Claude D'Amour, Rod McNair, Tom Diggles, Gerry Rious, Ron Fortier, Bill Thompson, Joe Omicioli, Tim Heale, Bryan Maille, Mike McParland, Daryl Holmquist, Tim Adams, Mike Huska." He pauses. "You talk about hockey being a team game, and I guess every sport says that. But with hockey, I can tell you, any guy I played with could walk in my house right now, and in two minutes we'd be right back to where we were all those years ago. You feel like you just saw them yesterday; you never forget. There's an instant familiarity."

chapter thirty-two

Becoming the Bigger Man

Brent Severyn

P ut it down to bad luck or lack of foresight, but the guy who roughed up Brent Severyn one night at the drive-in theater in Vegreville, Alberta, was making a bigger mistake than he knew. At the time, Severyn was a relatively slight 13-year-old, a kid who came from farming stock but who hadn't grown into the strapping Prairie lad of lore—yet. So he was relatively easy pickings when the local bully decided to have his late-night snack. Little did either of them know at the time that Severyn would grow up into an NHL defenseman, nor that later still he would transform into an enforcer who fought his way to being a part of the Dallas Stars team that won the Stanley Cup in 1999.

"I was the second smallest kid in my school in grade nine," he recalls now. "And this one week, things were said,

and word got around to me that the local tough guy was looking for me."

On that Friday night many years ago, Severyn and
a couple of friends went to the local drive-in theater. As
Severyn got out of the car, he saw his nemesis approach. "He
came right over and punched me," Severyn remembers.
"I went to the ground, and he kicked me in the face with
a steel-toed cowboy boot. I didn't put up any fight at all."

That was the last time anything like that would
happen. "I told myself that I would never not fight again," he
says, and he embarked upon a strength and conditioning
program that eventually saw him play in the NHL at a listed
210 pounds; in reality he weighed closer to 235. "I always
under-reported my weight in the NHL. I didn't want anybody
to know I was as big as I was," he confesses. Still fit past 40, the
current Anaheim Ducks radio color man says of his conditioning, "This is nothing. When I was playing, I didn't have
an ounce of fat anywhere."

Severyn's love of the game came from experiencing
hockey while his dad played in the local Senior league.
"I would go into that dressing room and smell the baby pow-
der that they put on the grips and tape of their sticks. I would
smell the hockey, and that's what gave me the love of the
game. The drive that took me to the NHL came later."

Shortly after the incident at the movies that changed his life, Severyn started to make a name for himself as a defenseman. It wasn't his size that got him noticed but his big slapshot. Soon he found himself playing in the WHL with Seattle, though his Junior career, like his later NHL campaign, saw him play for a number of teams. He played for Seattle, Brandon and Saskatoon before a two-season stint at the University of Alberta.

His Junior playing days taught him how to fight, and his university career taught him how to play. And all the while he lifted weights and gained strength and size, the drive-in incident having partly forged the motivation in him.

Severyn was drafted by the Winnipeg Jets in 1984. From there, he had a career that saw him play almost as many AHL games (297) as NHL ones (328). His big-league stops included Québec, Florida, the Islanders, Colorado, the then-Mighty Ducks and, finally, Dallas.

Along the way, he made the NHL debut that many dream about, against Montréal, in the Forum. It was a bit of irony for a kid who had had a full Montréal Canadiens outfit when he was young and had idolized Larry Robinson and Guy Lafleur in all their late-1970s glory.

But his real moment of saying "I have arrived" was the night he first played in Edmonton. For several years growing up, before his own hockey career had him participating in

70 games a year as a teenager, Severyn had attended Oilers games with his father. They always sat in the same spot, up high in the corner. The night he went to Edmonton while with the Florida Panthers in the 1993–94 season, Severyn got to the arena early, and while it was still empty, he walked up from ice level to those old seats and sat down. "I was in the very spot where I'd watched all those games, the great Oilers teams," he remembers, "and I thought about what this all meant to me."

Later that night, his parents and friends from Vegreville came to the game, sitting lower now, in seats he got for them, and he looked up from the bench to see them waving a banner with a message from his hometown on it. "Growing up where I did, in a small town in Alberta, you never know what will happen in your hockey career. You think, like every kid thinks, that you'd like to play in the NHL, but it's not real. You have to work hard; you're not spoon-fed anything, and I had done the work. Playing in Edmonton, I said to myself, 'Wow, this is real.'"

He played mostly as a defenseman until he got to Colorado and drew an assignment as the team's enforcer. It was a strategy that at the time helped him survive in the league, but one that ultimately probably cut his career short.

"You talk about playing with injuries," he comments. "During the playoffs, for example, the stars are said to play with injuries. But us third- and fourth-line guys play that way all season long. I had days when I couldn't get in my car. I had to take a half-hour shower just to skate. You break your nose in practice and you say, 'Oh, I'll just stick some gauze up there and go on.' That's the reality every day for a player on that part of the roster."

But the injuries didn't matter, because he was doing what he wanted to do. His reward was riding the wagon train with the Stars to the Stanley Cup in 1999. He commemorated that adventure with a tattoo of the Cup and his number, 17, on his ankle, something he's glad to show anyone who asks to see it. But he's also careful to set the record straight. "I was a part of that team, and I was with them during the playoffs, but I didn't play during the post-season, so my name is not on the trophy," he says.

His absence during the post-season didn't stop the team from including him in the celebrations, nor from giving him his day with the Cup at home in Vegreville. There, he and his friends ate pierogies—his favorite food—from the Cup in commemoration of the woman who had sent them to him on every stop of his NHL ride. Then, they drank warm pilsner beer out of the bowl, something that would have made his grandfather, who kept a beer handy on his tractor while he farmed, happy. The celebration was not without its physical cost, however, as Severyn had broken his back and his wrist, herniated a disk and sustained many other injuries over his career. None of that mattered in consideration of the result.

The ring he got as part of the win he gave to his father, though Severyn himself has kept some important mementos of his career. "I have my sweaters, the actual game ones, in my house in Dallas. To a player, those are things that really mean something. The other stuff, scrapbooks and the things from my early hockey days, are still in my parents' house in Vegreville. We had a one-story ranch house with a basement, 'the dungeon,' I called it, and that's where my room was. In fact, it's only recently that my parents told me they're going through all that stuff. I'll have a look at it when I'm in Edmonton with the Ducks one of these days."

Now retired and working for the Ducks as radio color man while also running a multi-faceted sports strength and conditioning business, Severyn enjoys his success and his family. But to say all of that leaves out one part of the story. It's the kind of *Brady Bunch* revenge moment that anyone who was bullied growing up, even once or twice, dreams about.

Several years into his professional hockey career, Severyn and his cousin walked into the Homesteader bar in Vegreville, and there sat his old tormentor. "All of a sudden, this guy who had been such a monster in my mind and tough as nails is right in front of me," he recalls. "I went over to him, and to my surprise, and I'm sure his, I towered over him. I'd had my growth spurt, and I'd spent years lifting weights." Meanwhile, his cousin was encouraging Brent to even up the old score. He had all of that NHL fighting experience to draw upon, after all.

"And I looked at the guy," Severyn continues, "thinking, 'Am I willing to waste my time to beat this guy up?'" What struck him about the situation was the pathos. "Here's this guy, and he's the same person he was when I left, while I've gone all these places and done all these things."

Severyn went back to the other side of the bar, joined his cousin for a beer and put the past behind him.

chapter thirty-three

Helicopter on Ice
Mick McGeough

T he more intense the game, the more heat the referees seem to take. The closer the play, the more likely you are to hear the boo-birds, the hecklers, the offers of eyeglasses, all made with elaborate gestures. Deep down, of course, everybody knows that most of the time the refs are right, that they are only human, after all, and that without them there couldn't be a game in the first place. But in the heat of battle, and sometimes afterward, rationality doesn't always prevail among the gathered die-hards.

From time immemorial, or so it seems to hockey fans, referees have been scrutinized for the calls they make or don't make. But only one is famous not only for the calls he made but also for the way he made them. Mick McGeough, who retired in 2008 after reffing nearly 1100 NHL games and more than 60 playoff contests, including the 2006 Stanley Cup finals, is perhaps the most flamboyant man ever to have worn the orange armband of officialdom.

Meeting him off the ice, anyone who had seen him ref an NHL game would immediately place him by observing the bulldog body and the full head of gelled hair. (He's proud to say that he was the last helmetless person—player or official—in the NHL.) Most, had they any desire to berate him for a call made 5, 10 or 20 years ago, would think twice seeing him up close. But any impression of ferocity doesn't last past "hello," because McGeough quickly disarms with a smile.

"Sure I had interaction with the fans, always did," he says. "You'd meet them in hotel lobbies, places like that. What would they want to do? Same thing they want to do now—talk hockey. Sometimes we'd become friends, maybe play a round of golf."

I ask him whether he's aware that a group on Facebook is called the "Mick McGeough Lasik Eye Surgery Fund." His eyes twinkle at my question, and he chuckles. "I didn't know, but hey, that's all a part of it. It is what it is. Have I made mistakes in my career? Absolutely," he says, drawing out the syllables of the last word. "But the good calls far outweighed the bad calls. If I did make a mistake, maybe it stood out a little more because I was a little flamboyant, a little different than most other referees, but that never bothered me. You go to your next assignment. A good official is one who can learn from the mistakes he made and move on to the next game.

"I really enjoyed going out there and performing, and a lot of the time doing some of these things, these antics, was almost subconscious. You get so involved in the game, and when you see a close play around the net, you want to make sure that everybody knows that it wasn't a goal. So maybe an extra wave-off, or a little flamboyant wave-off, it just became part of me. I always showed a lot of emotion on the ice, and I don't think it's a bad thing."

Fellow referee Rob Shick dubbed the most famous move the "Helicopter." The term refers to McGeough's trademark "no-goal" sign, where he waves his arms frantically while skating forward, one foot up in the air in front of him.

"You want to let the guys know that the puck hit the goalpost or it wasn't in, so instead of one wave, I would do three or four or five waves, maybe jump in the air a little bit, to let everybody know that it wasn't a goal. A little bit of showmanship, yeah, probably, but a lot of emotion went into all that," he says.

"I brought my intensity out to the ice every night. I took this job very seriously. Off the ice I was an easy-going guy, but when an hour before game time came, it was time to put the game face on, and our guys respected that, and the players respected that. I was never one of the most gifted officials in the league, but I worked my tail off and finally got to the top."

His career happened because, as the former Regina Pat says, "I was a hockey player with no skill. I had some brawn but no skill whatsoever, but it was fine. I knew I wasn't going to make it, but it was a good part of growing up. Every Canadian boy grows up playing."

He turned to refereeing more as an adventure than anything. He began his career as a zebra at 24 after having studied at university for a year while also playing hockey there. He quit school to take a job as a salesman for McMillan Bodell Lumber and at the same time had a friend invite him to work as a linesman in the Western Hockey League. He did that for one year, then became a referee in 1981. For four years, he refereed while working a regular job, earning $75 a game in the WHL, plus expenses. "You didn't do it for the money—you did it because it was fun; it was exciting to do a little traveling. At that time, I started to think about the prospects of becoming a professional. I actually never thought it could happen for one moment, until I got third or fourth year in the Western Hockey League, and then people start talking to you about it."

He got his big break by being invited to work the Memorial Cup in 1985. Of the seven guys who worked that tournament, six were signed by the NHL that year. Their names, some of which include Mike Cvik, Shane Heyer and Lance Roberts, would be familiar to most fans.

McGeough quickly developed a style of his own, one he explains with great precision. "I think, if you ask any hockey official, he'll tell you that there's a balance between the art of officiating and the rulebook. It's all part of one.

Back in the old days, we could interpret a little bit more. Not these days. Now they want penalties called. We could justify not calling a penalty in certain situations, and now it's pretty well cut and dried. But back when they gave us the latitude to do that, it was all part of the art of officiating."

The game changed for him and his colleagues when the league brought in the two-man system. "You had guys who had different game styles, and they were conflicting. Like anything, it took a while." He is glad to say that his assignments often had him working with some of his younger colleagues, because "they knew that I would look after them out there. I almost became like a father figure to some of these young guys, and I didn't like anybody laying a lot of crap on them. Sometimes you have to let them go on their own, but often you can look out for them and help them."

Explaining the trademark gestures he used to call penalties, he says, "I put a lot into it. I wanted the fans to know what a slashing penalty was, or what a hooking penalty was, so I used my signals, again maybe an over-exaggeration, but everybody knew, on the ice, exactly what was going on when I was calling a penalty. There was no mystery."

His style did get him into a little hot water every now and then, though McGeough's most famous moment—the Curtis Joseph bear hug incident during the playoffs in 2000—wasn't entirely his doing. "It was a real intense hockey game in Ottawa one night," he explains. "Toronto was playing there, and they had a fierce rivalry at that time. It was a tough call on a goal. I think it was a one-goal game, and Cory Cross carried Daniel Alfredsson over the line. Alfredsson hit the puck as they were going in, and it barely went over the line. They were complaining that it was goaltender interference, but I don't think they realized that Alfredsson was pushed. Anyway, Curtis was an emotional guy as well, and he came out of the net to protest the call I made. As he got close to me, he sort of slipped, and I landed right on top of him with his arms around me. Therefore it was seen on every television highlight show for about two weeks!"

At that moment on the ice, McGeough knew he had to do something. "I called a 10-minute misconduct," he says, but then he adds, "I didn't actually know what to call. I'd never had that situation before, but I knew I had to call something, so I called a misconduct. He didn't have to serve it, of course. And you know what? We got over it."

He continues to maintain good relationships with players in his new life as a referee coach working for the NHL. "I was in Anaheim recently, and Chris Pronger and I got to talk, Scott Niedermayer also. They might ask me about why something was done a certain way, what our approach was. They might just want to talk hockey." McGeough's OK either way. "I discuss this all the time with our young guys," he says, speaking of his new role. "It's not only going out there and skating hard, it's dealing with the coaches, the players, the media. It's part and parcel of the art of officiating."

As do players, officials prepare themselves both mentally and physically for a game. They've recently instituted pre-game meetings in the dressing room to discuss what will happen. "We talk about certain players, certain coaches and certain situations that might arise. We don't want to prejudge any game, but we want to know what to expect."

Once the game ends, it's time to forget. "I'm a big one for camaraderie. After the game, I'll encourage the guys to go out for a beer or a sandwich. Sitting in those hotel rooms doesn't do you any good. We spend enough time in there anyway. I think the guys need to go out and enjoy themselves and have fun." He says that on off-days in away cities, the officials golf or sightsee together to bond. "Travel away from home and away from loved ones is a big drain." About 70 percent of referees end up divorced. "No excuses, but travel takes a big toll."

McGeough sums up the life of the official by saying, "It's a commitment you have to make. You spend five or six years in the minor leagues. Back when I started, it was $26,000 to start in the NHL. Now it's $100,000 for a young guy to start, so at least you can make a good living at it. It's still no easier to recruit guys, though. I don't understand it, but it's a tough job, a very demanding job. You've got to be away from your family. You have to have a pure love for the game to do what we do out there." The typical schedule is 73 games a year, plus playoffs and pre-season, with a total of about 90 games the norm.

The payoffs, aside from the salary, are huge. McGeough hails from Regina and still maintains a home there, and he says that he gets nothing but positive responses from people in town. "I come from a small community, a city of 200,000 people, and I know a lot of people there. People look at you a little differently, have a little more respect for you, and being in the NHL was the greatest thing in the world. I can't tell you how much fun I've had and how many good people I've met in this business."

Not to mention achieving a certain amount of fame in the wider culture, and not only for those flamboyant gestures. McGeough has been quoted in as erudite a publication as the *New Yorker*, but he downplays that as a moment that might indicate that his career brought him to heights he couldn't have imagined. "It's just fun to talk hockey. It doesn't matter who it is, whether it's the *New Yorker* or the Regina *Leader-Post* or the Moose Jaw *Times-Herald*. It's just fun to tell people some of the stories we've had. I'm into this for a good story."

chapter thirty-four

A Hockey Guy, After All

O ne of the great things about having written *Growing Up Hockey* is that I've heard from so many people who have shared their similar experiences. This in turn has given me license to indulge in lots of hockey nostalgia about the game and my childhood. A lot more, that is, than what I did while I was writing that book.

So one day I got thinking about my old Brossard buddies, and I poked around on the Internet, hoping to find one. My first impulse was to Google these guys, so naturally I picked Ravi Ramachandran, figuring that of all the people in my neighborhood, he had the most distinctive name and therefore might pop up most easily. I was right. It took no time to find a person with that name, and looking at the bio posted at his employer's website, I noticed his birth year. I did the math. This had to be the same Ravi.

Turns out Ravi is the mathematical genius he appeared to be in elementary school, and now, 30-some years later, he's a professor of electrical engineering in the U.S. I emailed him and threw in several specifics about where I lived and a few memories of times we'd shared. Within a few days, I had an email in reply. We struck up a conversation, and I mentioned that I'd written a book of my recollections about how hockey had shaped my life.

As you might have picked up if you have read the Preface to *Growing Up Hockey*, the book contains memories of my childhood. The stories reflect the way I remember the events happening. But I was careful to say that I wasn't writing history.

Good thing, because my dialogue with Ravi over the next little while showed me how much I'd forgotten and how inaccurate some of my recollections were. In my memory, Ravi was a smart kid who was fun to be around, but someone whose life was far different from mine. His mom dressed in the traditional Indian sari, and his house smelled like an exotic, faraway land where food was spicy and delicious. (No slight to my mom's cooking, but onions were in our house only a handful of times, and curry, well, she wouldn't have had a clue what to do with it. Her baking was divine, though, so in the end it probably evened out.) Every time I went over there, I wished that the Ramachandrans would adopt me, at least at mealtimes.

I remember having Ravi over to my house a few times, but the details of what we did are sketchy. Was it homework? Watching TV? I didn't think our shared past had anything to do with hockey. And even after starting to prod my memory after this early email exchange, I was pretty sure Ravi didn't play on the street or on the ice.

So it surprised the heck out of me when he brought up a series of memories of the 1971 finals, won by Montréal with Ken Dryden in net. I consider the series my wakeup to hockey, the event that let me know that there was a world bigger than that of my family, and I've always felt that by virtue of being lucky to live in Montréal, I was part of the Stanley Cup win. But all I recall is that Montréal won it, beating Chicago. I vaguely picture Tony Esposito in net for the Blackhawks, but even that could be a false memory. I liked Tony O my whole growing up and certainly saw him play many times later, when I was old enough that memories would stick. Nothing else about 1971 comes back to me, except how I worshipped Ken Dryden.

But not so for Ravi. He remembers the number of games, the scores, the details. What he said to me was this:

Memory: 1971 series in which experts predicted Boston to win in 4.

Ken Dryden made his debut, won the Conn Smythe and led Montréal to victory over Boston in 7 games. Game 2 is particularly memorable since Boston was leading 5–1

going into the third period and we beat them 7–5!! We
went on to win the Stanley Cup [after] beating Minnesota
in 6 and Chicago in 7.

The 7th game versus Chicago is another true memory.
Chicago led 2–0 and we came back and won 3–2. It was
the days when Bobby Hull and Stan Mikita were stars for
Chicago.

Wow! This kid was seven when these events happened!
I didn't ask him if he looked up the facts before emailing me,
but I'm guessing from the other hockey memories he shared
with me that he hadn't. He just has an encyclopedic way of
keeping track of the past.

But Ravi surprised me even further. He told me stories
of times he had been at my place, particularly during the 1972
Summit Series. He recalls taking part in a gas station promo-
tion, to get fans involved, that went something like this: you
picked up postcards that said "Go, Canada, Go!" on them,
and you wrote down your favorite player's name and mailed
the cards off to encourage the guys.

Now, it's not like me to forget this kind of thing, but
I have no memory of these events. Ravi, however, hasn't for-
gotten, and I know his memory is accurate because the players
he named when he told me the story are exactly the ones that
I would have sent postcards to—Ken Dryden and Phil
Esposito. Ravi says we sat at my kitchen table and filled in the

cards. And although he didn't say so, I'm sure we also discussed the players, the upcoming games and Canada's world domination of the game, unknowing of the set of surprises that was in store for us in the days ahead.

He also reminded me that he had played a lot of hockey, on both the ice and the street. And he told me stories of how we used to play a version of the game at recess with a tennis ball that I brought to school every day. It was soccer with hockey rules and, given that we couldn't bring our sticks to school, it was our only recourse to the familiar world of hockey that filled the hours of our days whenever we were at home. Hearing his memories, I felt amazed at his powers of recall and was humbled that the years had obscured his central place in my young hockey life.

And because this renewal of our friendship took place during the 2008 playoffs, we started to discuss our team's chances. Unfortunately for me, the post-season was taking place in the abstract, because I was in England, and I had no access to hockey on TV. He asked me why, and I told him that the cable system we had didn't carry the NHL.

What Ravi didn't know was that four years earlier, I had been in the same boat, except that I didn't have a TV in the Oxford apartment. In a desperate attempt to see some games, I had bought a set and used it to tune in games that appeared on one of the BBC channels at 3:00 AM, a great idea until I received nasty letters from the TV Licensing police, who were going to raid my apartment and take me to court for my love of the game—well, from their perspective, for watching telly without paying the appropriate fees, because you need a license in England to watch even the non-cable channels. Now, on this second England trip, Gaby and I had a TV in our apartment, cable, a license and everything. I made sure of it. But there was still no hockey.

The first chance I got, I turned on the TV and checked the guide to find where the NHL games would appear. Nothing. As playoff time got near, I checked the listings again and still drew a blank. I searched the Internet and figured out that the games played on a special cable channel (who changed that since I was here last?), one that we didn't get. Skunked again.

Anyway, about the time I was conversing with Ravi, Montréal was winning its first-round series against Boston, so he became my hockey lifeline as we shared our enthusiasm for our favorite team. It's not that I couldn't discuss hockey via email with other friends or with people from the press world back in LA. It's just that none of them had grown up in Montréal. Their hearts were not torn when the Canadiens lost and didn't soar when the Habs won. With Ravi, it was different. He got it.

But as I emailed him, I also thought about the ironies in our friendship. We probably couldn't have come from two more different families. Neither of us lives in the old neighborhood any longer, nor even in the old country, for that matter. And my recollections of him from years earlier were of a quiet kid to whom hockey was invisible.

Talking with him again, however, I felt as though I'd reclaimed something I'd long lost. And I learned something, too. Hockey is big enough to bridge the difference between backgrounds, and hockey memories are not something that one person holds alone. They are a shared legacy. By adding Ravi's memories to mine, my sense of the past got bigger, and my childhood opened up to me in a way I hadn't realized it would when I found him three decades after we'd worshipped the Canadiens as boys.

The Wider World of Hockey

Anyone at least 35 has always known that the world of hockey is bigger than the NHL. We first learned this in 1972, when the Russians came over and gave us a good scare on the way to nearly beating the most invincible team of superstars ever assembled. Since then, the hockey fan's universe has widened to include the Olympics, the Russian Super League and other places where hockey is played at a high level, such as the Swedish Elite League, where NHL players often come from.

And don't forget the scope of the game as it's played in arenas all over North America. Anyone with kids or young relatives in hockey country understands that the lure of the Timbits Light Blues playing the Timbits Reds on Saturday morning at 10:15 can be as compelling, and the game action every bit as much worth discussing, as any professional contest. The level of play among the six-year-old combatants may be halting, but the goals are exciting anyway, and they only grow more glorious as bystanders discuss and relive them standing in the cold of the arena. These days, chances are that someone named Meghan scores goals as often as someone named Keegan, because, at least at the lower levels, hockey is now a sport shared between the genders.

Hockey exists in multiple worlds, with the NHL being merely the most visible. The experiences of the players in the rest of the hockey universe—in Europe, on sleds, in the minor leagues in the U.S. and Canada—show that the game means just as much elsewhere as it does in the NHL. Winning and losing comes down to what a team and its fans have invested in the contest. It might not be the Stanley Cup at stake, but no matter, because in the minds and hearts of the players, the end they strive to reach means just as much.

chapter thirty-five

These Guys Invented the Game

One of my students, a guy of about 25, came up to me after class one evening. I'd mentioned earlier in the course that I liked hockey, was Canadian and had played some growing up.

Dan approached me awkwardly, as if he wasn't quite sure what to say. "So you're into hockey?" was his opener. I wasn't sure how to respond. My old prejudices flared up. What did this guy know about my game? Was he another of those LA types who never played and who followed the game only because of the Gretzky era?

"Yeah," I said, "I like hockey. We all played growing up." Whenever this kind of conversation comes up in California, I attribute my love for the game to a more general cultural condition than to any special talent I might have had.

Especially since I didn't have any. "Do you follow hockey?" I asked, trying to remember what I had said in class that might have led to his question. We were studying contemporary California literature, after all.

Instead of answering my question directly, Dan said, "This year has been hell. My wife has been ready to kill me." I knew what he was talking about. It was spring 2005, and the season would have just been ending, had the lockout not occurred, with some lucky bunch of guys hoisting the Stanley Cup. Instead, there had been no playoffs, nothing. In desperation, I had joined the NASCAR nation. But that hadn't worked out too well. Indeed, I was casting about for something else to love, a long summer gaping before me. I nodded in acknowledgment of what he'd said.

This was the opening he needed. He started talking about the Kings. He knew the players, and not only the recent ones. He reeled off the names of the old players, even before the Gretzky era. In LA, that's a crucial test. Most people remember the Gretzky time—hockey was popular then, not for the game itself, but because the Hollywood set was watching games, and that bred copycat interest. But for a guy to remember that Butch Goring played in LA, or to know that Brian Kilrea scored the team's first-ever regular-season goal, well, that suggested deep devotion.

But because there was no game to discuss, I didn't quite know what to say next. "I suppose when you were growing up, you didn't play?" I ventured what I figured was a safe guess. Back when Dan was a kid, there wouldn't have been many indoor arenas around. Certainly the big Ice Station that my buddy ran out in the Valley, a model outfit with two pads and a smaller, practice sheet nicknamed "The Pond," wouldn't have been there.

"Not on the ice, but we played on the street, on tennis courts, on basketball courts, wherever we could. It was a regular Friday night thing. A big group of us would get together. We made goalie pads, since you couldn't really get stuff out here back then, and we just went crazy. Later, as we grew up, our girlfriends would come out and watch. We played on roller skates, too, if we had them." Dan related his hockey memories with the same earnestness he brought to the discussions of the novels we had been reading in class.

For a moment, I was distracted by the rag-tag image he presented, and I almost slipped into my familiar rant, at least in my head: *These Californians. Think they know the game. Think they can play the game. But they can't, and don't. Roller skates? Or had he said "Rollerblades"?* It didn't matter. Any real hockey fan knew that sneakers were the only proper footwear to sport during a street hockey game, whether it was being played on asphalt or somewhere else.

But then I realized that what Dan had said meant a lot more than what I had initially thought. He and his buddies hadn't played the game our way—the way we had played in my Montréal, and later Peterborough, neighborhoods. In fact, these guys had done something remarkable.

Although my buddies and I had older brothers, friends or bigger kids in the neighborhood to school us in street hockey and then, when the weather got cold, how to play on the ice, these guys in LA had no one. They literally had to invent the game for themselves out of almost nothing.

The rituals of our game—such as picking sides by tossing hockey sticks into the middle of the rink and then throwing them out to either end or starting play with the two centermen tapping their sticks on the ice and then up to touch each other's three times, or saying "Game on" and "Next goal wins"—were given to us by others. But Dan and his friends had created all the rules, practices and mores of their game alone. They'd had no models. And because they'd done that, they deserved credit as true fans and participants in the game, regardless of whether they'd ever been on the ice.

I looked at Dan standing there; I really looked. Although in some ways he was almost a different species than I was—different generation, different country, different pastimes—we were bound together because each of us, though in diverse ways, had spent his childhood trying to emulate a bunch of heroes who played a game that we could only dream of playing at the NHL level. My abilities were never a fraction of what even a third-line NHLer's would be, and Dan had never laced up a pair of skates in his life. For all our differences, however, we were the same, because our passion for hockey made us who we were.

"So you still play?" I asked. Although I doubt he understood the nuance of my question, what I meant was, "What you did qualifies as playing hockey. It might have looked funny if a bunch of Canadians had seen you play, but I'm giving you credit for what you did. You guys invented the game, adapting it to the circumstances in which you found yourselves."

"We're all married and stuff now," he began. I felt a letdown coming. "But we still get together once in a while," he added. Hearing him say that made me feel better. It might not be the same as me going home to Oshawa and getting into a street hockey game with the local brats, playing just like my friends and I did more than 30 years ago, but it was something. Dan and his friends had their traditions, and the game lived through them. Maybe that's even more remarkable because the Gretzky era in LA is long over, and there often hasn't been much to like about the teams the Kings have put on the ice over the years since. If these guys were carrying on with their version of the game, there was hope for hockey in this place.

Since that encounter with Dan, I've discovered that a lot of other hockey people live in California. Some of them, like me, are displaced Canadians who brought the love of the game with them. For us, hockey is even more alive here than it might have been had we stayed in our home country. The game takes on a heightened importance precisely because it's such a ready symbol of all that we miss about home. But others, like Dan, came to the game in their own way.

These inventors of the game never had a backyard rink or an arena where their parents took them at 6:30 AM on a Saturday to practice. They don't know how it feels to put on your new hockey jacket for the first time and read the patch on the sleeve that says "Right Wing." They never attended a hockey banquet. In short, their hockey experiences aren't the ones that seem so eternal and universal to those of us who grew up where hockey is the only sport that really matters.

But like some lost tribe or expatriate colony trying desperately to imitate the nearly forgotten motherland, these people developed their own rituals and practices surrounding the game, and these traditions are what bind them to each other and to the sport. Put them on the ice and they might skate around like a bunch of four-year-olds. But in their own element—under sunny January skies with the threat of winter rain—they do just fine. The game they play might not be ours in the way that we value so desperately, but it is theirs, and no less hockey for that.

chapter thirty-six

Getting Out in Time

Vaclav Nedomansky

He was one of the best players in the world, and the world knew it. At least, they saw it in those rare instances when they could glimpse Vaclav Nedomansky's talent during the yearly World Championship tournament from the mid-1960s and beyond. The rest of the time, "Big Ned," as North American fans later called him, was locked away behind the Iron Curtain, because his was an occupied country.

The system he lived under was oppressive. "Things just happened, and you couldn't really question it. There was no chance to think about it, because there was so much pressure in the Communist system," Nedomansky says. His only relief was hockey, though even that reflected the prevailing social conditions.

He spent his childhood during the height of the Communist era, and he first played hockey in Hodonín, Czechoslovakia, starting in 1955. It was decidedly unglamorous. Someone came into the arena's dressing room, threw a bunch of used equipment on the floor and told the boys to scramble for what they needed. Practice was in half an hour. Something as simple as a new stick was almost unimaginable. "We would try to buy a stick from an older player. There were one or two types, and that was all." His parents were working people, and thus a shortage of money combined with the scarcity of new goods made his hockey dreams hard to fulfill.

It's not that Nedomansky didn't dream of more. Because the rink where he played was new, it hosted the country's first summer hockey camp. The country's best team practiced there, and he would go watch. A couple of years later, sometime around the late 1950s, teams from the British National League visited and played games, and later on, Canadian teams did the same. Aside from that, no communication and absolutely no information was available from the outside world, except what the government allowed.

He soon realized that his only lifeline to the outside world was through reading the newspaper. "I was always collecting newspapers. I would get them from the place where they were published, there outside on the board. I was very much involved in sports. It was the most important thing for me. My father, he was a racer, racing on a motorbike. I asked

him, 'Can I play soccer and all these sports?'" Mr. Nedomansky supported his son's efforts, never imagining where they
might lead.

As a teenager, Vaclav played a couple of seasons on
a Czech 2nd League team, and then he graduated from high
school and went to Bratislava to study and play in the
Czechoslovak Extraliga. "Because I studied physical education
and biology, I went there—you have to go for an interview.
I was not thinking about university, but my coach called their
coach and set it up. I made the HC Bratislava team."

Over the 12 years he played for this squad, from the
early 1960s to nearly the mid-70s, he also spent time with
the Czech National team. For players in Europe at the time, the
World Championship served as the biggest showcase of their
talents, and Nedomansky took part 10 times. He was the leading scorer of the tournament three times and leading goal
scorer during four years.

His team won the World Championship gold medal
in 1972, breaking the Soviet Union's dominance, a victory
that he still cherishes. It was in this same year at the Olympics that he famously shot a puck over the boards right at the
Russian coach. "We knew all the Russians because we had
played against them for such a long time. They always put
pressure on us, and we really had a desire to beat them on
the ice. We played so many times, and I knew that whole
generation of players.

"We started to beat the Russians, like in the 1968 Olympics, where we beat them 6–4. We were in the Olympics again in 1972. It was a serious competition, but [Russian coach Anatoly] Tarasov was extremely impolite, and he was screaming at me, calling me names and so forth. I controlled the puck in front of the bench, and he started to scream at me, and I just turned and shot at him. A wrist shot."

His team eventually won the bronze medal, and the Russians took gold. That treasured medal and a couple of others have survived to this day. "When I won them, I got to keep them," he says. When asked where the medals are now, he replies with one word, "Shoebox."

His hockey dreams were coming true, but he'd had enough exposure to know that he would never be happy until he played against what he considered the best players in the world, and they were in the National Hockey League.

From time to time, the Czech National team made trips to North America, and his memories of those times are still vivid 40 years later. "My impression of Canada was that it was all hockey. That first time I went there, we played in 12 cities. I remember [like it was] today. Chicago, Victoria, Vancouver, Winnipeg, Saskatchewan, Edmonton, Toronto, Montréal—I played in Montréal against the Junior Montréal Canadiens. I scored two goals. Plante played for them; they had something like five guys from the older team, but we were beating those teams."

If he could have, he probably would have stayed in Canada at that time, but the Czech government made that impossible. "They would just take your passport, hold team meetings, keep you on team buses, and there was one guy who was police, or who was there to guard these people." He asked several times during this era of his career to be released to play in North America, but each of his requests was denied.

NHL people also gave it a try. "First of all," Nedomansky recalls, "I was asked maybe three or four times to stay in Canada and play. One year, 1974 actually, Cliff Fletcher and David Boyle went to Prague and tried to officially get me out, but they couldn't even get an appointment. They waited a week and then went home." It didn't seem to matter that part of the deal involved a big payoff to the Czech government.

Through it all, Nedomansky was entirely uncertain about his future. He was nearing the age when the team typically put players out to pasture, but he says that the government "didn't want to let me go even when I got [to that age] because of my education in biology. In addition, I was already working and publishing different material on sport." He was planning to teach at university, but unusual circumstances closed that door, too. The situation was bleak. "They took my passport and told me that for five years I could not travel. I had no idea what I could do. I felt like if they found out that I was looking to leave, they would kill me, just like happened to other people. It was becoming obvious that I was not going to play hockey much longer, but that I could not work. What was I to do?"

It was at this time that he took matters into his own hands, planning a vacation and packing his wife and young son into his Citroën 2CV. He had a separate passport, "for personal use," and the family left on July 4. "I had no idea what that day meant, but we left that day. I had two suitcases, and I was wearing a pair of shorts."

Once they got out of Czechoslovakia, he made a desperate phone call. "I called a West German number. I knew one guy who was a German-English guy. I don't know exactly who it was, but basically yes, I told him I'm in Switzerland. Guys from both the Atlanta Flames of the NHL and Toronto Toros of the WHA jumped onto a plane. I discussed the situation with both guys, and basically I made the decision based on, first, that Toronto is in Canada. Second, it was the World Hockey League [Association], but I found out that actually I would be suspended from the National Hockey League for 18 months because there was an agreement between the International Ice Hockey Federation and the NHL. Even players entering European countries couldn't play for 18 months." And so it was that, on July 13, 1974, he and his family arrived in Toronto so that he could play for the Toros. The additional benefit for him of playing on that club was that they had just signed two players he very much admired, Frank Mahovlich and Paul Henderson.

When the team moved to Birmingham after his first two seasons, Nedomansky went, as much for personal reasons as hockey ones. He says, "I spent one full season [down there] because I was attached to the president, to Mr. Bassett, to Mr. Eaton; they owned the club. But by then, the 18 months were over. On the 18th of November 1977, the Red Wings traded for me." And so, at 33, he played his first NHL game.

Sometime during the same season he had one last telling run-in with his Communist homeland. The Czech National team played the Red Wings in Detroit, and although Nedomansky was on the ice, his name was not mentioned on the Czech radio broadcast, only his number. He says, "I had in the first period four penalties; I broke my stick over their heads four times. But they still couldn't use my name. So on the transmission, they said I died in a car accident."

His NHL career, although it started when he was 33, lasted six years. He retired in 1983, having netted 122 goals. Adding his WHA and NHL outputs together, he played 673 games and scored 257 goals.

Two decades passed before he could go home again, and the government's harassment continued. "When I left, they sent me a letter that I should be going to jail. I was going to be punished. I lost all my worldly possessions. My mail, when I was sending things from Toronto, small presents, the police would steal that. I would send 20 items, and my parents would get three items, opened." He got to see his dad once, in 1987. The elder Nedomansky was given a compassionate visa for travel because he was sick with cancer.

He didn't see his mother for 20 years, until he went back home in the 1990s. And even then, knowing the history of the government there, he felt jittery. "I was holding my paperwork, waiting for somebody to jump me. I was very nervous," he recalls.

Nedomansky now works for Hockey Slovakia after doing stints as an NHL scout. One benefit of the renewed openness between Eastern Europe and the West is that his career is being recognized and honored. He is in the Hockey Hall of Fame in Slovakia as well as in the International Ice Hockey Federation Hall of Fame, headquartered at the Hockey Hall of Fame in Toronto. He has donated items to each institution. "I gave the IIHF some stuff because my team won the Spengler Cup and I scored a couple of goals—against the Russians again," he says. His voice reflects the bittersweet memories of a time when being an enemy on the rink also meant being at odds politically and ideologically. The two worlds of hockey—Europe and North America—now see players freely moving back and forth between them. An Iron Curtain no longer separates players from whatever opportunities they might seek in the NHL. As such, Nedomansky's experience will never be duplicated, but it stands as a reminder of a time when seeing the opponent as the enemy truly represented a life-and-death difference.

chapter thirty-seven

Coming to a New Hockey Country

Anze Kopitar

I n his first NHL game, Anze Kopitar picked up a puck at center ice, swooped in on Ducks defenseman Chris Pronger, went around him as if he was rooted to the ice and wristed a shot past a sprawled Jean-Sebastien Giguere. It was one of two goals Kopitar scored that night, and it immediately set the hockey world to talking.

The two obvious questions asked were, "Who is this guy?" and "Where did he come from?" The answer to the latter question was that Kopitar is from Slovenia, and he's the only player ever to make it to the NHL from that nation, which gained its independence in 1991 after being a part of the Socialist Federal Republic of Yugoslavia since 1945. It's a country of about two million people that sits north of Croatia and south of Austria. And the answer to the former question reflects something you hear over and over again when talking to players who eventually made the NHL. Kopitar is the product of a family with deep ties to one another and an ongoing interest in his progress in the game.

To North American ears, Hrusica, Slovenia, may be a long way away, but Kopitar's life was similar to that of a Canadian or American kid who makes the NHL, and his hockey initiation started when he was born. His father played for the nearby professional hockey team representing Jesenice, which has a history dating to 1948. A close approximation of the team's colors adorned the young Anze right after his birth.

Contrary to what some have said, Kopitar didn't exit the hospital wearing a Jesenice hockey sweater, but he did wear something with a clear sports connection. "Apparently it was like a red track suit that my grandma bought me. Those were the first steps. I wore that the first couple of minutes when I came out from the hospital. Maybe that was the sign for me to be an athlete," he explains.

His career didn't take long to get going, and this too has a familiar ring. He put on his first pair of skates when he was four and used them on his backyard rink. "I don't know if it was the case with every kid near me, but I certainly liked to skate," he says.

When most North Americans think of Europe, especially the former Communist Bloc, they probably imagine grim cityscapes with rundown towers of apartment houses. Kopitar's home was anything but that. "We lived in a house. We had the Alps there, so it wasn't like California where the houses are like five feet apart. We had a lot of land, so my dad made me a rink.

"Having ice in my backyard was really fun. I was on the ice all the time. My dad skated with me as much as he could. It was a great time. He and my grandpa made an ice surface maybe as big as this locker room." He's referring to the dressing room at the LA Kings' practice facility in El Segundo, California, which is larger than most NHL arena dressing rooms, measuring perhaps 40 by 40 feet.

"At first trying to skate, I was pushing a chair around, but after that I skated with my stick and started to play around," he recalls. It's an image as familiar as the one most fans have of Gretzky on his backyard rink in Brantford, or of the Staal brothers in Thunder Bay.

Within two years, Kopitar was playing on a tournament team. Like many who make their way in hockey, he competed with boys a year or two older than he was. His first grand success was in Villach, Austria, when he was six and a half. "I guess I was the best scorer of the tournament. I think I got 30 goals or something like that," he says. For his trouble, he collected the first of many trophies he would win over the years. "I still keep it at home. I keep all the medals and things. We still have the same house, and they're there."

He also collected hockey cards. "There weren't really any cards from the league my dad was playing in, but we collected NHL cards. It wasn't like here [U.S.], so there weren't a whole lot, but we got what we could and saved them."

Hockey was always a family affair. As a player and later coach of the Jesenice squad, Kopitar's father allowed young Anze to taste hockey at that level from his early days. "I really admired all the guys who played on my dad's team," he recalls. "Dad would take me to his locker room, and I would hang around there and sometimes get to skate with them after practice. It was pretty cool. They were a professional team. Not quite like this [the NHL], but still professional."

Back at home, he enjoyed a rich neighborhood life. "We played soccer; we played basketball; we played hockey," he says of his childhood. "It would just depend on how the guys would feel about playing. Obviously I wanted hockey first, but if the rest of the guys wanted soccer, we just played soccer."

The hockey was, as elsewhere, not restricted to the ice. Street hockey also permeated local town life. "We played all the time," Kopitar says, "me and my buddies. It was actually in front of our house, too. We had a parking lot, a driveway, where we played. I had the nets, the sticks and all that stuff, so all the guys from the neighborhood would come over, and we would just play hockey."

When he was 10, he did a homework assignment that may have been the first prediction of what his future would be.

"I wrote a book about a little guy dreaming, how he might come to the NHL and play here. Obviously when you're a young kid and you're playing hockey, you always want to play in the NHL. That's your main goal, I think, all over the world in the big hockey countries. I took that as an example and wrote 'Secret Dreams of Hockey Player Miha.'" The narrative was written in his native Slovenian. His English fluency began to develop shortly thereafter with English lessons in school, encouraged by his mom, an English teacher.

The next step in his hockey development was a familiar one—leaving home at an early age. In his case it was to Sweden, where he played in the Swedish Elite League at 16. "My parents were behind me all the time. I really have to thank them for that. It was really hard, because we were a really tight family. So having them see me leave home and move to another country was kind of hard for them, and especially for me. I loved hockey, and that's the only reason that kept me over there. If I hadn't felt really good about hockey at that time, I probably would have gone back home. There were some tough times, but I loved hockey too much to blow this chance."

His next transition came when the LA Kings drafted him in 2005 and brought him to California for their rookie camp in 2006, where he was so far above the other young players that it was obvious to everyone that he deserved a shot at the NHL roster. Then came that infamous first night against the Ducks that took place shortly after his 19th birthday.

In the three seasons since he joined the Kings, Kopitar has averaged close to a point per game, with a career-high 32 goals in 2007–08. He's at the core of a young Kings team and was named an alternate captain at the start of the 2008–09 season.

His transition to life in the big city has been smooth. "Once you leave home, you leave home anyway. It's a little bit more convenient when the flight is three hours to Sweden and you're there, than being on a plane for 14 hours to come to LA. But when you're gone, you're gone. It doesn't really matter, for me, where you are. My adjustment to California wasn't really all that hard."

He says that LA didn't at first seem like hockey country, but when he saw how many fans are into the game in California, he realized something. "This organization, we're bringing a hockey nation together. Everybody's really excited to play on any given night. When we're doing good, we're selling out every night, and so it's almost like Canada. When I saw that, I thought that this could be a hockey town for sure when you start winning."

You might think that such success and a new contract reportedly worth tens of millions of dollars would have changed the young man. But if you did, you'd be forgetting the strong family values he grew up with. His family has relocated to California to be with him, something he enjoys talking about. "Oh, yeah," he says, "My whole family is here right now, and my girlfriend also."

When asked whether he's aware of the frequent greetings that appear on Internet message boards from fellow Slovenian expatriates, he seems surprised, but he understands that, as a Slovenian, he is an important symbol for his countrymen. "The feeling of being the first guy is obviously great. It's an honor for me. I felt great when I played my first NHL game and was the first guy [from Slovenia] in the NHL. I was hoping to open a couple of more chapters in Slovenian hockey and show the guys back home that it can be done— and hopefully show this hockey world around here that some good players can come from the small countries. Hopefully, some more guys are going to come."

chapter thirty-eight

The Single Word, "Player"

Cammi Granato

C ammi Granato never questioned that she would be a hockey player. Although few girls played the game in the late 1970s, she declared at an early age that she would one day become a Chicago Blackhawk. It was a dream that didn't come true in exactly those terms, but her experience shows that even when the path is not clearly set out, hockey can take a person to amazing heights.

She played hockey with boys all during her growing up in Downers Grove, Illinois. Most of the time that wasn't a problem, mainly because she was among the best players on the team. Her goal each year was to be the scoring leader. Her career eventually took her to Providence College, Concordia University, the Olympics and the World Championship tournament, none of which was even a possibility when her hockey hopes were forming. But as a kid, Cammi didn't think about the obstacles. "I was obsessed with the game. Playing hockey was completely normal for me. At school I daydreamed about hockey all the time. Nobody could ever take that away from me."

Her hopes formed early. When Granato was four, she took figure skating lessons on a tiny ice pad next to the hockey rink, and one day when her mom became distracted while talking to someone, Cammi snuck out the open back door and stood next to the glass, pointing. "That's what I want to do," she said when her mother caught up with her. Like any figure skater, she wore a frilly costume, but as she says it, "Once I got to be five or six and had an opinion, I wasn't going to wear any of that stuff." Her parents kept their promise that if she finished her skating lessons that first year, she could join a hockey league, and she did.

Her on-ice career was a family affair. One night she scored a handful of goals, including one that she put top shelf. She was six, but most proud because her brother Tony, a future NHLer, was watching her play. Years later, when Tony was 16, he was given the job one night of driving 10-year-old Cammi across town to meet a ride that would take her to a game an hour away. As they went, they got into a car accident. Their mom, six or seven months pregnant, was with them. In the aftermath of the accident, all Cammi could say was, "Am I going to miss the game?" Newly licensed Tony ended up driving an enormous van an hour through the snow to get her to the arena. They arrived during the second period.

Life in the Granato family revolved around hockey off the ice as well. When Cammi was seven, they moved to a new house, and the kids immediately converted the basement into an arena. They took two plastic football uprights and turned them upside down for nets, then used tape to mark out goal lines, blue lines, a red line and goal creases. They had two goalie masks, the old, plastic, full-face kind. One was plain; the other was eventually painted the U.S. colors in honor of the 1980 Olympic men's gold medal.

Every day when the kids got home from school, they immediately changed into their play clothes—sweatpants with the knees worn through—and went downstairs. Brother Don's job was to post a list of who was playing whom on a corkboard attached to one wall.

"U.S. versus Russia," or "Blackhawks versus Minnesota" it would say, and the Granato kids would play, two-on-two, on their knees. The puck was a ball of tissue, taped up. The bench was an old mattress that sat in an alcove. They followed hockey rules, but with one addition. "If you got hurt, you couldn't tell mom," Cammi says. "It would get everyone in trouble. The rink stretched from wall to wall, and we checked, so it got rough. The only people who would play with us were our cousins. Friends came over and said, 'Wow, this is too much for us.' I remember getting banged around and sitting halfway up the stairs taking a breather." It was good training for what would become Granato's life outside the house.

Being female and playing on boys' teams was no big deal to her, and usually not to the people she played with, especially once they saw her skill level. Occasionally, though, the issue of her gender would come up, such as the time she was at a tournament for the weekend and had just dished the puck off during the first game. As she skated down the boards, a kid from the other team blindsided her, giving her a mild concussion and putting her out for the weekend. She was furious, and it didn't help that the boy came up to her near the end of the tournament and apologized, then said, "My dad told me to do that."

"I was mad that I hadn't gotten to play, and I thought, 'How crazy that a dad would tell someone to act like that,'" she says.

As she formed her goals in life, hockey was in the center, though she still wasn't sure where she might go with it. Then one day, when Cammi was 12, her mother asked her to come upstairs, into the living room, a place normally off-limits to the kids.

"You know, you're going to have to quit hockey at some point," she said. Cammi looked at her mom in disbelief.

"What do you mean?" she replied, crying. "Why can't I be a boy? Why do my brothers get to play? I'll never quit hockey!" She stormed out of the room. Her mom feels bad about it now, but her intention was not to dash Cammi's dreams. She wanted her daughter to choose a sport that might take her somewhere. Little did either know that hockey was to be the way Cammi would make her path in life.

Her goals became achingly clear when the family went to the 1988 Calgary Olympics to watch brother Tony play for the U.S. While watching the opening ceremony, Cammi didn't stop talking. She tugged her mom's arm. "I have to be here," she said. "What can I do? Could I play basketball?" She had been involved in other team sports and was searching for a way to make it to a future Games. "Do you think I could make the men's hockey team?" she asked. In those days, the squad was made up of amateur players, not NHLers as is the case now.

Around this time, Cammi became aware that some east-coast colleges had elite women's teams. She got a letter expressing interest from Providence College right when she was leaving off playing in boys' leagues. "I played Bantam for three years," she says, "because they changed the age divisions at that time. But when it came time to move on to Midget, I stopped. The guys were all getting bigger, but I wasn't." She focused on soccer and was all set to go to Wisconsin to play for the university team when Providence came through with an offer to play hockey in August 1989. Four years there netted her 256 points in 99 games.

Her next step was to play on the U.S. Women's National Team, which eventually led to the Nagano, Japan, Olympics in 1998, the first time women's hockey had been included.

The Olympic adventure started with a six-hour flight delay at the San Francisco airport. Once on board, she and her teammates kept talking about what the arena where they would play would be like. They arrived in Osaka and took a bus to Nagano, where they were whisked directly to credentialing. Granato's moment of realization of how huge it all was came when she looked at the pass hanging around her neck. "I'm official," she said to herself. Then it was off to a big conference room to get outfitted as part of the American team.

"You got a big shopping cart, and started around," she recalls. "Each station was for a different set of clothes. The first was for the opening ceremony, and you got a shirt, pants, shoes, socks, a jacket, the works. Then it was the medal ceremony outfit, then the closing ceremony. At each station, they had the whole gear. There was a tailor there to fit the pants. It was amazing. We all just pushed our carts around and laughed." The goodies went into duffel bags to be transported to the Olympic Village, but not before the team put on their medal podium jackets and had a photo taken.

That first night in Nagano, Cammi and her five roommates tried on all their gear for the opening ceremony and marched around the room practicing their waves. At the time, it was still surreal. "I'm going to absorb every second of this,"

Granato told herself. "It was the pinnacle of my hockey life, and I knew it."

When the opening ceremony came the next day, she stood with the others waiting to go down the tunnel to the field. Even outside, she could hear the noisy roar, and as they went down the chute, she could feel the wave of energy from the crowd. "I had dreamed so much and seen the 1980 Olympics on TV and watched the movie about the hockey team's gold medal so many times with my brother that we wore out the tape. It all came to this moment, walking into that ceremony. People had told me for so long, 'You shouldn't be playing because you're a girl.' But this was our day to celebrate."

After that, it was down to business, and the U.S. team won every game. The day they beat Canada 7–4 in the final preliminary game, after trailing 4–1 with 10 minutes left in the third period, they knew that they could win the gold medal. The final match was two days away.

"I couldn't sleep and couldn't eat for two days," Granato says. "I wrote in my journal, 'I can't believe that 60 minutes of hockey can mean so much—either a gold medal or complete devastation.'" They won the gold, and as team captain, Cammi was presented her medal first. Cammi's husband, Ray Ferraro, likes to say that it was the first Olympic hockey medal given to a woman athlete, ever.

"I had thought about the celebration if we won, the jumping and hugging, but I hadn't thought about the medal itself," Cammi recalls. "I looked at [the medals], all shined up and clean and stacked up really high as the presenters walked towards me." At the magic moment, she couldn't hold back the emotions anymore. Feeling the weight of the medal around her neck, she wanted to curl up into a ball and cry. That night, she and her roommates slept with their medals beside them.

Granato's career continued through another Olympics and nine World Championship tournaments, including the 2005 contest in Sweden, in which the U.S. team won its first gold. Then she was cut from the team without warning before the 2006 Olympics in Torino. "I had no idea it was coming," she says, "So I never got closure. I never had a last game, in the sense of knowing that hockey was coming to an end."

At the same time, her attention turned toward the goal of having a family, something she had put off to pursue her hockey dreams. "I missed so many years of family that it's an important focus for me now. One reason I'm not gearing up for a chance to come back and play in Vancouver in 2010 is because of my focus on family," she explains. In 2006, she and Ray had a boy, Riley, an event that has filled her life with more hockey than ever.

"Tonight," she says on the phone from Vancouver in the spring of 2009, "Riley and I are playing mini-hockey in the living room, there's a game from Red Deer, where my step-son plays, streaming on the computer, and my brother Tony's [Colorado Avalanche] game is on the TV." All this hockey is not just because Ray is a former NHLer and now broadcaster. Riley, even at two, seems to be forming hockey dreams of his own. In a reprise of his dad's habit when he was a kid, the little boy puts on his hockey helmet, stands straight up at attention and asks his mom to sing "Ho Canana," as he calls his national anthem. He sings along, and when it's done, he yells, "Game on!"

"Riley has no chance," Cammi says. "He's going to play hockey."

For her accomplishments in the game, Cammi Granato was awarded the Lester Patrick Trophy in 2007. The award, recognizing outstanding contributions to hockey in the U.S., gave Granato the feeling of belonging that only an NHL career might have otherwise. "I was being honored by the NHL, and that's a family that I always wanted to be a part of," she says.

The list of recipients reads like a who's who of hockey. Above her name are those of Steve Yzerman, a 2006 winner, and Brian Leetch, who won alongside Granato in 2007. But what's important to note is that beside each of their names, including Granato's, is a single word: "Player."

chapter thirty-nine

Hockey with a Twist

Jean Labonté

He grew up idolizing the Montréal Canadiens, but he didn't get to see his first game in the Forum until he was 17, and then not in circumstances he would have chosen. The tickets that got Jean Labonté and his brother in to see the Habs play the Penguins that night in 1987 came courtesy of The Montréal Children's Hospital, where Jean was being treated for cancer.

Six months earlier he had been a lifeguard, spending his summer in swimming trunks and wondering about the lump he'd found on his tibia. Now, with a diagnosis of osteosarcoma, a type of bone cancer, he was undergoing what would turn out to be a year's worth of surgeries and chemotherapy to rid him of the disease. It was a tough way to transition from childhood to young adulthood.

Not wanting him to lose his leg, Labonté's doctor suggested that the tibia be replaced by a long steel rod. Suddenly, the boy who had played baseball every season as a kid and enjoyed road hockey with his friends had a rigid leg that would keep him out of sports altogether. Jean fought for his life but went on. He attended CEGEP de l'Outaouais and then Université du Québec à Hull to study software design.

Three years later, in 1990, he broke the rod holding his leg together. Ironically, a few weeks before this happened, he had called his doctor to discuss amputating the lower part of his leg and removing the rod, which was hindering his movement. Now he had no choice, but neither did it feel like a renewed tragedy. It was a chance to do something he'd been thinking about anyhow.

He had his surgery and decided to get back to being active after learning to walk with a prosthetic leg. He took up what he describes as "a bunch of able-bodied sports," including golf, softball, rock climbing and badminton. Then someone mentioned sledge hockey. He'd heard about it before, having read a magazine article about the sport when he was in the hospital for cancer treatment. "That looks cool; I'd like to try that," he'd said to himself at the time.

The game, invented in the mid-1960s, sits players on sledges, or sleds, with their lower limbs straight out in front of them. Two skate blades are mounted below the seat and a runner is fixed underneath the front of the sled. Propulsion comes via two shortened hockey sticks with picks on their ends that players use to push themselves forward and control their motions in turns. Goalies are similarly equipped, except that they use a stick in one hand and a catching glove on the other. The glove has spikes so the netminder can move side to side. All players wear regulation hockey equipment.

Labonté's first attempt at getting involved in the sport came when he realized that the arena near his home in Hull had some equipment. He tried to reactivate the league there, as he thought it would be a good way to acclimatize himself to the sport so new to him. But Labonté was too busy with school commitments, and he let the hockey drop.

Then came his first post-university job, where he met the man who would help him take his athletic career to a height he might never have imagined. Hervé Lord was a longtime National team member, and he invited Labonté to Ottawa to play with the Sledgehammers, at the time a club team. Labonté accepted the offer, and as he learned the game, he found that he could hold his own as a defenseman. It was the start of his climb from novice to international-level player. "I knew from early on that that's what I wanted to do—play on the Canadian National team," he says. His objective was to make the squad and go to the 1998 Paralympics in Nagano. He made the team in 1996, a year in which several of the players were either hurt or engaged in other sporting pursuits, so there were several openings. "I made the team a bit by luck that year," he says. He soon found himself at the World Championship in Sweden.

Surprisingly enough, for a kid whose first vivid memories were of the Canadiens players jumping onto the ice in the last few seconds of their win over the Rangers to take the 1979 Stanley Cup, being a hockey player had not been on Labonté's agenda growing up. "I didn't grow up in that kind of family," he reports. "I could have played hockey if I had asked my parents to let me, but I didn't bug them for it, and so they never signed me up in a league."

He's making up for lost time now. His team won a Paralympic silver medal in 1998 and was fourth in 2002. They won gold at Torino in 2006 to reach the pinnacle of their sport, and while waiting for the medal to be put around his neck, he thought of his family: "my wife, my son and the sacrifices they've made to get me here. They don't get to come out and get a medal, but they deserve it just as much as I do."

That the sport is a serious endeavor is witnessed by Hockey Canada recently taking the Paralympic team under its umbrella. "That was a big thing," Labonté says. "It made us look at ourselves as elite athletes. We see ourselves as part of the hockey family now, playing the same game as the able-bodied Olympians." Anyone who has seen video of the National sledge team's games can attest to the special skill and training it takes to play the game at this level. You don't get a medal at the World Championship tournament or

Paralympics for nothing. But Labonté is still shy to claim pro-athlete status for himself.

"When we went on the Olympic ice in Salt Lake City in 2002, we were all looking around, thinking 'this is it—this is where they [the Canadian gold medal hockey team] played, and now we're playing here,'" he says. And he recalls being at an autograph session in Toronto and sitting next to Paul Coffey. "I said to myself, 'Oh my goodness. Look who's next to me.'"

But Labonté comes by his elite athlete status honestly. Consider the training schedule he is now embarking upon to prepare for the 2010 Paralympic Games in Vancouver. He lifts weights and uses a three-wheeled hand cycle for cardio training. He is also on a schedule of on-ice workouts that he does with some of the other players in the Ottawa area. (Some of the National team players do not live locally, so each trains on his own or with other players who live close by, and the team gathers a week or two before departing for major tournaments to practice together.) In addition, the whole team gathers every three to four weeks during their hockey season for a four-day on-ice session that features two practices per day.

For the run-up to the 2006 Paralympics, Labonté took three months off work to devote himself to training. For 2010, he hopes to get a six-month leave so he can focus exclusively on his game. He will work on all aspects of his conditioning, most especially strengthening his core muscles and increasing his endurance level. "It's a physical game. You can hit.

You just can't ram a player with the front of your sled," he says. "So you'd better have yourself in shape." That, plus dealing with the same pressure any other player feels—younger guys are waiting for their chance—drives the two-time captain of the Canadian team.

His coach, Jeff Snyder, once commented that Labonté is like a rock on defense, and the nickname stuck. Now "The Rock" hopes to spread the word about his sport and keep the gold medal in Canadian hands, especially with the Olympics and Paralympics taking place at home in 2010. It will likely be his last big tournament, and it's probably the last place he might have imagined—or even hoped—to find himself when he was growing up watching Guy Lafleur and Larry Robinson play. But when he's on the ice, he says, "I don't think about my cancer and those years of treatment and the complications. I think the same thing as any hockey player who wins a championship—about all the work, the ups and downs, reaching the pinnacle."

He goes on to generalize this attitude to all the guys he plays with. "Any of us, when we're in it, we don't think of the loss of limbs, and all that. We've moved on. This is our life now. Someone from outside might think about those things, but it's part of who we are. We may project an image to the onlooker of having half a body, but it's people from the outside who think about that. What we're thinking about is how to win the battles. Win that game. That's what matters to us."

Asked to sum up his career in sledge hockey, Labonté is clear about what the game means, not just for him, but for all its players. "The moments on the ice are different from everyday life. One player on our team never walked," he says, "but when he's in his sled—it's freedom. He can move like he wants. Once we sit down, it's our game."

chapter forty

Life in the Minors
Peter MacKellar

Peter MacKellar came closer to making the NHL than 99 percent of the rest of us, and probably closer than most of the guys who ever play at any level past house league. He spent four years in the Ontario Hockey League, having a breakout year at age 21, when he scored 40 goals and added 39 assists. From there he spent four years at the University of New Brunswick, where he earned a BA in addition to playing for the national champions, the Varsity Reds. The spring he was to finish school, Peter had an offer to play with the Tacoma Sabercats of the West Coast Hockey League. He went, and the taste of the professional hockey life he experienced with the team stayed with him.

In the summer of 2000, after getting his degree, Peter became engaged to his long-time girlfriend Shawna, and the two decided to do whatever it took to support Peter's hockey dreams. He had been impressed by how professionally the Sabercats organization treated him and his teammates. Upon returning to Fredericton, the calls and offers from numerous professional hockey teams—ranging from the American Hockey League to various other minor leagues—started pouring in.

One particular coach from Little Rock, Arkansas, was quite persistent in demonstrating his interest in Peter and even arranged for Peter to participate in an all-expense-paid tryout with the Boston Bruins' AHL affiliate team, the Providence Bruins. Thinking this was the most promising path for his career, Peter put his trust in this coach, hoping he would impress the Providence scouts and coaching staff.

After an unsuccessful tryout in Providence, MacKellar committed to the East Coast Hockey League team in Little Rock. He was very excited to play for a coach who was seemingly so interested and impressed with his skills. So he and Shawna packed up their Jeep and a U-Haul with almost everything they owned and began the journey down south into the unknown and unpredictable world of semi-professional hockey.

Upon arriving in Little Rock, Peter and Shawna met and connected with fellow players and their families. Peter posted several points in a couple of pre-season games and felt confident in his choice to play with the team. Despite his ability to put up some points, his excitement about the season soon faded. The shifting ways of hockey life unfolded before him when he received the dreaded coach's request to meet in his office after a morning practice. He and Shawna had been in their new apartment just a week.

Unsure of what to expect, Peter eagerly met with his coach only to be told that the team was releasing him so that they could afford to bring in another player.

Peter was in complete shock, all the while feeling let down by a coach he trusted and thinking of all of the promising offers he could have pursued but had passed up. Little did he know that this scenario was often the case in the minors; guys come and go, even on a weekly basis in some instances. Contracts are signed but often go unfulfilled. Peter went home to tell Shawna that their time in Arkansas had come to an abrupt end.

Together, they waited for another team to claim him off waivers, another process unfamiliar to the couple. Technically, he had to go to whichever team claimed him. In the meantime, MacKellar decided to take matters into his own hands and started phoning the other coaches he had spoken with earlier; however, many had already begun training camp and had filled most spots on their team.

The disappointment the couple felt was compounded by the fact that Shawna had excitedly accepted a position in special education with the Little Rock school district. Now, she had to regretfully turn down the job. Almost as upsetting was that she had just stocked up on $200 worth of groceries for their new home.

After a few days of talking to various coaches, the couple decided to head north to the Elmira, New York, franchise of the United Hockey League, but not before they gave their groceries away to some of the friends and families they had quickly bonded with in Little Rock.

Almost as soon as they arrived in Elmira, Peter and Shawna knew that the situation was not a good fit for them. Problems with housing persisted. At one point they were asked to live in a duplex that was being fumigated for fleas on the day they visited the property, which was located next to a pub boasting a large "Welcome Hunters" sign. Shawna stayed at the Holiday Inn for about a month while Peter tried to connect with his new team. However, although they were geographically closer to their families than they had been in the deep south, both had a feeling that their stay in Elmira would be short-lived.

While back home in Ontario over Christmas, they took time to reflect. Peter was sure he could find a spot in the game somewhere that would allow him some stability and a chance to enjoy a normal home life. The couple discussed what to do next, and Shawna recalled that one of the hockey wives from Little Rock had told her how much she and her husband had missed living and playing in Bakersfield, California, and how professionally the players were treated there. With these thoughts in mind, Peter phoned the head coach of the then-WCHL Condors. Peter's call to Coach Kevin McDonald was quickly returned, and within days Peter was flown to Bakersfield, where the coach would evaluate his skills and then fly in Shawna if he wanted to keep Peter.

Having been through several unfortunate situations with other teams, Peter appreciated Kevin's honesty and his up-front nature. Having had coaches such as Teddy Nolan, Mike Kelly and John Oliver, Pete had developed high standards for his coaches and expected nothing but the best from them. So, he played a few games for Bakersfield. He was at a New Year's Eve get-together at the infamous "John and Judy's" (die-hard Bakersfield fans who are the best at barbequing and supporting their Condors) talking to Shawna on the phone when Coach McDonald walked over and told him to fly her in because he would be there the rest of the season.

Peter was offered a decent contract, and upon her arrival, Shawna secured a position with the local Beardsley School District. But neither got too comfortable, because they knew that Peter's days with the Condors could end at any time. Still, Peter enjoyed the role of minor celebrity in a town that didn't have a lot of entertainment choices; at that time it had only one other professional sports franchise: baseball's Blaze. He did radio interviews, was a frequent guest on the team's between-periods TV spots during games, visited schools to talk about reading and hockey and also helped out with other local community events and charities.

Everything was good, except that this was not the NHL, nor was it the next step below that. MacKellar had made it to some degree. He was making a living playing hockey, but he wanted what every hockey player wants, and that's to be in the NHL. And so his quest continued.

He didn't expect to make a magic jump to the NHL. He knew the odds, and he understood the breaks—some guys who don't make it with one team hook on with another, have a good season or two, maybe even establish a solid career. Sometimes, it comes down to timing more than anything else, because, for every guy who plays in the NHL, there are three or four more who are just as capable. At this point in his hockey career, Peter still hoped that he might be that lucky one.

However, his days in Bakersfield ended when a new coach took over during the summer. MacKellar decided that maybe, at 26, he should move on to life after hockey. The couple moved back to Ontario. Peter continued to work out and focused on improving his graphic design skills by attending classes at Port Huron College in Michigan. But he couldn't bring himself to say that hockey was over, so he contacted some coaches and connected with Jim Latos, head coach of the Wichita Thunder of the Central Hockey League. Peter signed a contract with Wichita, Shawna secured a position with the local USD 259 School District, and off they went once again with a U-Haul, to give hockey one last good try.

Peter and Shawna quickly took to life in Wichita. Peter developed a good coach-player bond with Latos, Shawna loved the kids she was working with, and it didn't take long to make some wonderful community connections. The couple also started up a non-denominational Christian hockey ministries program. But life in the minors in Wichita wasn't without change. Toward the end of the season, the Thunder replaced Coach Latos, and Peter was traded to Tulsa, Oklahoma. Excited to play for former NHLer Gary Unger, Peter immediately bonded with his coach and new teammates. Meanwhile, Shawna remained in Wichita, visiting on weekends and holidays.

When the season ended in Oklahoma, the couple decided that they enjoyed living in the south so much that they would stay in Wichita for the summer. Then, as a new season was about to begin, they realized that the hockey dream was over. After all of the moving around and the many unpredictable encounters experienced in minor hockey, they figured it was time to head home to Ontario.

Looking back, neither Peter nor Shawna regrets the nomad years they spent in the minor leagues. Although it might have been nice to be in one place for an extended period of time, each city brought new experiences and opportunities.

Upon moving to Courtice, Ontario, Peter established a graphic design business, and Shawna put her degrees to work with the local school board. Peter found that the historic

Whitby Dunlops team, the very one that had won a miracu-
lous gold medal at the 1958 World Championship, was being
revived. He contacted team management, tried out and
immediately became the captain of the team—a position he
continues to hold.

It's not the NHL, but the Dunlops practice twice
weekly, participate in numerous community events and play
before lively home crowds weekend by weekend throughout
the winter. Then, at the end of the season, the team has the
chance to compete for the Allan Cup.

Although he would still jump at the chance to play in
the NHL, MacKellar is living a version of the hockey dream
that satisfies him, knowing that he did whatever was possible
to achieve his goal of playing at the highest professional level.
Perhaps most importantly, he now gets to play hockey in front
of his friends and family, including his three starry-eyed sons,
who hardly blink when watching him from the stands. To this
day, Peter never goes into the grocery store without remind-
ing himself that the comforts of a full fridge mean something
important, too.

chapter forty-one

Not Too Far for Heroes
Keijo Liimatainen

G rowing up in the 1950s, a kid probably couldn't be farther from the NHL and still know hockey existed than to be in Örnskoldsvik, Sweden. Geographically, thousands of miles would have separated a hockey fan there from the nearest city with an NHL team, Montréal. And even if you were a fan of the game, you would have been much more likely to follow local club teams in the Swedish Elite League or even the contests of the World Championship tournament held every spring or the Olympics every four years.

And that's exactly how Keijo Liimatainen spent his childhood. His local team was Alfredshems IK (now MoDo AIK), and his favorite player was Nils "Nicke" Johansson, a defenseman who wore number 4. Nils was a tall, gangly fellow who rarely came off the ice. In 1962, he led his team to the World Championship, a hometown guy playing for the hometown team, and Liimatainen was old enough for the win to capture his imagination.

It was about this time, too, that nine-year-old Keijo started a habit that would shape his future, both immediate and long term. Walking past the office of the local newspaper, he noticed that they posted the black-and-white photos originally used as shots for their stories. "Nice," he thought to himself. "I wonder what they do with them when they put up the new ones?" He decided to ask, and he walked in and talked to the young woman who was working there.

"I take them down and throw them away," she said in response to his question.

"Could you save them for me?" He wasn't sure at that moment what he would do with them, but a plan was starting to form in his mind. The woman replied that she would keep the photos in her drawer, and that when he saw new images go up, he should come in and ask for the ones she was saving.

A week later, back he went, and out he came with an envelope full of pictures of sports figures and people in the news. By this time, he knew what to do with them. He searched out the addresses of the people pictured and sent them their photos along with a note asking that they autograph them and return them to him. He had done his research and discovered that he could make the task easier for them by buying International Reply Coupons from the post office, so that returning the photos would not be at their expense. Often, he included a letter. "They were the kind of letters a nine- or ten-year-old would write, asking for advice or just telling them that I liked something about their careers. Now I look back at them and cringe, but back then it was pretty important to me," says Keijo.

His quest soon saw him getting autographs from people such as Jack Dempsey and Muhammad Ali to add to his growing collection. Each man also sent him a photo, something he hadn't expected. "It was very seldom that I didn't get something back," he recalls years later. "Often, they'd send back the picture, signed, along with a handwritten note thanking me for my interest in their careers. Of course I was thrilled, and I was practicing my English and also honing my research skills finding out where to get in touch with them. You had to be like a detective to find out where these people were back in those days. It was so exciting to walk home through snow and sleet and with the sky getting dark in mid-afternoon and find some mail. It could be mail from anywhere in the world. There must have been a couple of years when every week there were three, four things."

By 1967, he had been collecting autographs for five years, and hockey and running were Liimatainen's passions. At the time, Swedish TV did not cover the NHL. Results were printed in the paper, and the occasional goal was shown on a Sunday highlights show, but nothing else. But one week the photos from a story about Bobby Hull appeared in the paper's window. Keijo knew that they would soon be his, and he scrambled to find an address for the great superstar, whose career was known to him and his friends only in bits and pieces. "We would talk about him," Liimatainen says, "and imagine what it looked like to see him play. When I saw the story, I thought to myself, 'I need his autograph. He's a good player, let's see if he's a good person, too.' All I was hoping for was his signature on a scrap of paper—anything would have been wonderful."

A few weeks after he mailed a note to Hull, he received a card, a black-and-white autographed picture with a note on the back. It had a message responding to the queries in the boy's letter, and it was signed, "Good luck—Bobby."

One line of the note was particularly interesting. "No idol," it said.

Keijo explains: "What this is, is an answer to my question about what it was like being the idol to so many people. I guess he didn't consider himself an idol, and was saying so, but he certainly was to me.

"Anyway, I don't remember specifically, but the way I was raised, I would have sent a thank-you note for that first picture," he claims. "And I thought that was the end of it. Then out of the blue another envelope came." He got it out of the mailbox as soon as he got home from school, a complete surprise. "I looked at the postmark and said to myself, 'Bobby Hull again—what is this?'" On the envelope above the preprinted Chicago Blackhawks return address appeared the name, "Bobby Hull," in ink, the same as the signature on the other card. The lettering of Keijo's name was in the same hand, proving that the great man addressed his own mail.

He took it inside, and his mother came home shortly after to discover Keijo in the kitchen for his customary cookies-and-milk snack with the large manila envelope in his hands.

"Didn't you already get something from Bobby Hull?" she asked. Of course, he had, but inside this package was a note and two hockey newspapers, a copy of *The Hockey News* and one of *Sport Images*, the latter in French, plus a large black-and-white photo of Hull, again autographed.

The note enclosed said, "I was cleaning out my desk and I thought you might enjoy these." The date on the envelope was March 22, 1967, and the dates on the newspapers just a few days earlier. *The Hockey News* had been shipped to a Mr. Don Murphy, the Blackhawks' longtime PR man. The thrill Keijo felt was magnified by the fact that the gift was unsolicited.

"I'm sure I didn't do any homework that night. I couldn't read French, but I looked at every picture, and of course, I read over the other newspaper word-for-word before I went to bed and have kept it in the envelope all these years," Liimatainen says.

But the story doesn't end there. His love of sports and interest in sports personalities led to a career as a journalist, which Liimatainen still practices. About 10 years after the surprise package from Hull, the Winnipeg Jets came to Sweden to play some exhibition games. By this point, Liimatainen was writing for *Länstidningen*, in Södertälje, Sweden. He took the packet of papers with him when he went to interview the now-WHA superstar, and he had his photo taken with Hull.

He also got up the courage to ask the great man whether he remembered his spontaneous act of kindness, and Hull did. "And I asked him why, since I figured he got thousands of letters just like mine. He told me, 'Some letters you just remember more than others,'" says Liimatainen. It was an answer to a mystery that had always lingered in his mind.

In a further twist, Liimatainen got to confirm the story another decade later, when he was working on a crew doing a TV interview with Brett Hull, by this time making his own hockey history with the St. Louis Blues. Liimatainen told Brett what had happened with his father, and Brett responded, "Yep, that sounds like Dad. He was always particular to answer people."

Liimatainen mentioned that it wasn't one response but two, the second with the hockey papers. Again Brett Hull concurred. "That's my dad. If he likes someone, he'll reach out and do something unexpected." Then in typical fashion, he smiled a crooked grin and asked, "You still have that junk at home?"

Keijo smiled back, "I do," he said, "but I consider them treasures."

chapter forty-two

Full Circle and Then Some
Gary and Pete Dalliday

F ew towns love hockey as much as Peterborough, Ontario, does. The names that have come through the local Junior team are enough to fill the Hockey Hall of Fame all by themselves—Bowman and Neilson as coaches, Gainey, Millen, Pronger and two Staals as players, among many others. The fabric of the town is working class, though the big factories that sustained families for so long are now on their way out. But one thing that has remained constant for three decades is the man who has kept the locals up to date on what's happening in the world of hockey and with their beloved Petes.

Gary Dalliday had what many might call the prototypical Peterborough upbringing. A bit hardscrabble, he came from Bethune Street, legendary as the tough part of town. Like anywhere else, the favorite local activity was street hockey, only on Bethune, train tracks ran down the middle of the street. "Instead of yelling 'Car!' like you did everywhere else, we yelled, 'Train!' " Dalliday says, "I never did figure out whether I lived on the right side of the tracks or the wrong one."

He had what he describes as a "sip of coffee" with the hometown team (then called the "TPTs" because they were sponsored by the Toronto Peterborough Transport Company) in the late 1950s, playing for Scotty Bowman. He recalls Bowman one night yelling on the bench that he wanted some energy, and that the guys needed to get out there and hit someone.

Dalliday went out on his next shift determined to impress his coach. He watched while St. Catharines' Bill Speers came out from behind his net, gathering speed. As he reached center ice, Dalliday intercepted him. The ensuing collision left Gary barely able to get back to the bench. "I've been told," Dalliday says, "that play-by-play man John Danko said, 'Speers and Dalliday come together, and Dalliday's stick is up in the rafters in Garden City Arena. He's still holding onto it.'" Dalliday appeared in only a handful of games for the team, played some baseball in the local City League, and then settled down to life in the place that to this day he wouldn't dream of leaving.

When Dalliday's playing days were over, he took a job in a local plant. About the same time, he was starting to raise a family of three kids. His two sons both played sports, and it was through lacrosse that he got the break that made him a familiar figure to Peterborough sports fans and eventually brought him full circle by giving him the chance to broadcast the Petes' games.

He was attending a game of the Junior A Peterborough PCOs one day when he ran into a guy he knew from his son's team. The fellow asked him if he would mind helping out upstairs, and Dalliday said he would be glad to step in. He went up to the broadcast booth expecting to be asked to keep the stats. Just before the game started, though, the producer handed him a microphone.

Dalliday was astonished at what he was asked to do. But he found over the course of the season that he liked doing color commentary, and when the year was over, he missed it. "I was back to being Joe lift-truck driver at GE," he says. "And then I noticed that the local radio and TV stations, CHEX, had lost their sports guy. So I called up Don O'Neil, the program director, and asked him if I could have a shot." O'Neil told him to come to the station whenever he wanted to do some practice tapes. "That, for me, was every night," Dalliday says, "and eight or nine months later they offered me a job." When he decided to take it, he told O'Neil that he would never leave. It was a promise O'Neil reminded him of years later during a ceremony honoring Dalliday's 30th anniversary with the station, in 2005.

Dalliday served as sports director at CHEX until March 2009, when he retired. Still, this did not silence his voice for Petes fans. He retains his role on the Petes' broadcast team, a job he has held since 1996. His son Pete is the other half of the duo.

Pete comes by his skills honestly. When he was a kid, he was often found in his room, pretending to be his dad. "Good evening, ladies and gentlemen, this is Gary Dalliday with CHEX TV sports. Here's what happened in the National Hockey League today," Pete would say. When games came on TV, he'd turn down the sound and broadcast his own commentary to whoever was near enough to listen. Sometimes Gary would lend him his tape recorder and play the role of an NHL player, and Pete would interview him. It was all good practice for what was to come.

When CHEX's sister station KRUZ got the contract to broadcast the Petes in the mid-1990s, it was obvious to everyone that Gary, who had been covering the team as sports reporter on TV and radio, would be involved. The station further liked the idea of a father-son pair. What they didn't foresee was Gary walking into the boss' office and saying, "We're good to go. Pete is doing play-by-play, and I'll do color."

The first night they were together on the air, Gary did the pre-game, then threw it over to Pete. "I said something like, 'And for the first time, here's the new voice of the

Peterborough Petes, Pete Dalliday,'" he says. "Then I added, 'Here you go, son. Go get 'em.' There was a huge lump in my throat."

Since that time, Pete has shown that he shares his dad's hardnosed Peterborough work ethic. He's closing in on 1000 consecutive games, something a reporter at the local *Examiner* newspaper has determined to be an OHL record. The only time he almost missed a game was the day he lost his maternal grandfather, to whom Pete was really close. Gary and his wife, Donna, went to their son's house at around 8:00 AM to tell him that his grandfather was gone. Pete was shaken, but he decided that his grandfather would want him to work. That afternoon, the Petes played in Toronto. Gary says, "A few times during the game, I could tell by his voice that it was affecting him, but nothing was said."

As a team, the Dallidays are like any duo who have worked together for a while. "I know when to jump in, and he knows when I finish," Gary says. "The first year, I might say something like, 'You know, your mother wouldn't approve of that.' We've toned that down now, but we have our own routines. We like to throw in Peterborough stuff, or something about Pete's son. I'll say, 'I hear that Noah Dalliday is playing some pretty good hockey,' as if he were just another kid in town."

For her part, Donna Dalliday is likely to take her son's side in any friendly disputes. "She'll tell me, 'Why don't you keep quiet—he was going to say something,'" Gary reports.

With Gary being in his late 60s and riding the bus to away games, you might think that he would be tired of the grind, but that's nowhere near the truth. "In the old days," he says, "you called the bus the 'Iron Lung.' These days it's much better, with satellite TV and Internet on there. I have an MP3 player, too, though the music I listen to is nothing like what the young guys like. But I like going down the aisles and saying hello to the kids."

His role at times tends to be that of a father or grandfather figure to the players, rather than a broadcaster. He remembers one afternoon when he was walking along a hotel hallway in London and he saw Jordan Staal standing in the way. "What's up, big guy?" Dalliday asked.

Jordan's reply was immediate. "Oh, I'm going to be in trouble. I forgot my pants." It seems that the third of the hockey-playing Staal brothers and the second to play for the Petes had left his dress pants at home. The team is strict with its dress code, and Staal knew he would be busted when he turned up to the team meal later in the day in jeans.

"Grab your coat," Dalliday said, "we're going out." He shook off the boy's surprised look by saying "There's a mall right across the street." He took Staal there and found him a pair of pants. "They were nothing expensive, but you know, these kids don't have money. The biggest trouble was getting something long enough for him," Dalliday says. But he also recalls the boy's reaction. "'Thank you, Mr. Dalliday,' he told me. He said it over and over. Couldn't thank me enough. It shows you something about how he was raised." Later in the day, Jordan passed by on his way to the bus for the arena. "Looking good," Dalliday said. Staal just smiled.

Summing up his role with the team, Gary says, "I'm covering them, but I'm still an alumni and fan. I always wanted to be a player, but it didn't work out. For a kid from the tough-nosed section of Peterborough, I've done OK. I'm not much of a materialistic guy, but I've been treated well. I've had a few other offers over the years, but I never thought too long about any of them. I love Peterborough."

He plans to keep his position next to Pete until he is at his side for the 1000-game milestone. His hopes, too, are for another Memorial Cup for the Petes. "I think they can do it in the next couple of years," he says. "They have a lot of good kids coming up."

chapter forty-three

A Whole New Hockey World

Marcel Kars

Growing up in North York in the 1980s, Marcel Kars did what most kids did. He went to school, came home, played the occasional video game. But when his friends started getting into hockey around age six or seven, he stayed on the outside. In his family, the emphasis wasn't so much on hockey but rather soccer, which took first place because his parents had been raised in Europe. They had left the Netherlands shortly before Kars was born so that his father could take a good job with Paramount Pictures in Toronto.

As a child, Marcel had no inkling that in his 20s he would make a reverse migration to the city of his parents' birth and create a life for himself that had hockey as its center. But that's exactly what happened, and now, most mornings, he steps out of his second-story apartment in the historic

Jordaan District in Amsterdam, gets on his Vespa and speeds off to the gym.

Later in the day he meets teammates from his Amsterdam Tijgers squad for coffee in an outdoor café. Later still, the whole team gathers at the Jaap Edenhal arena for practice. On the weekends, they play their games. And yes, they get there on their Vespas.

During the season, the Dutch Super League, like other European hockey leagues, takes a break for international competitions, in which Kars plays for the Dutch National team. Competing for them has allowed Kars the chance to travel to places as far off as China and as near as Poland. That's one of the things that he values about the chance to play in Europe. "For the person who is inclined to travel, it opens up your mind to a whole new world," he says. "A lot of places in Europe are very close, allowing for easy travel. Games are mostly on weekends, allowing for a few days off sometimes, giving the players a chance to get away for a few days to Paris or Barcelona."

In the meantime, playing for the Tijgers means that he has a salary, his apartment is paid for, and that Vespa is also part of the deal. "They'd give us cars," he explains, "which is the usual perk, but there's no way you want a car in Amsterdam. The scooter gets you everywhere you want to go." He also rides a bike around town at times.

Sometimes Kars ponders what his hockey future might have been, the one closer to home, had he not had the luxury of the EU passport, courtesy of his parents' European heritage. "I probably would have played in the U.S., in the ECHL," he says. "Or maybe the Central League. It's a nice life. You get free meals, and golf. But you don't really get ahead. The money isn't enough to go anywhere on. And you have to remember, those guys play something like 80 games a year, and depending on where you are, those games can be an overnight bus ride away." Kars' friends who chose that direction for their hockey lives tended to do it for a while, but after two or three years the thrill started to wear off, and they gave up their hockey dreams for everyday jobs.

Kars' version of the hockey life, by contrast, has seen him play in almost every corner of the globe. But if his hockey career is more exciting than he might have imagined it could be, the dream wasn't something that formed itself in his mind as a kid. Going back to Europe to play, let alone live, was never in his plans. "My parents took me back a few times growing up," he says, "but I was a kid. I wasn't paying all that much attention to what was going on around me." Meanwhile, at some point the younger Kars started to do what the other North York kids were doing, and that was to play hockey. He was always good enough to play at the highest league level for his age but never great enough to think that he would make hockey a significant part of his future. His plan, when he started to realize he might excel at the game, was to use hockey to get a university scholarship. He was drafted out of Bantam by Sault Ste. Marie of the Ontario Hockey League but knew that playing in the OHL would mean losing his eligibility to play in the NCAA. He opted then to play Junior A tier 2 in Ontario for several years in an attempt to receive an American university scholarship. After several successful years, including one for the Aurora Tigers of the Ontario Junior Hockey League in which he scored 25 goals in as many games, he still hadn't received an offer from a big school like Michigan or North Dakota. He decided to play for the Barrie Colts of the OHL to gain some experience for the remainder of the 1996–97 season. Next, he went to school and played for the University of Guelph, which had won the national title the previous year.

During his time at Canadian university, at an age when most players find their peak, Kars continued to develop his skills. He had his moment of hope that an NHL shot might still be possible when, in the summer between his second and third years at Guelph, he got a phone call from the Washington Capitals. They wanted to bring him to camp on a tryout contract.

"There was a game on TV. We were losing 4–1, and I scored four straight goals to win the game," Kars said. He figures that's where he got noticed. "That summer I got a call and attended camp in Washington. You have to remember, they want to fill their camp, too. It's not like going there is any kind of guarantee." As it turned out, the tryout didn't get him an offer, so he returned to the Guelph Gryphons and finished out his university days.

The summer after his university career ended, Kars was invited to take an ECHL physical, but he was suffering from a shoulder injury that turned out to be a torn ligament. He required surgery, and for a year, his hockey life appeared to be over. Then, teams from the Netherlands started calling. "They know who the guys are who have a Dutch passport. There must be some kind of a network," he speculates. "They track you, and at some point they make you an offer."

So off he went, and after moving to his apartment and starting to play in his first season, he realized one day that he was living two blocks from where his dad had grown up. Not long afterward, he got involved in the lives of his younger cousins, who lived nearby. "I started them on hockey, and pretty soon they were all quitting football," he reports. "They got to liking hockey better." Having the chance to live and play in Amsterdam gave him something he never had as an only child growing up in Canada, a connection to an extended family.

Kars also did some other hockey adventuring, including playing a summer in the Australian Ice Hockey League. Because July-August is the middle of winter Down Under, it's perfect for a North American or European player on hiatus from his usual team to jet over and compete. "They treated me so well," he says. "You're not paid, but they take care of everything—meals, a place to live, a car. And they keep you happy, hosting events for the guys and helping us find work with local hockey clinics. Australia is quite big, so you fly to most away games, giving the players a chance to see the whole country." He played the summer of 2005–06 with the Newcastle North Stars, scoring 29 goals in 20 games (29-37-66) and leading his team to the Goodall Cup, a trophy that has been awarded since 1910.

However, Marcel spends most summers in North America working at hockey schools. When he's home, he gets together with old friends, talking about the game. "All of a sudden, you're back with your Canadian friends, talking hockey all day every day," he says of his summer ventures. But when fall rolls around, he always finds himself heading back to Europe to continue his hockey career.

Perhaps not surprisingly, he's considering making his reverse migration permanent. Before he settles down, however, Kars would like to play a few more years around the globe. He has played seven years in Europe, mostly in his parents' homeland but also in Italy and Germany. He also wants to explore the idea of playing a year in France and checking out the hockey scene in Asia. He continues to be a big part of the Dutch National team, competing every April in the World Championship. Travel is among his prime motivators for playing hockey.

When it's all done and it's time to move from hockey to something else, he's pretty sure he'll wind up back in Amsterdam. "For some reason, I always feel drawn back here. My roots are here; my family is here. Plus, the European lifestyle is a more relaxing one," he explains.

His hockey dream might be unlike any that he could have conjured up when he was a boy in the Toronto area, but Marcel Kars has created a hockey life that has led him to adventures stretching from one side of the globe to the other and, ironically, back to a home he probably wouldn't have found otherwise.

chapter forty-four

The Same Old New Game

Anytime you go to a hockey game in Southern California, you'll encounter a range of people—everyone from Mr. T to the super-rich to kids with shaved heads and "LA" tattooed on the side might be sitting in the stands at Staples Center. And each person has his or her own motivation for going, from the hardcore fans to the see-and-be-seen types.

But one night at the old Forum in the early 1970s, no one had a more interesting story, or a more desperate need to experience the rhythms of a game that had formed such a large part of his life, than European-born Danny Blaha.

Danny loved hockey and had played it all his life. When he was a kid, it had been on the pond near his house, and later, when his city built a rink in the park, that had been his destination every afternoon after school. Danny lived to get home, sling his skates over his shoulder and head to the rink. For him and his schoolmates, the ice was the place where friendships were created, broken and mended again.

His favorite position was in net, and he honed his skills with hours of frozen-footed games. When he went to college at age 18, he was good enough to play on the traveling team of the school where he studied electrical engineering.

Then in a flash, just after Christmas the year he turned 21, he moved to California. Once there, he took up residence in what he first thought was a cool part of town: Hollywood. People the world over thought of Hollywood as the planet's entertainment capital, after all. What he didn't realize when he moved into his apartment was that Hollywood the place and "Hollywood" the idea were two completely different things. The latter might have formed the glamorous backdrop to the dreams of stardom for kids who got off the bus in hopes of being discovered and made famous, but the latter was, especially 35 years ago, the seedy backdrop to a lot of broken dreams.

This discrepancy didn't affect Danny much, because he was going to school to brush up on his English skills and was too busy to take much notice of the people pushing shopping carts past his apartment building day and night in their attempt to survive on the streets. Hollywood was, for him, just a convenient place to park until he got a job that suited his qualifications as an electrical engineer.

What did bother him about California was that almost no hockey culture existed. Sure, there was a team, but nobody he met ever went to the games, and nobody played the sport themselves. Playing on outdoor ice was not an option; even indoor rinks were few and far between, and hockey simply wasn't a central part of the sporting subculture. But one day after Danny had been in LA a few months, his uncle, sensing his loneliness, got tickets for a game. The Kings versus the St. Louis Blues.

Together they drove to Inglewood, found the Forum and parked in the vast lot that surrounded the building. Danny noticed as they walked up to the doors that there were plenty of spaces in the parking lot. Once inside, they found their seats behind the net, midway up. He looked around. The crowd didn't seem terribly large.

Small crowd, he thought to himself in his native language. *But who cares? It smells like the arena in here. This is right.* He would eventually learn that the fans, who numbered a little over 6000, were about 10,000 fewer than had been there earlier in the season when Montréal came to town.

As the game started, he watched intensely. It was his first NHL game, and he wanted to see how the players skated, what their skill level was compared to the guys he had played behind tending net over the past few seasons in university. It was February, so the players were in the prime of condition, and they moved—fast. The shots, too, were quick and hard.

He wondered how the goalies handled the force with which the puck attacked them.

As the game went on, he started watching not the individual players, but the team play, and a feeling began to overtake him. Something here was different to what he knew. Something was wrong with their tactics.

A winger grabbed the puck at his own blue line and started up the ice with it, full speed. He seemed unaware of the man with him on his left, and when he got to the blue line of the opposing team, he reared back. "Slapshot," Danny predicted to himself.

It was. Only it wasn't on net, but 10 feet wide, into the corner. As it caromed off the boards behind the net, the skater crashed into the defenseman trying to handle the puck, knocking it loose and sweeping it into the slot just as the centerman, who had been with the winger crossing the blue line, got there after shaking off his check. He grabbed the pass and winged a shot toward the top right corner. Wide.

Play carried on with the defense picking up the puck and feeding it out to go the other way, and again, a winger carried it down, this time back to the end where Danny was sitting, and slapped it waist-high into the boards. Danny watched as the goalie turned his head to follow the bounce of the puck. A defenseman corralled it and froze it along the boards. The whistle blew to end play.

Danny looked around him, curious about the reaction of the others in his section to the pace of play. Nobody seemed to be discussing strategy with a seatmate, and the puck dropped before he could lean over to his uncle with a comment. Once again, the home team grabbed the puck and carried it up the ice, only this time Danny was ready. When they got to the Blues' blue line, he stood on his feet, cupped his hands around his mouth, took in the biggest breath he could and screamed, "Nahrat!"

The winger flung it into the corner anyway, oblivious to what was happening in the other half of the arena. "Nahrava!" Danny tried again, yelling at the top of his lungs. He got no result at his second attempt to remind the Kings that they needed to focus on the pass and not give the puck away every time they tried to enter the attacking zone.

As he sat down, Danny looked around him to find that members of the formerly docile crowd were craning their necks toward him. Their wide-eyed stares were disapproving, although from his point of view, all he had tried to do was scream encouragement at the hometown players.

What are you staring at? He couldn't say the words in English, but he thought them, in Czech, his native language. *Haven't you heard that passing the puck is a successful way to attack the other team's goal?* He didn't have any words to offer anyone, though, and so he looked to his uncle to gain a moment of relief. The man just smiled, as if encouraging Danny to enjoy the game on his own terms.

Danny got the message, but it didn't salve the hurt that was encompassing his heart. Here he was, thousands of miles from home, in a place where the sun shone all year round, with no ice to be had, and yet he had thought that the one thing he hadn't had to give up was hockey. Now he wasn't so sure.

Maybe the game, too, was gone, along with his family, his girlfriend and everything in his apartment back in Plzen, Czechoslovakia. It had to be that way, because he had escaped Communism, and he'd done so in a way that other, more famous, people had; he had "defected" by simply vanishing.

It had been on a bus trip, a Christmas vacation to Italy for which he'd managed to get an exit permit. One night on the way home, in Austria, he had slipped off the bus and disappeared, eventually making it to the safety of the U.S. with the help of his uncle in California. What he had were literally the clothes on his back and the expertise in electronics that he carried in his head, nothing more. No friends, no other relatives than Uncle, no ability to talk to people and little sense of what life was really like in the U.S. All he knew was that it had to be better than what he'd left, but the first couple of months had been frustrating.

Hockey, to him, had been his one hope for a bit of normalcy—a refuge where language differences didn't matter.

But now even that dream was dashed in a moment of embarrassment over his scene and frustration at the lack of proper strategy being employed on the ice.

The hockey he knew was the hockey of Europe in the days before the Russian Red Army team came to Canada in 1972 and showed the Canadian team—and its supporters— that there was more than one way to play the game. The hockey of Plzen Skoda, the Czech National team and those Russians, was a game of strategy, passing and teamwork. What he was seeing in the Forum, supposedly the best hockey in the world as played in the National Hockey League, was a game of individual effort and reckless abandon with the puck. The players gave the puck away so often that he wondered how anyone ever managed to score a goal.

Sitting there, Danny knew he faced a choice. Going home was out of the question. But he could do one of two things—embrace hockey as it was here or give up the game that had been so important to him all his life. He decided, as he watched the Kings losing 2–0, that if this was the only hockey there was, he'd have to get used to it. And as he sat there, he also realized that the language school on Sunset Boulevard was unlikely to teach him the vocabulary he needed here. If he was going to enjoy watching the games in the spirited way that was his nature, he had to learn hockey lingo in English on his own.

He leaned over to his uncle once more and inquired in Czech, "How do you say 'pass' in English?" And the next time the Kings rushed down the ice, Danny yelled again, only this time in his new language, "Pass the puck!"

It didn't matter, really, whether the players could hear him, or whether this was their style of game or not. What mattered was that by participating in the only way a spectator could, he was taking his first step toward embracing the North American version of the game. In so doing, he was saving the one thing that gave him some continuity while he adjusted to a life that was as different from the one he'd always known as "hra" was to "hockey." This time, nobody turned around to look at him.

On the way out of the arena, he bought a souvenir puck, and when he got home and scrutinized it, he noticed that on the back it said, "Barum." He was surprised. This was the brand he'd grown up with. As he read the other embossed letters, he became more shocked still. "Made in Czechoslovakia," they said. He realized that the hockey world, despite what he had seen on the ice this night, was a lot smaller than he thought, and he hardened his resolve to devote himself to the Kings. Nearly four decades later, Danny is still living in LA and is still hoping that the Kings will one day win the Stanley Cup.

Afterword

I hope you've found each of these stories interesting on its own. Even when writing about a player who is well known, my goal was to give you something new—a glimpse into a corner of that person's life that might otherwise be overlooked. But the goal of this book is greater than to fill in the gaps in the biographies of stars like Hull, Clarke and Kehoe. The idea, rather, is that you add these stories to the ones of the less-famous people I profile in order to enjoy the wide scope of the hockey world.

Whether the other areas of hockey as I have revealed them are new to you or not—the women's game, the broadcast booth, the minor leagues, European or other versions of the game like sledge hockey, and so forth—I hope that by seeing them in context with stories of familiar heroes, you will have gained a more complete sense of the different ways in which people construct lives in and around the game.

By extension, I invite you to write your own story and place it between the pages of this book wherever you feel it best fits. When you do, please consider it a part of *Living the Hockey Dream*, because had I known about your hockey exploits, I might very well have included them here. Better yet, send your story to me so that I can enjoy it. You can always contact me through my website, www.growinguphockey.com.

Researching on Your Own

For anyone interested in researching further, a number of great sources of hockey history are available online. The Internet Hockey Database, www.hockeydb.com, contains a wealth of information on player stats. Also fantastic as a background source is the Hockey Hall of Fame website (www.legendsofhockey.net). If you want to read old articles from *Sports Illustrated*, the SI Vault (http://vault.sportsillustrated.cnn.com) includes cover photos and page views of issues that go back decades.

Gabriela Moya

Brian Kennedy

Born in Montréal, Brian Kennedy spent much of his hockey-playing youth in Ontario. He went to school in the U.S. in 1981 and ended up in LA. He's been a hockey fan since the age of five and played hockey as a child, retiring three different times.

Brian holds a PhD in English and teaches at Pasadena City College. He is also a freelance sports writer, using his writing to get him everywhere from NHL locker rooms to the race shops of famous drivers of the past and present. He covers the Anaheim Ducks and the LA Kings, and in his spare time he rides a racing bike, practices karate and preserves memories. He still has many artifacts from his youth. He is the author of the bestselling book, *Growing Up Hockey*, an everyman's autobiography of anyone who has ever loved the game.

ALSO FROM
FOLKLORE PUBLISHING...

GROWING UP HOCKEY
The Life and Times of Everyone Who Ever Loved the Game
by Brian Kennedy

Many of us grew up scoring a thousand glorious NHL goals in our minds, and on our streets and corner rinks. We won the Stanley Cup over and over—in our imaginations. What happened to those childhood heroics? We packed them in a box with our hockey cards and forgot them.

Growing Up Hockey uses the heartwarming and comical exploits of a house-league third-liner to prompt us to re-live our memories of hockey glory. It shows that for those who love it, the game is never far away.

Bobby Hull, Frank Mahovlich, Wayne Gretzky—they're all here. But equally large are the neighborhood rink bullies, the Pee Wee league superstars and the obsessed NHL aficionados. Together, they create a hockey myth as grand as ever existed and as unique as each of us.

$19.95 • ISBN: 978-1-894864-65-7 • 5.5" x 8.5" • 370 pages

Available from your local bookseller or by
contacting the distributor,
Lone Pine Publishing
1-800-518-3541

www.lonepinepublishing.com